21st Century Airlines

T0305485

In *21st Century Airlines: Connecting the Dots*, Nawal Taneja addresses the challenges and opportunities facing the airline industry as it tries to innovate and create products and services that are radically different by 'connecting the dots' at four key levels: recognizing the implications of global events, improving cross-functional collaboration within the organization, working more closely with the travel chain, and providing much higher engagements with connectors within the social networks.

The book synthesizes insights gained from the experience of non-traditional businesses, such as Uber, that have no physical assets and that focus on scalability through platforms, as well as traditional businesses, such as Mercedes-Benz, that are transitioning from operators of physical assets to adapt to the on-demand and sharing economies. These insights show pragmatically that digitizing airline businesses would require digital mind-sets, digital technologies, digital strategies, and digital workplaces to explore new frontiers in value for both customers and airlines. Moreover, forward-thinking airlines need to consider working with bimodal organizational structures, in which one group optimizes current business models (network, fleet, and schedule planning, as well as revenue management) while a second group explores innovative ways to add digital features to physical products in order to provide a consistent experience throughout the journey.

The book is written for all senior-level practitioners of airlines and related businesses worldwide, as well as senior-level government policy-makers.

Nawal Taneja, whose experience in the aviation industry spans almost five decades, has worked for and advised major airlines and related businesses worldwide. His experience also includes the presidency of a small airline that provided schedule and charter service with jet aircraft and the presidency of a research organization that provided consulting services to the air transportation community throughout the world. On the government side, he has advised worldwide departments of civil aviation, finance, economics, and tourism in matters relating to the role of government-owned airlines and their management. Within the academic community, he has served on the faculties of the Massachusetts Institute of Technology (as an Associate Professor) and at Ohio State University (Professor and later as Chair of both the Department of Aviation and the Department of Aerospace Engineering).

21st Century Airlines
Connecting the Dots

Nawal K. Taneja

Routledge
Taylor & Francis Group

LONDON AND NEW YORK

First published 2018 by Routledge

2 Park Square, Milton Park, Abingdon, Oxon OX14 4RN
605 Third Avenue, New York, NY 10017

Routledge is an imprint of the Taylor & Francis Group, an informa business

First issued in paperback 2021

Publisher's Note

The publisher has gone to great lengths to ensure the quality of this reprint
but points out that some imperfections in the original copies may be apparent.

British Library Cataloguing-in-Publication Data
A catalogue record for this book is available from the British Library

Library of Congress Cataloging-in-Publication Data
A catalog record for this book has been requested

ISBN: 978-1-138-09313-3 (hbk)
ISBN: 978-1-03-217900-1 (pbk)
DOI: 10.4324/9781315107028

Typeset in Times New Roman
by Apex CoVantage, LLC

Dedicated to Angela, Matthew, Sophia, and Ravi

Contents

Figures

Table

Acknowledgements

I would like to express my appreciation for all those who contributed in different ways, especially Angela Taneja (my business research analyst), Peeter Kivestu (transportation and logistics industry consultant at Teradata), Dr. Dietmar Kirchner (formerly SVP at Lufthansa and now senior aviation advisor and co-chair of the International Airline Symposium Planning Committee), and Rob Solomon (formerly SVP and chief marketing officer at Outrigger Enterprises and now co-chair of the International Airline Symposium Planning Committee), for discussions on challenges and opportunities facing the global airline industry and related businesses.

The second group of individuals I would like to recognize include, at:

- Abbotsford International Airport – Parm Sidhu;
- AIMIA – Evert de Boer;
- Air China – Zhihang Chi;
- Airlines Association of Southern Africa – Chris Zweigenthal;
- AirlineTrends – Raymond Kollau;
- Amadeus – Monika Wiederhold;
- Austrian Airlines – Andrea Pernkopf;
- Aviation Strategy – James Halstead and Keith McMullan;
- British Airways – Alex Cruz and Glenn Morgan;
- CAPA – Centre for Aviation – Peter Harbison, Derek Sadubin, and Binit Somaia;
- Digital Frontier Partners – Chris Stevens;
- Emirates Airline – Rob Broere and Christoph Mueller;
- Finavia – Katja Siberg;
- Finnair – Katri Harra-Salonen and Juha Järvinen;
- Google – Rob Torres;
- HNA Aviation Holdings – Wang Lei;
- Hong Kong Airlines – Dianchun Li;
- IATA – Stephan Copart, Eric Leopold, and Juan Ivan Martin;
- jetBlue Technology Ventures – Raj Singh;
- Journera – Gary Doernhoefer and Jeffrey Katz;
- Lufthansa – Christian Langer;
- Metro Trains – Robin Barlass;

- oneworld – Dennis Tierney;
- Passenger1 – Chris Moss;
- Plug and Play – Amir Amidi and Kevin Wang;
- PricewaterhouseCoopers – Jonathan Kletzel and Bryan Terry;
- Sabre – Stan Boyer, Vinit Doshi, B. Vinod, and Arnaud Voermans;
- Siemens – Stefan Jenzowsky;
- SITA – Arthur Calderwood, James Peters, and Terence Tucker;
- Tigerair-Scoot – Trevor Spinks;
- United Airlines – Amos Khim and John Slater; and
- Volantio – Azim Barodawala.

Third, there are a number of authors whose work and ideas have been referenced throughout this book. They include Marshall Van Alstyne, Megan Beck, Sangeet Paul Choudary, Aswath Damodaran, John DiJulius, David Evans, Jeff Gothelf, Vijay Govindarajan, Nicholas Johnson, Jim Kalbach, Richard Koch, Paul Leinwand, Alan Lewis (with Dan McKone), Greg Lockwood, Barry Libert, Cesare Mainardi, Joseph Michelli, Alex Moazed, Charles O'Reilly III (with Michael Tushman), Geoffrey Parker, Joshua Cooper Ramo, Ben Reason (with Lavrans Løvlie and Melvin Brand), David Rogers, Richard Schmalensee, Ken Segall, Josh Seiden, Arun Sundararajan, Adele Sweetwood, William Taylor, Peter Thiel, Jerry Wind, and Todd Zenger.

Fourth, a number of other people provided significant help: at The Ohio State University – Robert Mendez, Cynthia Overly, Ishwar Shreram, Delsi Winn, and Brad Wendel; at Routledge of the Taylor & Francis Group – Guy Loft, Senior Editor, Aviation|Health and Safety; Kevin Selmes, Senior Production Editor, and Matthew Ranscombe, Editorial Assistant, Aviation|Health, and Safety); at ApexCovantage – Kerry Boettcher and Will DeRooy.

Finally, I would like to thank my family for their support and patience.

Foreword

Saeed Amidi

Founder and Chief Executive Officer
Plug and Play Technology Center

When I founded Plug and Play in 2006, my dream was to create an ecosystem encouraging open innovation and collaboration between startups. Through my past experiences in real estate, I learned that working alongside optimistic and energetic people who wanted to conquer the world only encouraged me to be more like them. When considering my next venture, I knew that no matter what I was doing I wanted to be immersed in this culture. This dream and desire led me towards converting an old Philips semi-conductor building in Sunnyvale, CA, to build an innovation platform/accelerator for connecting startups with corporations.

Not a day passes when I'm not amazed at how large our once small family has grown based on the demand from startups. To date, we're operating out of 22 locations globally, collaborating with more than 180 corporations; last year we accelerated more than 350 startups and invested in 162 of them. By structuring our programs into 11 industry-specific verticals and bringing together the major stakeholders, we're able to truly bring value to all parties.

Each one of our verticals runs a three-month program where the startups have access to business opportunities, whether it be their first pilot or a new customer; corporations have access to a global network of emerging technologies tailored to fit their organization; and venture capitalists, like ourselves, are provided an avenue to find their next unicorn. So far, we've been able to invest in PayPal, Dropbox, Lending Club, and Guardant Health through these efforts.

In 2015, my nephew Amir Amidi came to me with the desire to start a program focused on the travel and hospitality industry. Drawing from his four years of experience in the industry, he felt it was a space ripe for disruption due to its fragmented and risk-averse nature. I wholeheartedly agreed, using my experience as a traveler and recognizing the lack of modernization as well as the inherent friction.

From an investment perspective, a traveler's journey has not changed much over the past couple of decades and in some cases has worsened due to global volatility. The travel industry is phenomenally vast, contributing to about 10% of global GDP. However, this hasn't translated into the rapid adoption of innovation we've seen across other industries, wherein lies an investor's opportunity. I missed Airbnb by a hair, and I swore I wouldn't miss the next opportunity.

So in 2016 we founded our Travel & Hospitality Vertical, and it has been what one might call a 'slow burn'. Around the office we joke that creating a culture of innovation within any corporation is like turning a plane on the tarmac. I suppose we should have assumed that an industry which literally turns planes on the tarmac would have put our little analogy to shame. Although we're proud of the work we've done, I'd be lying to you if I said it hasn't been sluggish.

At a high level, our role is to help our corporate partners tap into innovative technologies to increase revenues, decrease costs, improve operational efficiency, and build brand loyalty through significantly better customer experience. Based on the contents of this book, Nawal Taneja is convinced that emerging technologies can enable the airline industry to achieve these goals. Through our global network, we have become very good at identifying disruptive technologies that can turn an industry upside down in a relatively short time. Our goal is to invest in these technologies and inform our corporate partners of industry-wide threats and opportunities created by disruptive innovation.

As I write this, we've been able to successfully accelerate 60 startups. Despite tremendous results in this metric, the area in which we have not excelled is investment opportunities and industry support. In total, we have 14 phenomenal partners including AccorHotels, Carlson Wagonlit Travel, Changi Airport Group, Gatwick Airport, JetBlue Tech Ventures, IATA, LATAM Airlines, Lufthansa Innovation Hub, Panasonic Avionics, Pittsburgh International Airport, Swissport, Travelport, TUI Group, and Turkish Airlines. In terms of investments, we've had the opportunity to invest in six startups we truly believe will impact the travel industry.

This may seem like a phenomenal amount of progress over the last year and a half, but the striking parallel we draw internally is to our own Insurance Vertical. Slightly younger in their efforts, this vertical has accelerated 20 less startups through their program. However, they boast more than 40 corporate partners including some of the largest carriers, brokers and reinsurers in the industry. Clearly, the insurance sector recognizes the potential disruption in its sector and has become very proactive in identifying disruptive technologies to help adapt to the changing environment.

Admittedly, I oversee 11 of these industry-specific programs, and as a result I have a bird's-eye view, but from my perspective the insurance and travel industries do differ in many ways: i.e. mission critical tasks, maintaining ground and air operational logistics, managing hard assets, and perhaps most importantly profit margins. However, I can't help but draw a comparison between the standard practice of putting Band-Aids on mortal wounds and cultural resistance to not just innovation but even modernization.

From the conversations I've had with not only people from the aviation industry but others, airlines recognize this problem but don't see a clear path to solving it. Illuminating an avenue towards finding that solution is the single thing I'm proudest of doing during my time with Plug and Play. By the nature of our business, we're able to place the major stakeholders from an industry together in one room to discuss truly innovating the very nature of their business along the lines discussed by Nawal Taneja in this book.

One of the questions I'm mostly commonly asked by the people I meet is, "What tangible value does Plug and Play bring to their partners?" It's not hard for me to see, as I was the first believer. There is no other place in the world where you'll find the innovation teams and executives from Lufthansa, Gatwick Airport, and JetBlue working together to change the nature of the game. This is what we refer to as 'open innovation', an activity that is critical if the airline industry is to transform itself.

Plug and Play's Travel Team has a simple mission statement: Our goal is to speed up the rate of adoption across the travel industry by creating an ecosystem bringing established and influential corporations together with the world's best innovators. In the near term, incremental innovation needs to be proven, but in the long term we will find the true disruptors.

Silicon Valley, USA

Foreword

Peter Baumgartner

Chief Executive Officer
Etihad Airways

A good deal of the small talk I enjoy – and on occasion endure – is spent discussing the various merits of airline business models. From the incredibly lean Spirit, to the opulence of a private jet business, and every shade in between. The discourse in the airline industry over the last two decades has been dominated by the impact of low-cost airlines on legacy carriers. I think every airline CEO has some modelling work in their drawer which explores the various merits of launching a low-cost subsidiary.

And yet I increasingly believe that this debate, still comfortably the dominant ideological debate inside the airline industry, will be obsolete by the middle of the next decade.

To understand why, you have to go back to the reasons why low-cost airlines sprang onto the scene in the first place (and I appreciate that I am conveniently leaving out plenty of other major factors, for the purposes of brevity). With a very low-cost base they could serve – and in fact act as a major stimulator of – a price-sensitive group of customers who didn't value some of the layers of product 'forced' upon them by airlines. Those low-cost carriers stripped all that wasn't strictly necessary originally. They succeeded – as they still do – from the clarity of communication that brings. Flights were a commodity. Websites and GDSs were unable to convey the better products available, even if a customer might have valued the additional features 'full service' provided. Therefore 'single product, single purpose' airlines thrived.

What began to happen next was more interesting. Low-cost airlines realised that they were attracting more than just price-sensitive leisure travelers; business flyers were choosing them too. They understood that the increased yields possible from these travelers warranted some additional cost. They retimed some flights to appeal to them in order to grow that base. They added some additional features. Some were free, some were charged for. We even saw low-cost airlines invest in loyalty programmes, often held up as a typical unnecessary expense offered by flag carriers.

At this point we begin to see the impact of this decade's dominant force: the disrupting force of technology to allow the industry to sell to two different customers on the same flight quite different experiences.

There are three primary components at play here. Firstly, the increased communication capability of booking engines, allowing airline customers (or agents) to see what they are buying. Natural technological progress has been accelerated in recent years by the standardization efforts of IATA and their New Distribution Capability (NDC) initiatives. These improvements increasingly allow a flyer to weigh the features of the airline against the price charged, and then in turn against other airlines – a trend that has increased with the introduction of more sophisticated OTAs and aggregators. Crucially this has another related impact: Customers are also able to see what they are not going to receive in their ticket price and are able to purchase additional ancillary features to suit their needs during the journey.

The second major factor is the increased ability to recognize a customer and serve them a different product proposition. That is perhaps most easily achieved at check-in, and most challenging onboard the aircraft. But there are many in the industry doing this with increasing levels of success. Of course, the low-cost carriers' FFP investments have more to do with securing customer data for this purpose than they do any old-fashioned ideal of 'buying loyalty'.

Thirdly, and least well understood, has been the increasing sophistication of airline merchandising capabilities. This 'mid layer' between our core systems and the channels is, I believe, the reason I will be having far fewer conversations about airline categorization in five years' time.

This third element solves a central conundrum, perhaps best explained by relaying a discussion I had with an economist friend. He explained to me his biggest concern with our industry. At the time, most full-service airlines offered three products; Economy, Business and First Class. He viewed this as utterly inefficient. My friend explained that there must be a million different customer segments, each demanding something slightly different. Perhaps only a handful of passengers genuinely wanted to pay for exactly what we full-service airlines were offering. Those who wanted less than our product proposition were the segments we were wasting money on. Those who demanded more than our core 'cabin' proposition would have been happy to pay more. In both cases there would be a relatively high chance of customers moving to a rival airline if that airline had a product more closely aligned with their demands. In most industries, my friend explained, there would be many, many product options available. Very few companies would limit themselves to three.

Like most airline professionals, I had plenty of answers for him. Most involved explaining the complexity of trying to do anything else and the manpower required to maintain anything other than a three-cabin proposition, both in creating the offer and delivering it.

So what has changed? Technology has dramatically altered my view. Merchandising technology now enables us to build repeatable rules to serve different customers in a variety of ways based on thousands of variables. And big-data solutions are now very affordable, allowing us to collect and store customer information and to use it in real time, at the point of initial transaction or whenever it is relevant throughout the journey.

Now, if my small talk had gotten this far it normally means that I'm not speaking to someone running an ecommerce site. Or for that matter anyone who lives in Silicon Valley. To speak openly, it is just far too embarrassing to define such a future with someone who would probably believe my five-year vision to be seriously lacking in ambition.

But we all know that what I am describing is hard to deliver in our industry. NDC hasn't moved as quickly as we would like, meaning we are still often limited by the least adaptable platform in our often complex IT architectures. Even the most nimble airlines need willing partners in other parts of the industry ecosystem, and there are always vested interests. Frankly, a major barrier can be navigating traditionalists inside your own company when it's clear that the organization must evolve to use the available technology.

For now, let's leave aside the challenges and engage in a little creativity. How flexible could a single airline's proposition actually be? Is it feasible that we might have five variants of economy seat on the same aircraft, from the minimum safety requirement to something exceeding a premium economy product (if my network planning team members are reading this, let's leave the cost of fleet complexity for another day). Certainly five levels of baggage allowance don't frighten me. Variable IFE levels and the flexing of catering quality – from nothing to a premium option – are already well-tested by a variety of airlines. As you can begin to see, looking at individually varying product components offered little to concern us.

Which leads us to wonder, what else will constrain our future state? Service delivery will benefit from automation, making any impediment temporary. The booking channels will become vastly more sophisticated and rich – as they have in almost every other industry.

What's left? Again we are left to challenge our ability to pull all these disparate components together and work out how to sell them – what most of us call 'merchandising'. Difficult? Well, we once led the world in our ability to sell the core seat. No other industry managed inventory with more sophistication and with greater volumes of transactions. We took inventory management from the hotels, and we refined it to a level of complexity that was looked upon by other businesses as we ourselves glance enviously at the ecommerce sites today. We just lost our way when our margins became so slim that we had to disinvest from innovation.

But I am hopeful our industry will solve this. There is clearly sufficient motivation. Over the course of Nawal's last ten books, he has plotted dramatic changes in this industry. This latest text describes even greater singularity of purpose among my peers to ensure that airlines embrace the opportunities offered by digital disruption. That upside is again best explained by my economist friend. Whoever uses digital capabilities to solve the industry's obvious (to him at least) mismatch of supply and demand will benefit from efficiency savings and revenue upticks, while in turn improving customer satisfaction.

That will mean lining up customer needs and an airline's customer proposition with incredible precision. It will mean every single customer onboard an aircraft receiving subtly different propositions. If that's the case, I'm confident that my small talk will shift from discussing which airline model is right for this or that airline to passionate debate over who is delivering all the business models in a single airline.

Abu Dhabi, UAE

Foreword

Stephen Brobst

Chief Technology Officer
Teradata Corporation

In Silicon Valley we say that in the 21st century there are only three possible choices for an enterprise: (1) there are those that are already data companies, (2) there are those that will soon become data companies, and (3) there are those that will cease to be relevant in the marketplace. In the digitally transformed economy, organizations must learn to harness data to create new customer experiences and to establish new models of doing business. Being digital is no longer an option – it is an imperative. In his work *21st Century Airlines: Connecting the Dots*, Nawal Taneja creates a framework for the next generation of mobility by foreseeing evolution in the mindset, technologies, strategies, and workforce for digitally enlightened enterprises.

In this new world, we must capture data in real time and act upon it immediately with the intelligence born from deep learning algorithms. In the world of advanced analytics, we envision the concept of *The Sentient Enterprise* as a means of exploiting the digital tsunami as described by Taneja in this book. The core foundation of *The Sentient Enterprise* is self-awareness through capture and exploitation of data assets. There are five stages of maturity typical in the realization of *The Sentient Enterprise*. The first stage is one of agility. Disruption in the digital economy is not an event, but rather a state of continuous change. Staying competitive means continuous invention and re-invention of business models and algorithms for exploiting data assets. Annual strategic planning cycles and long delivery times for creation of new business capabilities will not be successful in the digital economy.

The second stage of maturity toward realization of *The Sentient Enterprise* is capture and exploitation of behavioral data. These are the interactions below the level of transactions. Not just that a flight ticket was purchased, but every click and every search that led up to the purchase of the flight ticket. Every interaction prior, during, and after the travel experience must be captured. Monitoring of social media and other sources of sentiment throughout the travel experience is critical. Behavioral data also includes use of IoT (Internet of Things) sensor data to track passengers, luggage, and assets through the travel experience. Behavioral data is not just about consumers, but also about employees and machines.

In the third stage of evolution, we use data to facilitate collaboration in the ecosystem for delivering products and services. Data is shared throughout the enterprise and even beyond traditional enterprise boundaries, to consumers and partners. A sign of advanced maturity in collaboration is when there are more users of data outside the enterprise than within the enterprise. The enterprise itself contributes to and makes use of open-source collaboration models to create and share advanced analytic capabilities such as machine learning algorithms. We also make use of crowdsourcing to capture and catalog organizational knowledge as well as to implement advanced analytics.

Creation of analytic application platforms represents the fourth milestone in the journey toward *The Sentient Enterprise*. While data is at the core of the digital enterprise, its value cannot be monetized without the creation of platforms for delivering the value of the data assets within the enterprise. The analytic application platforms must be able to "listen" to data in real time and translate events within the enterprise into actions which optimize customer experience and the use of corporate assets (human and machine). The analytic application platform must be designed with continuous enhancement and deployment in mind (with alignment to the agile enterprise ideas described earlier).

Automation of decision-making capability is the final stage in maturing toward *The Sentient Enterprise*. The use of data and self-learning algorithms to make decisions provides better, faster, cheaper, and more consistent decision making than what is possible with human decision makers. The role of humans is in the development and deployment of the advanced learning algorithms, but not in the front-line operational decision making within the organization. Only when decisions are demanded outside of the trained experience of the automated decision-making algorithms will humans be asked to intervene to provide operational intelligence to the enterprise.

The notion of platforms with autonomous decision-making capability will be critical in the digital economy. In the future, consumers will make use of individual decision-support platforms to interface with the providers of goods and services. Doc Searls at the Berkman Center for Internet & Society at Harvard University envisages a concept wherein every consumer will have a personal VRM (Vendor Relationship Management) platform that will interface with the CRM (Customer Relationship Management) platforms of commercial enterprises. Traditional models of commerce will be transformed as decision-making platforms disintermediate traditional buying and selling interfaces. It is likely that commerce will be turned upside down as consumers take more control of the experience through use of auctioning from the buyer's perspective. Rather than piecemeal assembly of travel components, the consumer will (via the individualized decision-support platform) define the desired experience, and then "packages" of products and services will be acquired in an automated reverse auction. The individualized decision-support platform will evaluate proposed options – vendor CRM solutions using past experience (encoded as data), defined preferences (encoded as data), reviews (encoded as data), and so on (encoded as data) – to make informed choices.

The winners in the digital economy will not be the enterprises that manufacture or own physical assets; rather they will be *The Sentient Enterprises* that have accumulated data assets and built the application platforms with embedded algorithms for intelligent decision making aligned to breakthrough customer experiences and new business models. Those that focus on the acquisition of more aircraft will lose out to those that focus on developing platforms and analytic algorithms for scheduling, maintenance, and matching of consumer desires to optimally make use of these assets. Even the business model for aircraft manufacturers will evolve – from the old model of selling large assets to charging for outcome-based services in which analytic algorithms are continuously enhanced to improve service levels and profitability extracted from manufactured assets.

The airline industry is certainly not alone in its disruption from the digital forces of the 21st century. Every industry is being re-invented as you read this. For example, in the banking industry, the FinTech revolution is likely to be as destructive as the financial crisis itself was just ten years ago. Near-term digital disruption in banking is occurring as platforms using advanced analytic capabilities replace traditional channels for delivering financial services. The FinTechs are re-inventing the consumer banking experience with new platforms for social lending, mobile payment services, robo-advising, data monetization, and so on. Longer-term disruption will take place as core banking systems are transformed by blockchain technology. The use of blockchain technology will allow completely digitized contracts that will eventually make obsolete the trusted intermediary role that banks now leverage at the center of their business model. Outside of financial services, leaders in manufacturing are re-inventing themselves to create intelligent devices ranging from smart cars to smart toothbrushes that are capable of capturing data and monetizing the data via analytic algorithms. No industry will be untouched. My final thought for you is a piece of advice from my favorite race-car driver of all time – Mario Andretti once said: "If everything seems under control, you are just not going fast enough!" Enjoy the ride.

Silicon Valley, USA

Foreword

Andrés Conesa

Chief Executive Officer
Aeroméxico

Through my career in the industry and running Aeroméxico for the last 12 years, I've learned that while staying ahead of the curve and building flexibility should be a core objective of every successful business, it's not in any industry more relevant than in the airline industry. Due to its complexity, heavy regulation and global nature, airlines are constantly forced into adapting to the new environment (which keeps changing at an incrementally faster pace).

The first and most important lesson that the industry taught me was to never underestimate the importance of flexibility and to consistently encourage my team and everyone in the organization to pursue innovation and think outside the box. Using my own history, I came to this fascinating world of aviation by great fortune over 13 years ago: My original task was to help the Mexican government sell CINTRA, the controlling company that grouped two of Mexico's most important airlines, Mexicana and Aeroméxico, and I was appointed CEO of the latter. Some months after my appointment, in 2008, the industry was hit by the financial crisis, a significant currency depreciation, an increase in oil prices and, particularly for the Mexican market, a public health emergency: a perfect storm. The Mexican industry went through a severe crisis, that led to the bankruptcy of 11 airlines and a complete overhaul of the ones that remained.

A similar but global trial is in sight: an increasing penetration of technology in our lives, the rise of personalization, the ubiquitous availability of information and intricate networks of people connecting in seconds an idea to the world are shaping a challenge never before seen for the industry and pose a key test to the big players. While the days of merely transporting passengers are far gone, we witness a change in which even satisfying the demands of our customers is no longer enough; our "traditional practices" and "standard processes" are being called into question more than ever, and to ensure we stay ahead we need to go beyond.

Customers have evolved faster than the industry, and, thus, we need to ensure our companies are fit and adaptable enough to embrace the shift ahead and find the best and most efficient ways to respond.

Using technology and data as our best tools to predict and respond to changes in behavior, consumption patterns and satisfaction drivers for our customers, we need to provide the right training to the hands that use them and empower them to find new ways to stay ahead of the curve. While old processes can easily be optimized with innovative products such as booking robots, luggage tracking, enhanced security processes and optimized in-flight purchases, the market will keep demanding personalization, on-time response and curated products at a rate that the industry might struggle to keep up with.

In this book, Nawal Taneja sheds light on the most impending changes the industry is going to face and provides a detailed map on how organizational structures, ideas and barriers will need to be adjusted from the inside for each airline to be able to fulfill the promise it makes to its passengers.

At Aeroméxico, we feel excited about the current trends in the industry, and every day we find new ways to connect the dots, seeking to shape the best end-to-end experience for our passengers and in turn continue to be the line that unites Mexicans and Mexico to the world.

Mexico City, Mexico

Foreword

Barbara Dalibard

Chief Executive Officer
SITA

The 21st century could not be a more exciting time to be at the intersection of air transport and information technology. Technology has driven transformation in air transport many times before, and it will continue to disrupt the industry in the future. As we see in this book by Nawal Taneja, technology has an all-important role to play in 'connecting the dots' across our industry – a task on which SITA has focused ever since its inception over 60 years ago, in providing information and communication technologies that have helped to transform the way the industry works. Indeed, the company was founded by the industry to share data communications among airlines, making technology and innovation available for the benefit of the entire global community, while reducing the total cost of ownership.

That in itself was a transformative application of technology for the air-transport industry. We have seen many examples since. One obvious example is e-commerce. In 1995, SITA's software partner company made e-commerce history with the launch of the first website able to complete travel bookings and take payments in real time via the internet. Called 'Cyberseat' by British Midland, it was described as "the world's first Internet system that will allow you to book seats and pay with a valid credit card online".

Again in the 1990s, we saw the arrival of another technology set to shape air transport of the future when, in 1996, the world's first electronic visa system went live in preparation for the Sydney Olympic Games, leading to SITA's position today as the world's foremost border-management provider. Safety and security have always topped the air-transport industry's agenda, and developments in advanced passenger information systems, as well as the evolution of biometrics, have been instrumental in joining up the dots at the border.

In 2008, SITA became the only IT provider to gain US government approval to transmit passenger data at check-in. It made a huge difference for airlines flying internationally from, over, or to the US, as prior to aircraft departure they could meet requirements to submit passport and travel-document information for passengers and crew. Now we see further advances in border management, with the widespread adoption of automated border and passport control gates and kiosks, making use of increasing biometric capabilities. Ongoing developments are meeting ever-increasing border requirements of governments and airlines, at the same time limiting costs for the air-transport industry.

At the airport, we have witnessed increasing improvements in passenger processing, baggage management and airport operations – again due to the application of IT. Owing to increasingly 'intelligent' airports, we are getting even better at exploiting collaborative decision-support systems. SITA's own experience embraces Integrated Airport Operations Control Centers as well as mobile resource management, with the empowerment of mobile workforces. This is a perfect example of 'connecting the dots', since it relies on connectivity, data availability and analysis to get clear views of operations, while enabling workforces to operate with unity and cohesion, becoming better informed and able to act responsively and efficiently. We have worked with many airline and airport customers around the world to pioneer proximity sensing technologies – including low-cost transmitting devices (beacons) to connect passengers and 'things', as a building block towards the IoT. This is benefitting workforces as well as giving insights into passenger flow and behaviour at the airport.

Another example is the work with airlines around the world of our in-flight connectivity and connected-aircraft business, SITAONAIR, to unlock vast amounts of critical data from the cockpit, cabin and aircraft engines, to enhance performance and service. This makes the aircraft another node on the network of the IT department. Taking a 'nose-to-tail' focus considers the big and long-term picture that eliminates silos among various airline departments and removes platform-dependency through a coherent IT and communications platform integrating aircraft and ground systems. This again is truly joined-up thinking, allowing the airlines to remain in control of their operations and associated critical IT components, giving passengers seamless connectivity on the ground and in-flight, helping cabin crew to improve passenger service onboard, furnishing real-time access to flight information and documentation in the cockpit, and enabling aircraft data management in-flight and on the ground.

The pace of change

In all of these areas and more, SITA has proven, and continues to prove, that technology has the transformative power to connect dots – linking systems, people, stakeholders and aircraft. But there are more major technology and trends shifts to come. And the pace of change is now faster than ever. Aviation should experience a near doubling of passenger demand over the next 20 years – rising to 7.2 billion passengers traveling in 2035 (IATA). We are now seeing ever-greater expectations around the passenger journey, increasing pressure for faster and more streamlined operations capable of handling more capacity, new business models and ways of working, and the building and planning of hundreds of new airports.

Technology itself is forcing the pace too. Every day we hear of tech advances – from data analytics, machine learning and artificial intelligence (AI), to blockchain, wearables, virtual reality, drones, robots, and more. According to the World Economic Forum, we are witnessing the 'fourth industrial revolution'. This refers not just to *one* ground-breaking technology profoundly disrupting the status quo, but to *multiple* trends and technologies – often inter-related, and each colliding and converging with the other. Alone they bring great promise. Together, they present formidable disruptive potential. The WEF refers to technology that solves one problem, such as GPS and mobile, now combining to unlock new sources of value.

The trends are reinforced by higher spending on air-transport IT. SITA's latest IT Trends Surveys (www.sita.aero/ittrendshub) find that for 2017, 52% of airline CIOs predict increasing operating spending and 57% expect rising capital spending. In the meantime, over the last three years airport CIOs have seen their budgets increase on average by more than 8%. These figures correspond closely to leading analysts' forecasts of growth in air-transportation spending on IT and communications.

A connected community

These technologies present 21st century aviation with huge opportunities. The technologies connecting our consumer world are also connecting the world of airlines and the wider air-transport community. As we see in this book, the industry has no choice but to turn to technology to 'connect the dots' across organizations and operations within the travel chain, making air-transport practices, processes and each step of the journey more intelligent and responsive. Whereas technology was once sought for marginal gains in efficiency and service, today it is seen as imperative to changing the economic and operational fundamentals of the air-transport industry.

SITA's Airline, Airport and Passenger IT Trends Surveys show that industry IT investment is laying the groundwork for a more connected community. The vast majority of airlines cite significant spending on business intelligence and cloud computing platforms to make greater use of data, while over two-thirds are channelling their money into the Internet of Things (IoT). Widespread IoT adoption is some way off, but the technology is gaining traction in some areas, such as fuel and engine monitoring, where better information is helping airlines optimize flight operations. As the community moves towards greater connectivity – including high bandwidth wireless and mobile communications – we will see growing investment in other IoT areas to manage the aircraft environment, manage equipment, track crew status and more.

As investment plans are made, SITA's remit as an air-transport provider and innovator is to help the community to manage and embrace new technologies, trends and innovations – to deploy the right technologies in the right way to deliver benefits. This is expressed through our purpose of 'transforming air travel through technology, for airlines, at airports, on aircraft and at the border'.

'Digitization'

One of the biggest disruptions that will shape air transport's connected community is a very 21st-century-sounding phenomenon called 'digitalization', or, more concisely, 'digitization'. In short, this refers to air-transport organizations establishing digital platforms on which to build their operations, develop the passenger experience and determine the journeys of the future. SITA is deeply involved in this industry transformation, as airline and airport customers embark on digital infrastructure programs that will underpin their operations and the services of tomorrow.

Data, 'the new oil'

Digitization goes hand in hand with data. Of course, the air-transport industry has been enabled by data since its earliest days. Data has always been its lifeblood. But the technology-driven innovations of the last 20 years have now extended the reach of data to all aspects of the industry, especially the interaction with passengers throughout their journey. At the same time, existing industry processes are being greatly optimized, if not completely transformed, by the impact of data-related technologies. The proliferation of technologies such as beacons, Near Field Communications (NFC), wearables and smart devices provide the means to both collect data and share it with stakeholders.

In this book we hear about the criticality of platforms for acquiring and managing data, the importance of behavioural information and journey analytics, the need to exploit the industry's transactional data, and the opportunity to use data to increase our knowledge of customers. It is clear that data – ever increasing volumes of it – sits at the heart of the industry's operations, be it transactional, operational or even social.

Data has the potential to add ever more value at every touchpoint and at every interchange between airlines and their passengers, as well as airports, ground handlers, border agencies and other stakeholders who make the journey happen. Industry operations – including up-to-the-second intelligence and analysis to smoothen passenger flow, track bags, clear borders and speed up aircraft turnaround – will increasingly depend in their entirety on big data and analytics capabilities. This will all be available across the IoT, both on the ground and in the air. In this new digitized environment, 'data is becoming the new oil'. This will be nothing short of a revolution for the air-transport industry.

Sharing and bridging

As a community provider, SITA 'naturally' has access to large volumes of air-transport data – along with experience in unlocking and handling huge 'lakes' of data through Application Programming Interfaces (APIs), as well as airline, airport and government systems. In fact, today we bridge as much as 60% of the air-transport industry's data exchange among airlines, airports, aircraft and border agencies. This is a long-standing pedigree – part of SITA's DNA since its inception. Commencing with teletype messaging, SITA has responded to the need for, and in many ways led the development of, data sharing and processing for the air-transport industry. The range of data streams transmitted by SITA and the data assets it maintains is broad, covering much of the current scope of the industry, from messaging for air-transport stakeholders, airport management and airport operational databases, to baggage and border management and much more.

Having always been in the data business, SITA is a vital component in the sharing and exploitation of that data. Our long-time role of sharing and bridging among organizations within the air-transport community has become more critical than ever. This is why, with access to data from across the industry's operations, we are further exploring advances in big data and data mining, business intelligence and analytics, predictive disruption management, baggage processing technology, the IoT, the cloud, blockchain and more. I am particularly excited about the IoT. In the rail business, for example, where I worked for many years, it became clear that the IoT has the potential to enhance everything from fleet management and customer relationships, to operations at the station. It is the same in air transport. The IoT will revolutionize the airport, the fleet, the cockpit and cabin – everything.

It is SITA's responsibility to ensure the air-transport community benefits by encouraging and enabling data sharing. This includes bridging divides and improving processes within and among industry players, as well as exploiting data to offer new services. Ultimately, this will help us to do things better as an industry, deepening our understanding of the interconnections and operations in air transport, while enabling change for low-cost, hybrid and full-service carriers, as well as for airports of all sizes. We articulate our role in this revolution through our vision to 'make air travel easy, every step of the way'.

Use cases

There are many examples of how new and emerging technologies will make travel easier, but let me cite just three. First, I can see great value in deploying an integrated industry-wide platform for collecting, storing and analyzing data to ensure a single version of the truth, so that when passengers glance at their mobiles for the latest flight or gate details there is complete consistency in status reporting between, say, airline check-in agents and airport Flight Information Display systems or apps. Such a platform would create new value by fully exploiting and maximizing the potential of the industry's data through aggregation, analytics and collaboration – as an enabler for 'intelligence-based action' using business and operational intelligence that exploits the emerging capabilities of the IoT, AI and ambient computing.

Second, there is also potential for a common industry AI platform. Though AI remains in its infancy, its promise is huge. AI offers the ability to intelligently and rapidly leverage data to improve decision making, along with the use of robotics as the means to automate physical actions based on those decisions. An AI platform calling on multiple data sources from across the journey, as well as external providers and enterprise data systems, offers the possibility of feeding all stakeholders' systems – whether airline, airport operator, ground handler, Air Traffic Control or border agency. It is easy to imagine the impact such an AI platform might have on the evolution of predictive air-transport systems, passenger-services robots, AI and smart machines in airport operations, aerial-drone inspection and many other likely use cases. SITA has already taken exploratory steps in the areas of an air-transport community disruption-warning system, a baggage robot (called Leo) and aircraft-drone inspection.

My third and final example is identity management and the exploitation of blockchain, which is becoming known as Distributed Ledger Technology (DLT). Through enforcing trust digitally, this nascent technology promises huge advances in making air travel easy. SITA is evaluating different use cases within air transport, one of the most revolutionary being to make blockchain the basis for virtual or digital passports in the form of a single secure token on mobile and wearable devices.

The combination of blockchain, mobile technologies and biometrics offers unique possibilities that simply have not existed before. This could reduce complexity, cost and liability around document checks during the passenger journey – as travelers need only be identified once at the start of the journey, be it at an airport kiosk or the bag-drop. It is another perfect example of SITA's ability to share and bridge across players responsible for the passenger journey. Such an approach would eliminate the need for multiple travel documents, without passengers having to divulge their personal data. Already trials are underway at major airports as part of SITA's Single Travel Token program.

These three examples alone illustrate what I said at the outset: that this really is an exciting time to be at the intersection of air transport and IT. As we in air transport become increasingly connected and networked, and as we embrace the new and emerging technologies that are becoming available to us, then greater data sharing from a business and technological standpoint – along with the ability to exploit that data effectively – will inevitably make 'connecting the dots in our industry' a reality.

Geneva, Switzerland

Foreword

Michael Garvens

Chairman of the Management Board
Flughafen Köln Bonn GmbH

The future development of aviation throughout the world will primarily be determined by a mega-trend: digitization. The networking of all spheres of life plus technical advancement is radically changing the mobility of people on the ground and in the air – and all this at a breathtaking speed. It wasn't so long ago that drones or flying cars were simply elements of fiction in books and films. The manufacturers are still somewhat "outlandish". However, so much meticulous work is being carried out on future technologies in the high-tech labs of the digital giants like Google and Uber. This does not mean that commercial aircraft will disappear from our skies – quite the contrary. Worldwide aviation will increase. Nevertheless, we have to think about mobility in a whole new dimension.

Aviation is one of the most important sources of innovation, and it has always been a driving force behind change. Change is our constant companion, and it is gathering speed all the time. The digitization and mobilization of our society plus the globalization of transport operations have triggered a dynamic which, despite all the technological advancement, we have never seen before. And this is just the beginning of the digital revolution.

We will soon see how seamless travel will be raised to a whole new level, how the way from A to B will be offered with various means of transport in different variants by just one single integrator. And perhaps we may even witness mobility becoming free of charge for the individual because a third party finances this mobility in return for access to customer data and new advertising markets.

Similarly, transportation of goods will also be revolutionized. Amazon just recently bought an airport – this shows clearly where things are heading. Starting off as an online dealer, the enterprise is becoming more and more an independent integrator – as mentioned by Professor Taneja in Chapter 6 of this book – which can organize the entire supply chain itself. At the end of the supply chain, the shipments are delivered to the customer fully automatically via drone, or collected. Technically speaking, with smaller parcels this is already no problem.

There will also have to be dramatic changes at our airports. On short- and medium-haul routes, a lot of the time we gain in the air is then lost on the ground. So we have to rethink the concept of the airport; the keyword here is 'Airport 4.0'. At Cologne/Bonn we aspire to be up-front. Why can't you check in your baggage via an electronic bag tag from home or from the car park? Why not standardize the shape and size of luggage so that it can be loaded automatically – perhaps with a price discount? Why can't we speed up the security check process using "trusted traveller concepts" – or iris recognition? Why do we not install Bluetooth transmitters in the terminals so that the passenger can be individually guided through the airport live via an app?

The key to all this is customer data. The value of this is immense. Facebook paid $19 billion for WhatsApp. At that point, WhatsApp had 450 million users. The superstars of the Internet economy are all frontrunners among the top ten international business enterprises – including Apple, Google and Facebook. Currently it looks as if the asset owners are more likely to be among the losers. The paradox is that they are the ones who actually make it possible for the countless online portals to be successful. Airbnb does not own one single hotel, and Uber does not own one single taxi. And yet the value of this transport service is estimated at $70 billion. That might seem crazy, but it does say a lot about the digital future speculations.

An airplane is now a symbol of prosperity for many people and no longer just a status symbol for the privileged. In Europe a major contribution to this has been made by the low-cost carriers. The launch of low-cost flights was a real game changer; it made flying affordable for many people. In the meantime this business model has become standard in European aviation traffic. And the concept will also revolutionize the long-haul market. Cologne/Bonn, with Eurowings, is the first airport in Germany to have such an offer. This is just the beginning of low-cost, long-haul flights, but I am convinced that it will be a huge success story.

With digitization, fiction and reality have come closer together, and quite often it is difficult to tell the difference. Many things which, from today's point of view, would only seem conceivable in the distant future can actually be reality tomorrow. We will witness how in urban areas means of transport will be even more closely networked and will communicate with one another in real time. Autonomous driving will become a matter of course, we will see how our transport infrastructure becomes smart and all systems are linked together. This is also the solution to meeting urban challenges, in particular in the urban conurbations where ever more people have mobility requirements.

It would seem that in Germany we are a bit unhurried and painstaking in this respect. Whereas the huge VW corporation is investing 1 billion euros in digitization, little Uber spends some 10 billion. According to a survey carried out by the industrial association Bitkom, 80 percent of business enterprises in Germany believe that without a definite digitization strategy they will not be able to survive. At least three out of four enterprises already have such a strategy. This shows that the idea of digitization has hit home in all businesses – also in the aviation business.

To meet the challenges of digitization, we need smart products and a high-performance infrastructure which will perfectly meet the needs of both passengers and airlines. At the same time, airports and airplanes still have a tremendous attraction for many people. And this, despite every innovative spirit, should not be forgotten. Digitization can speed up processes in terminals and make the time between arriving at the airport and take-off as pleasant as possible. It can also make it possible for passengers to "shop" in-flight and have their purchases delivered to their homes. However, at the end of the day no app can replace the fascination of flying.

Cologne, Germany

Foreword

Rob Gurney
Chief Executive Officer
oneworld

Aviation has arguably had the single biggest impact in shaping today's world, from geo-politics to social behavior.

Transportation is the conduit that connects communities, cultures and trading partners, be they nations or businesses. Aviation helps create experiences for people that just a few years ago simply were not available.

The real cost of air travel will continue to fall, offering even more opportunities for people to travel, with demand roughly doubling that of the economic growth rates. The airlines that have the vision and agility to seize these opportunities will be among the leaders.

But it is not just about transportation. Airlines will continue to strive to connect their brands with customers both in a pragmatic and an emotional sense. This is essential as competition for consumer head space intensifies with digital disruption. Two decades ago, the internet was the disruptor. Tomorrow, will the disruptor be artificial intelligence, virtual reality or something we are not even aware of today?

Just think for a moment about the impact the companies that have grasped the digital revolution have had on our everyday lives. Google, Amazon, Uber, Airbnb, and other companies have made buying and selling and comparing consumer offerings as easy as clicking a button. And changed the ways customers interact with the marketplace. This point is discussed by Nawal Taneja throughout this book.

Airlines are heavily vested in developing customer aspirations and fulfilling purchase requirements. After the purchase is complete, airlines are uniquely positioned to support customers as they prepare for travel and as they embrace the travel experience through the airport and onto the aircraft. Throughout their journeys and after, customers share their experiences through social media. The customer becomes the airline's advocate – or not.

Against this background, many airlines have a great deal of catching up to do.

The companies that extend their brand relationship, presence, scale and data to diversify revenue streams into both adjacent and non-adjacent businesses will be the most successful.

Those that fail to grasp this transformation will face being consigned to history.

New York, NY

Foreword

Peter Harbison

Executive Chairman
CAPA – Centre for Aviation

Incrementalism vs disruption: the future, in brief

The structure of senior executive management generally is that it is contractually driven, inspired by bonuses for short-term share price increases, where cost reduction is usually a significant dynamic. The very short-termism of that profile tends towards encouraging incrementalism, where conventional measurement tools can be applied and where any risk of seriously rocking the boat is suppressed.

Management in aviation has some of these characteristics, but with many overlays. The industry is heavily regulated, from both a safety and a commercial perspective. Hence the highly intrusive role of government effectively encourages existing airlines to seek to manipulate competition in their favour, either to sanction anticompetitive activities "in the public interest" or to prevent entry by others.

The combination of these generic and specific factors means that there are many barriers, managerial (internal) and external (such as government intervention) to innovative thinking. Self-disruption is a no-no. It is high-risk, and its results tend not to show until the current executive's contract has been terminated – probably for not reaching target share-price goals.

Even where there is a willingness to confront the future, the mere nature of the airline is of a series of silos of activity, with only modest communication and – more importantly – decision-making capability. Where, for example, the changing retail features in the marketplace demand large expenditures on IT solutions, it is still all too common to confine the response to being one for the IT silo (typically a cost centre).

As Dr Taneja's thesis outlines, incrementalism is one outcome. It is essential – for example, in ensuring cost levels on like-for-like operations are constantly reduced, in an intensely competitive industry. But that focus does much to inhibit longer-term, strategic change.

Many of the tools available to management in other industries are not available either. The fundamental limits on cross-border ownership greatly constrain logical moves to combine with other companies in what is after all one of the most international of industries.

Meanwhile, on the wider market a company such as Amazon spent over $3 billion on engineering over the past three years. Apple, Google, Facebook, Airbnb and many others are also investing heavily in defining traveller profiles and using massive resources to mine the data in ways that are increasingly threatening to the airlines' "ownership" of their customers.

But, as Dr Taneja highlights, the tsunami is coming. Many, if not most, of the fundamentals of other industries – from photography to media, to telecoms, to music, retail generally (think Amazon), taxis, accommodation, payments – were swept away in the flood long ago. Yet aviation lies anchored in shallower waters. There is no other industry that comes close to having so many septuagenarian brands still coursing the skies.

Now, the two fundamentals of the airline industry are about to be uprooted – in tandem, as they are interrelated and, in some sense, feed off each other:

- **The regulation of flying.** Ownership and control rules (O&C) are being overturned steadily by a combination of "cross-border joint ventures", cross-border equity investments, and the rising influence of the new markets of China and Asia-Pacific. Removal of O&C transforms the bilateral market access system that has lasted 70 years.
- **The selling of tickets.** New (non-aviation) retailers, armed with highly specific data and the skills to exploit it, are about to take on the role of selling end-to-end travel, of which the airline segment is only one part. Meanwhile airlines are confined to (usually) poorly exploited data about (only) their own customers, and to infighting with intermediaries: GDS companies, OTAs, metasearch, and others.

The result: a vastly different industry, one where airlines become mere pipelines, and where retailers become the platforms for sales.

By addressing the heart of these issues, Dr Taneja is doing a great service and continuing a distinguished line of academic and commercial exploration.

Sydney, Australia

Foreword

Jeffrey G. Katz
Chief Executive Officer
Journera

Management guru Peter Drucker is credited with saying, "What gets measured, gets managed." I started my airline career at American Airlines more than 35 years ago and worked there when it was run by legendary airline CEO Robert Crandall, who believed firmly in that saying. And when you measure, you generate data. Later, I became president of Sabre Travel Information Network – the distribution side of Sabre – when it was still owned by American and operated the largest privately owned computer system in the world. At American, I learned the value of automation and the power of data.

Beginning in the 1970s, the airline industry built a system of distribution based on private networks and enormous mainframe computer power that presaged the internet. Twenty years before Google was founded in 1998, a travel agent sitting nearly anywhere could use a desktop computer to determine the airlines, schedules, flights and fares on a given date for flights between any two cities in the world. This kind of online shopping is commonplace today, but it was revolutionary at the time.

Then the pace of change increased, with server-based computing gradually replacing mainframes. But the low-margin airline industry failed to generate the capital needed to replace the legacy infrastructure, and the technology leadership in sales distribution fell behind the wave of new internet-based merchandising by companies like Amazon. For the decade starting with the millennium, airlines found themselves selling a commodity through an aging technology infrastructure that reinforced the lack of product differentiation.

Next came the focus on direct distribution. The travel industry was an early adopter of internet distribution, with two online travel agencies launched in mid-1996 by Microsoft (Expedia) and Sabre (Travelocity). The industry's successful conversion to global electronic ticketing made the internet an ideal channel for travel sales. Shopping for travel requires an organized way to search and select among multiple alternatives for air, hotel and other services, with no need for the physical delivery of anything. The low cost of operating a website allowed the individual travel industry participants to develop their own online distribution channels, and they began encouraging travelers to buy directly from the source. With control over their own distribution channel, airlines and hotels began to offer more product differentiation.

The emphasis on direct distribution forged relationships between the providers of travel services and their customers – relationships less dependent on traditional travel agent intermediaries. At the same time, the number of channels consumers could use to reach the travel industry increased, working against the development of supplier-direct relationships. The strength of online travel agencies like Expedia and Priceline.com has grown through consolidation and sheer size. Savvy travel agents fought back, focusing on business travelers and diversifying the services they could provide beyond the simple shopping and booking to maintain relationships with corporate travelers. Today, the development of new information channels such as metasearch site Kayak, or TripAdvisor, which started as a travel review site and has recently added booking, and the entry of giants such as Google and Facebook challenge the travel industry's efforts to preserve and expand direct customer relationships. At the same time, air travel has learned from the hotel industry, and now both merchandize a differentiated product. Airlines unbundled traditional components of air transportation such as seat assignment and checked baggage, and they invested in additional amenities such as sections of 'economy-plus' seating, in-flight entertainment and onboard Wi-Fi.

These trends come together today in what promises to be an epic contest for the consumer. At one extreme, travel-service providers could become mere utilities with diluted brands, specializing in providing the physical services of transportation and hospitality, while completely reliant on intermediaries for sales, marketing and merchandizing because those entities have won the hearts and attention of consumers. At the other extreme, travel-industry players could claim ownership of their own product and service information and invest in innovative ways to reach customers with tailored, personalized offers of products and services that are highly correlated in content and timing to the preferences of the modern traveler. In any case, the fuel for the current contest is clear – it is data. "Data are to this century what oil was to the last one: a driver of growth and change" ("Fuel of the Future," *Economist*, May 6, 2017).

Over his many years in this industry, Professor Nawal Taneja has chronicled the trends in travel distribution summarized above in his many previous books. This volume, *21st Century Airlines: Connecting the Dots*, is perfectly timed as a guidebook to the current clash over data and how the use of data will shape the travel experience. There are two main elements of the data contest: the data you own, and the data you can get. The first gives you leverage if you can hold and mete it out sparingly on terms you set. The second, the data you can collect, gives an enormous advantage to companies that touch consumers in broad, daily ways.

Travel companies own essential information about their own products, services, schedules, routes, locations and prices. In the traditional economy, airlines and hotels pushed that data out for free in efforts to attract customers. In the data economy, that information has intrinsic value. A consumer wants to know and compare. Any independent party selling travel has to have access to travel-service providers' data to provide the shopping service, like the raw material inputs to a manufacturing process. Control of the flow of this data gives the service providers leverage in distribution channels from the supply side. As Professor Taneja discusses in this book, strategic partnerships employing multi-sided platforms that disseminate data pursuant to rules set by the owners of the data is one promising approach to establishing its value while gaining access to data from other sources. Together with Boston Consulting Group, I have co-founded a company named Journera using this model. Journera allows travel-service providers to make their data available to others on terms they set, and it facilitates data exchanges between the service providers – air, hotel and car – that are engaged for a traveler's journey so that each can better address that consumer's travel preferences.

On the other hand, companies like Google, Amazon and Facebook collect enormous volumes of data about individuals through multiple channels. And they have become expert at consolidating and analyzing it, giving them extraordinary insight into the demand side of travel consumers. They *know* the customer, can aggregate demand and tilt that demand in the direction of any chosen supplier or the highest bidder. The more these companies integrate into the daily life of consumers generally, the more likely they are to be the starting point for travel shopping and remain an intermediary between the service provider and the consumer.

How will this battle play out? Will the travel industry be able to control access to its supply-side data, or will economic pressures continue to compel them to grant access for free and pay the intermediaries for access to their aggregated demand? Will consumer knowledge and the demand-side advantages of the big internet players be eroded as travel-service providers find independent ways to harness and apply consumer data? The stakes are high, and the contest is in its early days. Professor Taneja's work offers a useful guide to the strategies and spoils at stake as the travel industry flies into the new data economy.

Chicago, IL USA

Foreword

Sean Menke

President & CEO
Sabre Corporation

So many things have changed in the airline industry since I started in the business more than 20 years ago. But what hasn't changed is the fact that airline managers are always trying to use data to know how their airline is performing relative to other airlines, how they are serving their customers, how their aircraft are performing, how much revenue they could make from selling a certain seat at a certain price . . . as a matter of fact, that's probably what you were doing at some point today – trying to connect all the data points to make a decision. So, it's fitting that Dr. Taneja would name this book *21st Century Airlines: Connecting the Dots*.

I now sit in a somewhat different chair in the business, as CEO of Sabre, the leading technology provider to the global travel industry. While there is much academic and business leader discussion on how a new generation of companies like Starbucks, Facebook and Amazon are using data, Sabre and our airline customers are harnessing the data in more sophisticated ways as well. I'd like to give you a sense of what we are thinking about at Sabre, and how we are helping airlines around the world connect those dots – especially between your commercial and operations departments – with the help of some inspiring thinkers.

> *"These days no one can make money on the goddamn airline business. The economics represent sheer hell."*
> **– C. R. Smith, former CEO, American Airlines**

Critics of the airline industry are quick to point out how consolidation has led to lack of competition, poor customer service and higher prices – but that characterization clearly paints an alternate reality from your world spent fighting for every customer while managing against higher operating costs across fuel, labor, airport landing fees, or any other category of spending. There is also a considerable amount of pressure on pricing from low-cost carriers, and even then, full-service carriers and LCCs alike are seeking differentiation in the marketplace, with customized products and services to maximize revenue and drive greater unit revenue performance.

With razor-thin margins the historic rule, airline managers are trained to from their first day on the job to drive efficiency. What is needed is a fully integrated system to connect all of an airline manager's solutions to do just that. The right routes, the right schedules, the right customer data, and the right pricing tools roll up into the ability to fill every seat and drive the maximum revenue from each customer. Just like the precision required on the operating side of your business, the revenue side must continue to be more exact, more sophisticated and more integrated. Whether it be the LCC identifying new routes that can quickly become profitable, or the full-service network carrier looking to move that customer into a premium seat and more flexible fare bucket, we design our solutions to anticipate your next generation of needs with the help of data and predictive analytics.

> *"There are a lot of parallels between what we're doing and an expensive watch. It's very complex, has a lot of parts and it only has value when it's predictable and reliable."*
> **– Gordon Bethune, former chairman and CEO, Continental Airlines**

A seamless operation keeps customers, employees and investors happy. Our solutions are designed to provide end-to-end resources relying on data and technology to coordinate across passenger processing, airport operations and in-flight decision-making. Conversely, an airline's ability to respond to changes and manage disruptions is key in ensuring that customers have the best possible travel experience, while also protecting the airline's profitability. Again, what is needed are operations tools that bring intelligent decision support and alert-based management, as well as automation that will allow an airline's team to focus on the critical issues at hand. This will enable airlines to manage complexity and to respond to changes efficiently – from planning through the day of operations. We are focusing on connecting the commercial and operations platforms to support end-to-end solutions – so everyone has a clearer picture – the same picture.

> *"In God we trust, all others must bring data."*
> **– W. Edwards Deming, statistician**

If we are really going to embark on a digital transformation, we need to embrace the opportunity. The precision required to run a safe and efficient airline was really the model for modern-day data analytics that many other industries now claim as more proficient. At Sabre, we have no intention of giving up the leadership role and working with our airline customers to make sure they also continue to be ahead of the pack in utilizing technology and data to generate growth and business success. As a former student of Professor Taneja, I continue to rely on my classroom experiences with him to make decisions in my career. And with this book, he provides us all with additional proof points to keep us focused on where we need to go.

Southlake, Texas, USA

Foreword

Musa Zwane

Acting Chief Executive Officer
South African Airways

Leadership of any organisation is challenging at the very least. It demands that one achieve an increasingly elusive set of objectives in order to meet the expectations of one's shareholders and stakeholders, who are forever looking for alternatives and increased returns on their investments. All these demands make the challenge of managing an airline more daunting for most of us, and if there is one wish that we all have, it is that we must have a trusted friend to turn to whenever we need assistance.

That trusted friend for most of us in the airline industry is Nawal Taneja. He has been very helpful in the way that he so freely shares his vast knowledge and worldwide experiences with all of us. Reading his books and articles in different publications makes the job much easier and encourages us to keep our focus on the most important objectives of our businesses. His latest offering, *21st Century Airlines*, comes at an opportune time when we all need the latest thinking on how best to approach these ever-changing times. From the introduction, which deals with the heart of the matter, changing customer expectations, to the very end, where we are encouraged to "re-think the airline business for the digital era", we are taken through a journey of rediscovery and exploration of the airline-industry landscape, where the multitude of changes and challenges are masterfully presented, analysed and framed in a conclusive approach that allows every leader to take as much as possible from the "Takeaways". Fast food for the mind and busy executive indeed!

Within South Africa, which is currently going through a period of low economic growth, the focus is on improving sustainability of the airline business and driving initiatives to contain and reduce costs whilst encouraging growth and improving yields to increase profitability. Whilst the global airline industry has experienced unprecedented profitability over the past two years, the focus in our region is to reverse trends of overall negative profitability. Within Africa, the priority is also to expand the airline network, with increased city pairs between destinations and increasing consumer choice. Liberalization of the African skies remains an important goal, with the objective of increased frequencies, aircraft utilization and reduced unit costs a priority. Notwithstanding, the industry in South Africa is responding to increasingly savvy consumer expectations, with the implementation of improved self-service offerings placing more emphasis on personalized offerings and control of the journey in the hands of the customer.

Within Africa in general, the innovative disruptors have established their platforms, and they are fast becoming a part of everyday life – talk about the adoptive audience created by the fast-growing middle class in Africa. For airlines operating in emerging markets, such as ours, throughout Africa, the constant challenge is to balance the provision of a competitive and world-class service with the ability to invest in new high-cost initiatives.

With the above in mind, the beauty of this book is that it handles the complexity of managing "21st century airlines" with so much detail that one is confident to apply the knowledge immediately without any hesitation. We are indeed very grateful to have a thought leader such as Nawal Taneja whom we will always be glad to have in our corner. Congratulations on a well-thought-out and thoroughly researched book.

Johannesburg, South Africa

Foreword

Xie Haoming

Chairman
HNA Aviation Investment Group & Hainan Airlines

The airline industry is a data-intensive industry that can benefit from recent increases in digital, Internet and e-commerce technology. This technology can improve airline knowledge of customer purchasing and travel behavior. In the years to come, this knowledge may be the biggest driver of increased airline revenue and profit levels. Travelers can benefit from this technology by being able to purchase from airlines those additional products and services that they value. The use of technology to provide high-quality, diversified and personalized service enhances the overall air travel experience.

Digitization also accelerates transformation within the travel value chain. In the past, the value chain was shared by airlines, GDSs and offline travel operators. However, nowadays, the value chain has gradually covered every travel detail, including travel aspirations, travel plans, searches for travel products, reservations, destination services, on-the-way services, post-travel evaluation and social networking – a comprehensive and changing tourism ecosystem is gradually formed. With more segments in the ecosystem, the value chain has been extended by further refined service processes, intensified integration of online and offline suppliers and additional participants, such as Google, which launched real-time travel booking services, and Airbnb, which plans to enter the fray with air tickets, hotel reservations, etc.

With the development of IT, the conflict between large volumes of data and human being's limited information-processing ability becomes increasingly fierce, which results in two main obstacles in the digitization of airlines: one is that data is isolated as internal IT systems are incompatible with each other; the other is that IT technology is out of line with the business process. Thus, the establishment of information centers through self-building and outsourcing will be necessary to achieve compatibility of data systems, and IT experts who are proficient in business and familiar with the airline industry will be more valuable than traditional IT staff. Intelligent travel based on software talent and IT technology will need to become airlines' core competitiveness.

As for China, China has the world's largest online population, where change in lifestyle is taking place through digital products and social media. More importantly, according to McKinsey, the size of the middle class in China was at around 225 million households in 2016, compared with just 5 million in 2000, using an annual income of 75,000–280,000 yuan ($11,500–$43,000) as a yardstick. It is predicted that between 2016 and 2020 another 50 million households will join the ranks of the middle class. The growing Chinese middle class not only promotes prosperity of China's domestic market but also generates a consumer base that has strong purchasing power in the international market. In 2016 the number of tourists from mainland China traveling abroad increased by 6%, to 135 million, with total overseas consumption of $261 billion, which is $11 billion higher than in 2015, which is leading to an enormous increase in traffic demand.

Under this situation, Hainan Airlines is aiming to be a world-class global travel lifestyle carrier which meets the demands of the middle class and is changing the existing travel mode through the integration of the Internet and the construction of a travel ecosystem. In the first quarter of 2017, Hainan Airlines launched service on Chengdu–Los Angeles and Chongqing–Los Angeles routes, which have started a new chapter of expanding our network from southwest China to the US and led us to become the carrier which operates the most routes between mainland China and North America. Hainan Airlines now operates 57 international routes in total, including 12 in North America, 11 in Europe and Russia, 12 in Asia, 5 in Australia and 17 charter routes. The capacity on North American routes saw the largest year-over-year growth increase, given the growth rate of ASK was 87% higher compared with the same period last year.

Hainan Airlines is the only carrier in mainland China that was awarded the SKYTRAX Five-Star Airline award for the sixth consecutive year. It has already adopted initiative actions on social networks, created a high-quality website, developed a mobile app and WeChat online service for passengers and improved their travel experience. WeChat is an instant messaging application which has the largest user base not only in all of China but in all of Asia. In late 2016, the airline released its mini program version 1.0 on WeChat which provides a native app-like experience. By scanning a QR code, passengers can check flight information, get automatically issued certification of delay and help with changing a flight. In addition, we built a "Voice of the Customer" (VOC) management system for improved communications and interactions with passengers. Service-related departments collect information on various aspects of passenger services, including complaints and satisfaction of passengers, and build up key indicators of service, such as the overflow ratio of the airline's hotline when disruptions occurred, the average time of refund, the error ratio of baggage service, the ratio of foreign matter in in-flight meals, etc. And a database which contains all the information above is established to continuously monitor our service quality. By classifying and analyzing information, the management system can efficiently identify potential service risks, facilitate corrections, share service-management experience and strengthen pre-service risk control.

In 2017, Hainan Airlines came in third in the latest JACDEC Airline Safety Ranking, rising from fifth place in 2015. Digital-safety management is important for us. To systematically integrate the core of safety management, we have prioritized the establishment of a digital safety platform. We have established an information-driven safety performance model and designed index and key process checklist databases. Learning from BOWTIE and TEM, we have designed an information base of possible hazards. We also have introduced big data in our Flight Quality Analysis System to achieve retrieval, measurement and analysis of QAR data with standard models and norms. And the airline also introduced its Boeing 787-9 aircraft equipped with onboard Wi-Fi technology to allow passengers in-flight access to the Internet.

This new book by Professor Taneja has inspired us to think about what airlines can do to not only adapt the rapidly changing digital technologies but also actively develop better products to improve their customers' experience and achieve transformational strategies based on their own visions, their available resources, and their abilities to aggressively develop technologies. He gives in-depth thoughts on the environment and challenges that airlines are facing in the digital era and provides valuable insights on adapting to the new reality in which airline managers need to take a deep dive.

Hainan, People's Republic of China

Preface

This book starts with an assumption of an oncoming tsunami – the equivalent of a seismic wave in the global airline industry – and the need for airline leaderships to connect the dots to transform their businesses. As in the case of a tsunami, the sea wave might appear to be relatively small and way out in the sea, but it increases rapidly as it approaches the shore, with the capability to destroy huge settlement areas in a short period. Similarly, the global airline industry is perhaps anticipating only minor changes, but the forces of change could become extremely powerful, creating the likes of a tsunami, with enormous potential impact on existing players in the marketplace. Such a tsunami could be the result of powerful converging forces, such as changing consumer expectations, the emergence of platform-based and networked businesses, the proliferation of "smart" consumer technologies, and the spread of cross-border joint ventures and equity arrangements, all of which connect with consumer networks and consumer databases.

Executives at airlines are clearly aware of the forces of disruption and the need for transformation based on what is happening not only in other business sectors (technology, entertainment, retail, and so forth) but also within the broader travel sector – for example, the hospitality sector and the air-taxi sector. This variation in the response of airlines to disruption is understandable given the variation in the complexity of operations, the variation in regulations, and the variation in the geographical networks. Just from the viewpoint of the complexity of the airline business alone, there is much concern about how to manage in the rapidly and pervasively changing environment. For example, which of the major changes should a given airline or group react to, embrace, or prioritize? There is also the ongoing debate as to whether transformation can or should be initiated from the inside or the outside. In light of these perspectives, it is understandable that most transformational initiatives so far have related to enhancing the value of physical *existing* products. For example, initiatives taken in recent times include:

- a new fare structure or a new branded fare,
- a new cabin configuration – for example, direct-aisle seat configuration in business class in intercontinental markets,
- a new app on mobile devices to provide customized information or to bid for an upgrade to seats in premium cabins,

- an easier-to-navigate web site,
- upscale amenity kits and/or meals planned by well-known chefs for passengers in premium cabins,
- delivery of boarding passes on mobile devices and more self-service check-in facilities at airports,
- flight attendants equipped with mobile devices to obtain and provide relevant information to passengers based on their situations, and
- the use of analytics in predictive maintenance and fuel management.

Although all these incremental improvements are clearly beneficial and are in the right direction from the viewpoint of customers and profitability, within each airline the pace of change and the potential profit gains have been uneven. More important, these initiatives have not created anything that is radically different. The situation is best put in perspective by Peter Thiel, author of the book *Zero to One*. Many companies, according to Thiel, develop products or services that take "the world from 1 to *n*, adding more of something familiar." However, what is needed is for a business to develop and create something new that would take the world "from 0 to 1."[1]

This book, *21st Century Airlines: Connecting the Dots*, addresses the major challenges and opportunities when it comes to creating products and services that are radically different by connecting the dots at four levels.

- At the first level, CEOs are undoubtedly connecting the dots based on their observations of global events – much more rapid, and in some cases fundamental, changes in political frameworks, regional economies, demographics, people's desire to travel, and so forth. Consider just two examples: it is becoming slightly easier to form cross-border joint ventures and equity arrangements, and there is potential for an open-skies agreement between the US and China.[2]
- The second level of connecting the dots relates to the need to break down the silos within the airline organizations so that planning can be undertaken at the cross-functional level to improve the bottom line through greater agility. In addition to the cross-functional integration, there is a need to develop one version of the data truth, a process produced and controlled by the finance department.
- The third level of connecting the dots is to work much more closely within the travel chain – airlines, airports, distributors, and so forth – to improve the quality of service and experience provided to customers throughout the entire journey. This initiative requires the development and adaptation of a carefully thought through data strategy, given that data is becoming a currency.
- The fourth level of connecting the dots is to work, to the extent possible, within a business platform framework to serve customers at a much higher level of satisfaction (for example, offering solutions, not products) and accessing and allocating funds to generate higher and sustainable margins. Connecting the dots at this fourth level also means connecting with the connectors.

For example, since most people are now making connections through the likes of Facebook and Twitter, leading businesses, in turn, are now connecting with Facebook and Twitter. As Trevor Spinks points out in Chapter 7, the dominant GAFAA players (Google, Amazon, Facebook, Alibaba, and Apple) know and communicate with consumers better than airlines. Technology is now available to help airlines connect the dots more easily at all four levels.

The first two chapters provide an overview of the coming tsunami from two perspectives – the information-armed, always-on and demanding consumers and the platform-based and networked businesses that are data- and analytics-driven and deploy digital and cloud-based technologies.

- Chapter 1 discusses the first force, related to the changing needs and expectations of consumers and consumers' capabilities to comparison shop. Consumers are moving beyond a search for smartly designed products and services and are now looking for solutions. Their expectations are shaped much more by their experience from other business sectors (technology, entertainment, retail, and so forth) than by the services provided by different airlines. New technology is not only empowering consumers to make smart decisions relating to purchase and experience, but also helping businesses make smart decisions about how to develop and market products and services in the new digital environment. Moreover, consumers are deploying digital methods to express and satisfy their needs.
- Chapter 2 discusses the impact of the rise of platform-based and networked businesses and how they facilitate the exchange between consumers and producers by helping people think differently about value and value creation. This chapter also provides a glimpse of data-driven technologies that can help businesses develop and market products and services while providing authenticity, seamlessness, and personalization. The combination of these two forces alone – rising consumer expectations and platform-based and networked businesses – is creating a powerful competitive force, an opportunity for the emergence of powerful digital intermediaries known as "matchmakers."[3] Third parties, with the use of "smart data," could easily disrupt the sales and marketing component of air travel.

Chapters 3 and 4 deal with ways to remove conventional planning constraints within the airline industry to reduce the long conventional planning-cycle times and to make the planning process much more agile. This increase in agility will help an airline re-balance its core functions to optimize its core products by experimenting and learning through meaningful engagement with consumers.

- Chapter 3 presents some examples of ongoing and dramatic improvements that can be achieved in the area of network and schedule planning as the result of several factors. The first factor is the availability of new analytical modules for optimizing slots and code-shares, for example. The second factor is the integration of all planning modules, old and new, in the portfolio. The third factor is the use of financial data that is more accurate, timelier, and more robust. Invigoration of planning systems along these lines can lead to an optimization of the physical assets of an airline even with the use of traditional *physical* hub-and-spoke systems. These improvements, however, are evolutionary. To make dramatic improvements, on the other hand, calls for the use of dynamic scheduling and the establishment of *digital* hub-and-spoke systems.

- Chapter 4 illustrates a similar rationale for re-strategizing the management of revenue. The first part of this chapter highlights a few significant limitations of the current revenue-management capabilities. The second part discusses the development of dynamic pricing, dynamic inventory, and dynamic redemption to produce value for the airline and for customers while significantly reducing the complexity of shopping for and buying airline tickets.

The next two chapters discuss some aspects of re-designing services to focus more on the customer's experience and to capitalize on the opportunities emerging within the digital environment, leveraging behavioral data and emerging technologies. The discussion relates to the use of data and technologies for three groups – customers, competitors, and partners – to explore new frontiers in value in the digital era and, soon, the cognitive era. These initiatives will enable an airline to move further from physical to digital products and to focus on outcomes, not products and services.

- Chapter 5 presents some thoughts for using customer-focused and information-driven insights to re-design processes and systems – from the viewpoint of the entire journey and with an emphasis on experience – and to manage customers more proactively, during normal operations as well as during operational disruptions. Within the design framework, although it is critical to leverage emerging technologies to engage with customers, staff, and partners, the design team must not overlook the value of human interaction to the customer's experience. The key design criteria are real-time information and services.
- Chapter 6 introduces the idea of re-thinking the airline business for the digital era (1) to utilize technologies that can enable an airline to move further from physical to digital products and (2) to focus on outcomes, not products and services. Focusing on outcomes and not products and services is a clear difference between how value was defined in the analog era (by businesses) and how it is being defined in the digital era (by customers' changing needs). This chapter provides four key ingredients for success in the digital environment: a digital mind-set, digital technologies, digital strategies, and a digital workforce. It provides some examples of digital strategies that can be explored by lower-cost lower-fare carriers as well as by full-service carriers. The chapter ends with a few thoughts on the potential new forms of transportation.

The final chapter provides the viewpoints and perspectives of practitioners who work in different business sectors, in companies based in different parts of the world, in different functions within their businesses, and at different levels within their organizations. This diversity of perspectives may help you imagine radical opportunities for airlines.

This book synthesizes insights gained from the experience of non-traditional businesses (such as Uber), as well as traditional businesses (such as Mercedes) that are transitioning from operating physical assets to providing a service and an experience. These insights show that the process of digitizing a business involves much more than acquiring the needed technologies and re-locating some traditional functions under the umbrella of e-commerce. It requires even more than a change in corporate culture. It calls for a different mind-set and a commitment to re-think conventional processes and systems by improving connections within the enterprise and externally with its customers and partners while exploring new frontiers in value by connecting the airline within the travel chain and supplier ecosystem.

This book is intended for senior-level practitioners of differing generations of airlines and related businesses worldwide (airports, distributors, vendors, financiers, and so forth), as well as government policy-makers. Why government policy-makers? At airlines that continue to be wholly or partially owned by governments, or controlled by governments, or bound by governmental rules and regulations, an appreciation by policy-makers of the value of digital transformation can lead them to facilitate changes that will benefit consumers, employees, and stakeholders. The material is presented at a pragmatic level; in some places, it is presented in the form of questions, to promote critical thinking about the viability and stability of current business models, as well as new business models.

Notes

1 Peter Thiel (with Blake Masters), *Zero to One: Notes on Startups, or How to Build the Future* (New York: Crown Publishing Group, 2014), Preface.
2 "US-China Open Skies: A Window in 2019 – Alignment of Airline Partnerships & Airport Infrastructure," *Centre for Aviation, CAPA*, Aviation Analysis, April 29, 2017.
3 David S. Evans and Richard Schmalensee, *Matchmakers: The New Economics of Multisided Platforms* (Boston, MA: Harvard Business Review Press, 2016).

1 Responding to changing customer expectations

Understanding customer expectations and behaviors is hardly a new concept, given the insights it provides for developing and delivering innovative products and services. What is new, however, is the need to understand the speed and the areas in which customer behaviors and expectations are changing. Also, industry professionals need to keep up with new ways of engaging and interacting with customers in order to understand and respond to these changes. Not that long ago, many airlines thought that they knew what consumers wanted, and, based on that belief, they communicated their perceptions of value propositions to consumers in the traditional marketing seller-to-buyer direction, and with influence exerted by the seller through mass marketing.

Now, with the proliferation of new technologies and social networks, businesses must have two-way communications with segmented sets of consumers through their networks to learn about consumer values and to communicate their values to consumers. The focus of communication is now not just information on the features of a product, but also the experiential aspects, as these also influence behavior. From that context, airlines are beginning to have some control of consumer behavior through the provision of experience. In the long term, this will be helpful, since customers behave, to some extent, in response to their experience. If a consumer is frustrated with an airline, she will look for services offered by another airline, assuming she perceives differences among airlines. As such, leading airlines see that experience is becoming not only more important, but also necessary in engaging and interacting with consumers to receive input on the delivery of experience as perceived by the airline and as received by the passenger. As a result, airlines are transforming their business models.

As Raymond Kollau summarizes in his contribution to Chapter 7, today's connected and empowered consumers' expectations can be described by three attributes: on-demand, real-time, and end-to-end. As for businesses, whereas in the past they focused on internal operations with the objective of moving down on the economies of scale curve to reduce costs, now the focus is more on economies of scope and on increasing margin to become more competitive and more profitable.[1]

Super-connected travelers

It has become clear that in recent years, travelers' expectations and demands have been changing rapidly, based partly on the products and services provided by leading businesses in a digitally connected world characterized by on-demand and sharing economies. In this super-competitive environment, sellers have been learning to fulfill buyers' needs by delivering purchased goods more quickly, by making entertainment content available on mobile devices, and by providing a wealth of information. In broader terms:

a   Buyers are seeking smartly designed products and services with emphasis on authenticity, a seamless experience, and personalization.
b   Buyers are deploying digital methods to express and satisfy their needs, and they are using a wide array of social networking channels and apps.
c   Buyers want to shop more effectively, and they expect a product to be available anywhere.
d   Buyers are increasingly looking for content through digital devices, and they are shifting from "mobile first" to "mobile only."
e   Buyers are moving beyond searching for products to seeking solutions to their problems, and they are beginning to have a short attention span.
f   Buyers are rapidly adopting the voice interface.

To complicate matters, businesses are dealing with multi-generational groups with more significant differences among them with respect to consumer expectations. For example, not long ago, the focus was on baby boomers, but now it is on millennials. This shift in focus is understandable, given that millennials are expected to compose up to 75 percent of the workforce by 2020. Therefore, designing products and services to meet this group's expectations is important. However, other groups, such as people in their fifties (between the millennials and the baby boomers), should not be overlooked. This segment has a sizable base and significant spending power. By the time you read this, nearly 50 percent of the US adult population will be age 50 and older, and those people will control about 70 percent of the country's disposable income.[2] Although part of this wealth is in the hands of the baby boomers, much of it belongs to those in their fifties. And, although those in their fifties are quite familiar and comfortable with the use of technology, as consumers they are very likely to go for "value over luxury." In the airline industry, this could imply new travel options, such as the use of low-fare carriers in long-haul markets and the use of alternative accommodations provided by Airbnb and many others.

An airline, of course, can dive deeper into an identified segment. For example, the millennials segment does not represent a homogenous group – there are wide variations within the group, just as in any other generation. Even among millennials, not everyone lives totally in the social media space – Facebook, Google, Instagram, WeChat, Snapchat, Twitter, and so on. In addition, not everyone is looking for visual content. The implication for airlines is that they need to be more careful about simplistic categorizations. Just as, in the past, the categorization of travelers into "business," "leisure," and "visiting friends and relatives" turned out to be too broad, the same is now true for millennials, fifty-somethings, and baby boomers. Similarly, just as economy, business, and first-class cabins were sufficient to meet the needs of most consumers, now consumers want more choices. These choices may not be in the physical products, but they need to be in the digital space.

In any case, the travel behavior of different groups has not stopped changing. Consider the implications for businesses of the change when consumers went from desktops to mobile devices, requiring a total re-design of web sites to fit the new, smaller format. Consumers have increasingly been making bookings through the mobile channel – a channel that is simple but effective. Going deeper, consumers are not just booking through the mobile channel; they are looking for improved user experiences, such as better control throughout the journey. Consumers are already starting to adopt wearable technologies, not to mention the use of voice interface. What are the implications of the widespread adoption of such technologies?

Consider another segment of travelers that is looking for packaged travel. For this segment, the need for the use of travel agents does not go away; rather, the need for such services is re-vitalized. A consumer might have been influenced through social media by reading about the experience a colleague had when bicycling in Iceland. How does this desire become part of the travel package? Consumers want to be able to select the components of the trip (air travel, hotel accommodations, ground transportation, and sightseeing) and the brands, not to mention the timings for the booking as well as service features. Whereas in the past, packages produced by travel suppliers may have created value in terms of lower prices, they did not provide convenience, flexibility, or, possibly, even the brands. As one example in terms of convenience and flexibility, a consumer may have flown on an acceptable day but might have desired to return on a different day when the airline had no service, requiring the use of a different airline, even if that airline had a lower brand value.

Corporate travelers

Consider another segment: corporate or business travelers. Before we discuss how the behavior of corporate travelers has been changing, it might be helpful to look at the past framework of corporate travel. Typically, travel managers at large corporations negotiated favorable rates with suppliers – airlines, hotels, and car-rental companies, for example. Travel suppliers provided significant discounts depending on the value of the travel generated. Why did suppliers offer lower rates to corporations? Corporate travel may represent 10 percent or less of the total number of passengers transported by an airline, but this small segment may represent in the neighborhood of 50 percent of the airline's revenue. Travel managers also engaged travel-management companies (TMCs) to display content, access inventory, and make bookings via global distribution systems (GDSs) at rates negotiated by corporations with the suppliers. The TMCs also took care of travelers during their travel and, in some cases, managed the reporting of travel expenses for corporations. See Figure 1.1. Corporate travelers were expected to use the services of the preferred suppliers, and the TMCs tried to monitor travelers' compliance with the corporate travel policies.

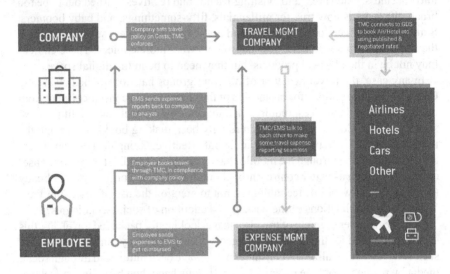

Figure 1.1 The typical current ecosystem of corporate travel (Note: EMS stands for expense-management system.)

Source: Christopher Moss, Passenger1

Although the typical corporate travel framework worked reasonably well, a number of concerns have been raised in recent years. From the perspective of an airline, although this segment provided a large stream of revenue, it involved not just discounted rates but also significant distribution costs and less direct control over the customer's experience, partly because of the lack of sufficient data on customers. On the part of frequent corporate travelers, many put themselves under tremendous stress. Their travel was in some cases painstaking, in other cases not particularly interesting, and they were required to comply with the corporate travel policies to control travel budgets. The situation was acceptable in that at least the travel took place in a relatively calm political environment. Now, corporate travelers are more connected (to social channels, for example), and they increasingly expect personalized services that maintain the productivity of the staff but make the trips more enjoyable. In other words, travelers want to satisfy their corporate objectives as well as their personal needs and life styles, and this is especially true of younger travelers.[3] Personal considerations are particularly important to them when they are traveling in dangerous or politically unstable regions.

Although business travelers were hardly a homogeneous group before, diversity within this group has been increasing, calling for airlines to engage with individual customers and provide them much more personalized services. Increasing numbers of corporate travelers are willing to participate in the sharing economy and utilize apps to meet their needs. For example, many are beginning to use apps to acquire ground services, such as Uber, and to utilize unconventional accommodation facilities, such as Airbnb. In the case of air travel, they are now more likely to use services provided by lower-fare airlines – for example, Southwest and jetBlue in the US and Norwegian and easyJet in Europe.[4] This trend is particularly evident in the younger generation of travelers. They want much more control over their travel experience and can use their mobile devices and apps to achieve this control. Sellers of travel services recognize the trend that corporate travelers are willing to consider alternative services and are beginning to re-configure their portfolios. Within the low-cost airline sector, eight low-cost carriers in Asia have formed the *Value Alliance*, discussed below in this chapter and in Chapter 6. Within the hospitality sector, the AccorHotels group has increased the number of partners to offer a much broader portfolio of products and services. See Figure 6.1 in Chapter 6.

These changes mean that the management aspects of corporate travel managers are also changing. Managers must now meet not only the cost-related needs of the business, but also the greater needs of the business, such as staff retention. Each traveler is very different and must be treated differently. Now the travel manager needs to look at each traveler's needs as well as the needs of the corporation – for example, the need to ensure compliance with corporate travel policies. Figure 1.2 shows a potential scenario of an ecosystem that has an embedded "Digital Agency" that connects corporate travelers with suppliers directly while providing a link between corporate travelers and travel managers on one side and expense-management systems on the other side. The needs of corporations and corporate travelers vary by corporation and by region. Corporations based in North America have different priorities relative to those based in Europe and those based in Asia. Even within a region, there may be vast differences.

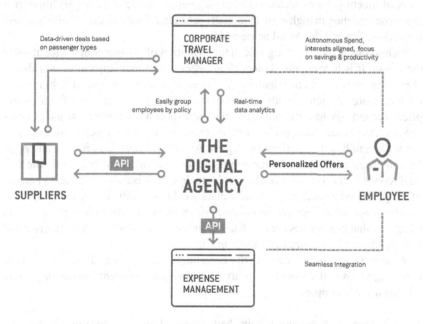

Figure 1.2 One potential scenario for the ecosystem of corporate travel
Source: Christopher Moss, Passenger1

The globalization of consumers

Consumers all over the world are becoming increasingly global. As such, consumer behaviors and expectations are being analyzed on a global basis. Let us consider consumers in Asia for a moment. Growth rates for products and services in Asia are expected to be very high, and there is increasing competition among Asian airlines and airports. Dianchun Li, in his contribution to Chapter 7, talks about the booming population and economy of the Pearl River Delta region of southeast Asia and how it has led to enormous growth in activity at two regional airports, Shenzhen (SZX) and Guangzhou Baiyun (CAN). Consequently, the big Hong Kong International Airport is facing stiff competition not just from new airports but also the rapidly expanding airports in the region.

Now let us consider consumers in Africa, where a middle-class segment is simply looking for reasonable schedules and fares in many markets. Consider passengers who need to fly between Algiers, in Algeria, and Doula, in Cameroon (about 2,300 miles). As of June 2017, there were no nonstop flights between these two cities. Royal Air Maroc offered a connecting flight at $544 (one way) that took 13 hours and 40 minutes, while Turkish Airlines offered a connecting flight at $699 that took 22 hours and 35 minutes. Compare that to flights between Manchester, in the UK, and Istanbul, in Turkey (about 2,100 miles). In this market, Turkish Airlines offered two daily nonstop flights taking 4 hours and 5 minutes, and British Airways offered connecting flights at $271 that took 7 hours and 40 minutes. Then there are middle-class segments (such as those in South Africa) in which technology-savvy consumers are looking for personalized services with self-service options. Airlines need to find ways of meeting the expectations of all segments – those traveling within Africa and those traveling in high-growth markets between Africa and the Middle East and between Africa and the Asia-Pacific region.

Technology is playing a big role in the evolution of consumer behavior all over the world. It is helping consumers shop faster, given that consumers worldwide "feel" that they are busier than the previous generations and need help making choices more efficiently with respect to tradeoffs between product features and price. Technology has also led consumers to expect a more seamless path to purchasing. As a result, the worldwide marketplace is becoming much more dynamic, but with significant variations by region. As Google describes it, consumers, at least in the affluent regions of the world, are living in the era of "micro-moments." And Asia is becoming affluent at a rapid rate. In fact, it is estimated that 85 percent of the predicted growth in the middle class worldwide will come from Asia.[5] The ramifications for airlines are enormous. For example, Trevor Spinks points out in Chapter 7 that group sales are much larger in Asia compared to North America and Europe, driven by the market growth in China.

What are some other reasons why consumers' behaviors and expectations are changing all over the world? To start with, their environment is changing. Here are just a few examples.

1   Changes are occurring within their culture. For example, more people are eating out during major holidays in the US. Dining out is going mainstream

given that (a) an increasing number of restaurants are starting to pay attention to distinctive and satisfying experiences, (b) mobile devices enable consumers to quickly decide where and when to dine based on reviews from trusted sources, (c) more and more apps are available to make reservations, and (d) social media is playing a major role ("Instagrammability"). Variations of this trend exist worldwide. For example, in India there is huge demand for the fashionable products offered by Starbucks.

2   Consumers want to see more personalized responses to their informational requests for service on a contextual basis, as well as the availability of actual services that are seamless and consistent. They want to be able to engage with suppliers via their mobile devices and be able to view the content through videos. In the case of travel packages, consumers want much more flexibility in the choice of components and contents.[6]

3   Consumers appear to be willing to provide data to suppliers and intermediaries if there is a fair exchange in value, such as the availability of improved services, if not personalized services. They do not want to be bombarded with irrelevant banner ads or creative sponsored messages, even though they now have the ability to block ads.

4   Consumers want comprehensive and location-based services. Think about the desire of consumers to pay with digital wallets. Think about the desire of passengers waiting at departure gates to use their mobile devices to have food delivered to them as they wait.

What insights can be gained from the experience of other business sectors?

1   Based on a survey conducted by Accenture, the financial sector is moving toward:

   a   micro-segmentations of customers to allocate resources and to develop products,
   b   re-imagination of the customer's experience using analytics,
   c   changes in the distribution mix (bank branches vs. digital banks, for example),
   d   development of loyalty through a combination of implicit and explicit schemes (advice vs. points, for example), and
   e   integration of strategy to offer an "Everyday Bank" value proposition.[7]
       Depending on the financial service required, consumers want recommendations; they want to be able to consult colleagues, other users, and experts through social media. The value is in finding a solution to a problem – a solution that could relate to an actual product feature, relate to information, or simply reduce stress.

2   The hospitality sector is no longer just influenced through traditional forms of marketing, but influenced through recommendations and reviews from "trusted sources." Consumers want transparency. For example, will there be a charge for using the Wi-Fi in the hotel room, the gym on the property, or the shuttle bus to and from the airport? Some consumers want ways of

authentication besides user names and passwords. Consumers want end-to-end customer engagement, not advertising, unless the advertising is relevant and helpful.

3   Consumers of the entertainment sector are expecting businesses to use software that consumers in the lets the businesses know if they are looking for something that is not available.

4   Forward-looking technology businesses are looking for insight into what consumers want, when they want it, and how they want it to be delivered. Businesses are even trying to know what consumers want but cannot yet articulate. In the 1980s, when Sony developed the Walkman; in 2000, when Sanyo introduced the camera phone; in 2010, when Apple embedded Siri in its iPhone; and in 2016, when IBM facilitated the development of Connie, the hotel concierge, did consumers know that these were the products they wanted?

Clearly, technology is changing consumer expectations and consumer behavior, which is beneficial in general. For example, technology has made it easier to book travel online. Technology also allows consumers to do much more research in a timely manner and to seek out suppliers that provide personalized services. The shopping and booking processes will improve when suppliers make it easier to navigate their web sites on the small mobile screens that many consumers now use. Besides apps, suppliers are beginning to offer "smart apps" and technology-enabled teams that provide 24/7 services. A new segment of technology that is likely to have a major impact is related to voice search and artificial intelligence, discussed in Chapter 6.

However, a concern is now emerging that consumers, including travelers, are dealing with too much information and too much technology – digital overload – not just in their travel but also in their everyday lives. Consequently, there is a segment, perhaps small, that is looking for human connections and human touch. For this segment, if there is a component of technology that enhances the human connection and the human touch when it comes to travel, it will add much value. Consider, for example, travel to countries that require visas. Although some countries may claim that the process is simple, it is not. Therefore, an airline advertising just lower fares may not be able to attract sufficient travelers to particular destinations if there are concerns about visas, terrorist attacks, political instability, and currency-exchange challenges. For example, in 2016, the terrorist attacks in France, the political instability in Turkey, and the diminished value of the British pound all impacted inbound or outbound travel. In addition, travel was affected when, in late 2016, cash was rationed in India after the government authorized the demonetization of most of India's currency. Would not travelers to India have benefited from the information that upon their arrival in India at the beginning of 2017 there would be cash shortages and long lines at the ATMs and banks? Can airlines help provide travelers with such information?

Implications for, and responses of, airlines

Travel suppliers are obviously monitoring these changes in customer expectations to respond with appropriate products and services. The travel industry is very large, and it is growing. Air travel, just one sector alone, is growing very rapidly. The number of passengers flying worldwide is expected to grow, according to IATA, by 4.1 percent per year, resulting in 7.3 billion passengers flying by 2034. China is expected to become the world's largest market, overtaking the United States. Given the size of the market and its growth, as well as its geographical distribution, suppliers of travel services are struggling to keep up with the changing behavior of travelers evidenced, for example, by the fact that alternative accommodations are growing rapidly. Consider some additional implications for airlines and some initiatives already underway. Let us start with some specific implications for airlines.

1   In order for an airline to provide personalized service, the airline has to know and recognize a person. The challenge is finding out not just what is relevant to a particular person but what is relevant to that person at a particular time: the factors influencing a particular consumer's travel decisions and how are they changing; the destination(s) being considered. The outcome desired is a personalized and consistent service delivered on a contextual basis through meaningful interactions. Since consumers even want a mobile experience that is seamless, airlines must focus on the design of the mobile web site or an app on a mobile device, and marketers must become well informed on different aspects of mobile search – organic versus paid, for example. There is a significant difference among different segments looking for seamlessness in service – for example, among those looking for seamless service at different touchpoints versus those looking for solutions in the context of "micro-moments."

2   An airline's marketing department needs to be able to access and influence the emerging consumer segment. The airline needs to know consumers' physical and digital locations, before it can use predictive marketing and cognitive-computing techniques to go deeper into actionable customer insights. Digital marketing can play a major role in analyzing changeable consumer behavior that now seems to be influenced more by recommendations from relatives and friends via social media than by digital advertising. Consequently, the questions are "How are travelers consuming digital content?" and "How is the mix of sources for travel planning changing between search engines, family and colleagues, and social media?" Consequently, the basics of conventional marketing must now expand in the areas of "acquisition, engagement, and monetization," aspects to encompass digital marketing.

3   The challenge is not having access to consumer data but knowing how to organize it and interpret it. Specifically, an airline needs to be able to gather and interpret a consumer's signals relating to behavior to understand the consumer's needs before designing the appropriate responses. These signals

provide answers to behavioral aspects – for example, to (a) shoppers who book early (e.g., 30–60 days ahead) versus late (e.g., less than 30 days), (b) the difference between the amount of money spent and the type of ancillary products purchased, and (c) the effectiveness of digital advertising relating to helping consumers decide on their destinations and on ancillary products and services.

4   Even though technology is available to help businesses gather and synthesize information on consumer behavior, and even though some airlines may have the expertise to gather information on consumer behavior, there is still the challenge of organizing the business itself to learn from the analysis of behavior and respond with appropriate offers.[8] For example, is an airline's marketing group organized to engage effectively with "social influencers" and bloggers? The key for the organization of an airline's marketing department is the ability to not just develop and deliver value, but measure value. This task is not easy, as value now includes experience-related elements that are difficult to measure. Based on insights from other business sectors, metrics are now available that can measure the value of an increase in engagement.

5   Airlines need to deploy "smart technology" that increases efficiency and productivity for airlines and human intelligence for the customers. Consider a system that can connect corporate travelers directly to airlines' passenger service systems (PSSs). Such a capability could (a) display rich content, (b) collect the needed data to enhance the customer's experience, (c) reduce distribution costs, and (d) increase ancillary revenues through the sale of customized products and services – specific meals, meet-and-greet services, access to specific parts of airport lounges for work or relaxation facilities, and so forth.

6   The common threads among the five implications listed above are the acquisition of data, the deployment of customer analytics, and social intelligence to improve the customer's experience and the airline's profitability. However, businesses should not "abuse" data. Regulators are becoming increasingly concerned about the privacy of data, particularly within the European Union.

To varying degrees, both traditional and low-cost low-fare airlines (LCCs) have already been transforming to meet customers' needs and increase the efficiency and productivity of their operations.

Full-service airlines

In an effort to become even more competitive, a number of airlines around the world have been expanding or developing their lower-cost subsidiaries. In Europe, Lufthansa and Air France have been expanding the capacities of their subsidiaries, Eurowings and Transavia, respectively. International Airlines Group (IAG), which had been expanding its lower-cost subsidiary, Vueling, recently added a new player – Level, which will provide long-haul services from Barcelona, Spain (a Vueling hub) to destinations such as Buenos Aires, Los Angeles, Oakland,

and Punta Cana. The frequency will be less than daily, and the announced fares will start at around 100 euros. In the US, the three majors have introduced Basic Economy products. These fares do not allow, for example, full-sized carry-on bags. Passengers will be allowed only small personal items that can fit under the seats. From the point of convenience, airlines have now begun to offer services in secondary markets. British Airways offers a nonstop flight to San Diego from London. Hainan Airlines has nonstop service from Beijing to Manchester, and Singapore Airlines flies nonstop from Manchester to Houston. United Airlines has started nonstop service from San Francisco to three Chinese cities: Chengdu, Hangzhou, and Xi'an. These services will undoubtedly increase with the availability of more slots at Beijing and Shanghai Airports, possibly after the new airport is built in Beijing and after there is an open-skies agreement between the US and China.

Outside of subsidiaries, networks, and schedules, traditional airlines are now offering preferred seats, preferred boarding, and fare-locking options, and soon they will offer boarding passes on smartwatches. As for self-service features, passengers can check in online, and they can use iBeacons to navigate airport terminals and receive location-specific messages on mobile phones. Some specific examples of the non-airline-seat product features are:

- KLM has developed the "Meet and Seat" mobile app, which enables passengers to communicate through their social networks with fellow passengers on the same flight. The idea here is simply to improve the customer's experience.
- Some airlines have been developing technology to enable passengers to see on their mobile devices the information being displayed in the terminals. The app, Qview, developed by Qantas, can display on a passenger's mobile device the information available in the airline's lounge – boarding gate and time, for example. Initiatives are underway to improve the customer's experience in the areas of shopping, booking, and self-service. In the area of shopping, the focus is on responding more intelligently to searches and making the selection, as well as making purchase processes more transparent and easier.
- Scandinavian Airlines has announced the opening of "City Lounges" (in downtown Stockholm) for the airline's frequent flyers to use work areas (temporary offices) and network with other frequent flyers.
- Delta has announced a capability for passengers to scan and track their bags using a mobile app, "Track My Bag."
- Virgin Atlantic is offering seats located in areas designated as "snooze zones."

Developments within the low-cost sector

Within the low-cost low-fare airline sector, there have been five major developments. First, penetration of low-cost low-fare airlines is increasing in areas where it has been minimal. North Asia, for example, has had minimal LCC activity (less than 10 percent of the total capacity) relative to southeast Asia. Consider the development of LCCs in Asia. Japan, for example, which has had low penetration by LCCs, is beginning to see an increase in activity, given some relaxations in its aviation policies starting in 2012. There are some LCCs already (Jetstar Japan, Peach Aviation, Skymark Airlines, Spring Air, and Vanilla Air), but more are planning to enter the marketplace (AirAsia Japan, for the second time). The major developments helping the expansion of low-cost services in Japan are:

1   Some airports are beginning to make decisions to open up their facilities to accommodate LCCs. Three major airports – Osaka Kansai, Okinawa Naha, and Tokyo Narita – have already built low-cost carrier terminals (LCCTs), and a fourth one – Nagoya – is planning to do so soon.

2   The government is seeing the value of LCCs in fulfilling the potential for an enormous increase in inbound tourism. It is reported that the government has set a target of about 40 million visitors by 2020, almost double the number in 2015.

As in other parts of the world, new accommodation facilities are emerging in Japan. For example, the traditional Japanese inns (ryokans) are being recreated (Hoshino Resorts) and beginning to be used by foreign visitors, promoted by LCCs such as Peach.[9] Japan is not the only market with low-cost low-fare airlines. For example, Vietnam Airlines, a major airline that now transports more than 20 million passengers a year, with a fleet of aircraft approaching 100, has developed a large low-cost subsidiary: Jetstar Pacific, which operates about 15 aircraft. Another example is the potential expansion of low-cost carrier VietJet, since its launch in 2011. According to a recent analysis by the Centre for Aviation (CAPA), from the viewpoint of airline services, Vietnam was the fastest-growing market in Southeast Asia, and one of the fastest-growing markets in the world in both 2015 and 2016.[10]

The second major development in the low-cost, low-fare airline sector is that a number of low-fare airlines– WestJet, Norwegian, and Scoot, for example – are expanding their services in long-haul markets. Ireland-based Norwegian Air International, a subsidiary of Norwegian Air Shuttle, announced new service in a number of transatlantic markets from secondary airports in the northeast US (Hartford, Newburgh, New York, and Providence) to three airports in Ireland (Cork, Dublin, and Shannon) and two airports in the UK (Belfast and Edinburgh) beginning in June 2017. The big news is that Norwegian is planning to serve these relatively low-density markets with the new-generation narrow-body aircraft with 189 seats – the Boeing 737 MAX 8. Norwegian has announced that these markets will be served initially at one-way fares as low as 69 euros and with a frequency of less than once a day. Although these services will undoubtedly divert traffic, they will stimulate significant traffic given the low level of fares.

Another example of rapid expansion relates to the two airlines based in Iceland: Icelandair and newcomer WOW air. Icelandair has been serving the market between North America and Europe as a sixth-freedom carrier for a long time. Figure 1.3 shows the route map constructed from the data available on Icelandair's web site at the beginning of 2017. WOW air started operations in 2012 and has been expanding its network, which also connects North America with Europe, with connections at Keflavík International Airport in Iceland. Figure 1.4 shows WOW

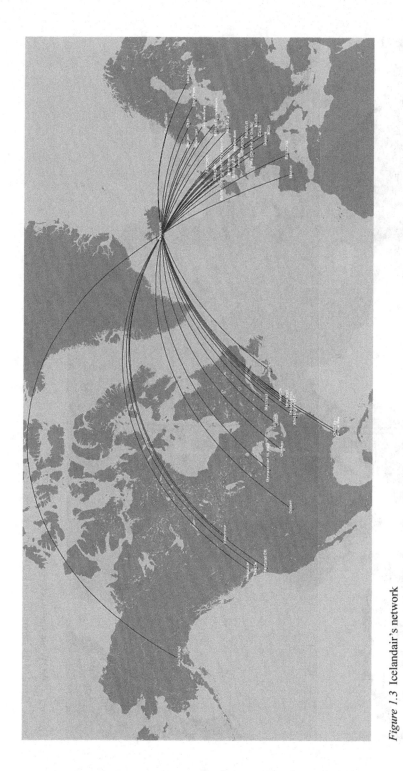

Figure 1.3 Icelandair's network

Source: Based on the information in Icelandair's web site, February 2017

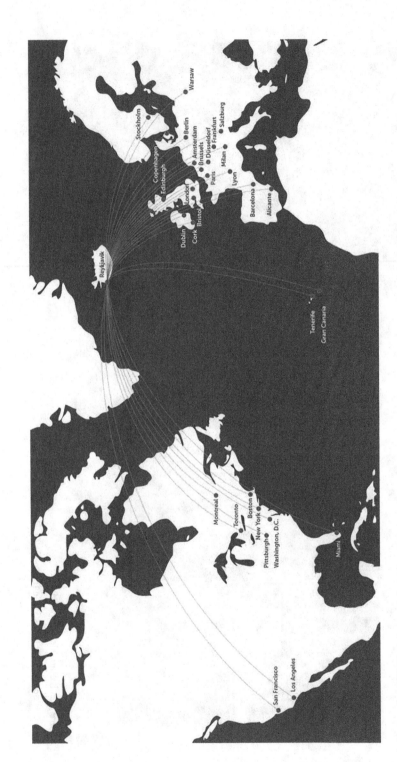

Figure 1.4 WOW air's network

Source: Based on the information in WOW air's web site, February 2017

air's network as of the beginning of 2017. Both carriers have been gaining market share, based partly on the increasing levels of capacity offered, competitive fares, and, in recent years, a growing inbound demand in Iceland.

The third major development in the low-cost low-fare sector is the continued expansion of existing LCCs in Asia. According to Tony Fernandes, the founder of AirAsia, these airlines are changing "how people work, live, and play" in Asia. AirAsia, in fact, started with the slogan "Now everybody can fly." Currently, estimates show that the AirAsia group of airlines alone transports more than 50 million passengers per year. Some estimates place the percentage of the capacity offered by LCCs in southeast Asia to be approaching 60 percent, with major players such as Lion Air (based in Indonesia and operating over 100 aircraft), Cebu Pacific (based in the Philippines and operating about 50 aircraft), and Nok Air (based in Thailand and operating about 35 aircraft). The penetration achieved by LCCs has led traditional carriers to develop their own low-cost subsidiaries – Tigerair and Scoot by Singapore Airlines, for example. LCCs have had an enormous impact on inbound tourism for countries such as Singapore and Australia, and traditional airlines obviously are anxious to participate in the growth.

The fourth major development is that the market for low-fare airline services is so ripe that some LCCs have developed a strategy to grow their share, in light of the competition from the lower-cost subsidiaries of traditional airlines: they have formed their own alliance. In Asia, eight low-cost airlines have formed an alliance called Value Alliance. Formed in May 2016, the alliance comprises the following members: Cebu Pacific, Jeju Air, Nok Air, Nok-Scoot, Scoot, Tigerair, Tigerair Australia, and Vanilla Air. This alliance may facilitate the movement of passengers in long-haul markets in the region – for example, by enabling consumers to book on any one of the eight airlines from a single web site and allowing each airline to upsell and cross-sell its products. In a similar development, Ryanair and Norwegian have just announced that they will use London Gatwick as a connecting hub between Ryanair's short-haul and Norwegian's long-haul flights.

The fifth major development is the ambition of some lower-fare airlines to divert a reasonable share of premium traffic from the full-service carriers. Norwegian, for example offers a Premium Economy cabin. AirAsia X and Scoot offer "quiet zones" in their cabins. JetBlue offers "Mint." Korea-based Jeju Air lets passengers buy empty seats next to the seats they will be traveling in, for extra comfort. Jeju Air can even sell its "Sleeping Seat Package" for passengers traveling on its long-haul flights. Even Ryanair has begun to offer Business Plus service, which includes more flexibility (changes to day before or day after flights), fast track through airport security, reserved priority seats and priority boarding, and a higher baggage allowance. In Chapter 7, Keith McMullan and James Halstead provide excellent insights on the challenges and opportunities facing low-cost low-fare airlines offering schedule services in intercontinental markets. They first describe the three basic kinds of long-haul LCCs and the main arguments put forward by traditional carriers as to why they will have difficulty in gaining any significant market share. They then list a number of factors for success in the marketplace and the potential share of the market that the long-haul LCCs could obtain.

The previous examples clearly show that airlines have been looking deeply into what matters to their customers and how to design and offer the desired products, services, and experience. However, the strategies must now go far beyond the aspects relating to networks, schedules, and prices. The traditional airlines have begun that process, evidenced by the examples presented, relating, for example, to KLM, SAS, and Qantas. The leading airlines must now consider opening up to the ecosystem to improve the customer's experience right from the design perspective. The deeper dive in this process involves gathering information on individual customers on a huge number of variables in real time to predict behavior and to make the right offer to the right customer at the right time. The goal is not only to improve the customer's experience but also to generate ancillary revenues. Nevertheless, it requires a careful approach. Would the customer view this as simply a real-time approach for increasing sales or providing helpful information for improving the customer's experience? Although airlines have always had enormous amounts of transactional data, now they are beginning to collect data on customer behavior through digital interactions. Vast quantities of data can now be handled more efficiently, as the costs of storage have come down. Consider the discussion by Stefan Jenzowsky of Moore's Law in Chapter 7. Customer data and customer analytics, particularly those employed during various stages of a journey, can now synthesize the customer intelligence data to help an airline make relevant offers and improve the customer's experience throughout the journey.

Airlines do realize that consumers are highly empowered with information and apps that make shopping for air travel easier. However, it is also possible that consumers are overwhelmed by the information they already have and by the many sources of additional information that they may, in fact, have become stressed, leading to a slowdown in the decision to make purchases. This could easily be the case with higher-cost trips and complex itineraries. It is possible that some consumers will even not be clear about their needs. In some ways, providing more options makes sense, but it could lead to uncertainty and a slowdown in the final purchase decision. It is true that the services of airlines such as Jetstar, Norwegian, and Scoot are valuable, just like the services provided by Airbnb in the hospitality sector and Uber in the ground-transportation sector. But the availability of lower airfares and alternative hotel accommodations and ground-transportation services could give travelers some opportunities to explore more and new destinations on their own, especially these days, when travel can be facilitated even more with the use of technology provided by such organizations as Groupon Getaways, Living Social, and Snaptrip.

Consequently, airline managers can now take advantage of opportunities coming from more information on the expectations of newer generations of consumers. Every passenger is different, from the one who wants to be recognized and treated on an extremely personalized basis, to the one who simply wants an extremely easy shopping and booking experience, to the one who simply wants on-time performance. Can multi-industry insights help? Consider what brands such as Amazon, Apple, and Starbucks have achieved.

Takeaways

- The pace of change regarding consumer expectations has been and will remain greater in business sectors outside of the airline business. In the airline business sector itself, many of the changes in consumer behavior and methods of better serving consumers have not come from within the airlines' mainstream organizations or culture.
- Airlines are beginning to appreciate that their strategies must now go far beyond the aspects relating to networks, schedules, and prices. They recognize that customers want smartly designed products and services with emphases on authenticity, a seamless experience, and personalization. The challenge, however, is not related to knowing the need for such products and services, but rather how to develop strategies to produce and deliver these services desired by customers and that are profitable for airlines. In the case of corporate travel, for example, travelers want to satisfy their corporate objectives (cost management and work productivity) as well as their personal needs and life styles, especially younger travelers.
- These initiatives call for airlines to get closer to customers. Although getting close to all generations of customers is not a new concept, it is now becoming easier in the digital environment, for two primary reasons. First, it is becoming easier to follow the customer all the way from the trip-preparation stage to the post-trip stage. Second, it is now possible to use customer-journey analytics to develop information on customer behavior and to identify context-based actions as well as, to some extent, be able to predict the outcomes.
- Customers are looking for outcomes and solutions, not just products. If that is value, how can it be defined? Furthermore, if the value of a product also includes experience-related elements that differ among consumers and different trips for the same consumer, how can value be measured? What an airline can do is observe, through multiple channels, its customers' behaviors as they purchase and use its services and try to identify the transactional and behavioral aspects that relate to value and then try to measure the attributes that can be measured using new metrics.
- The key to the creation of additional value, for both customers and airlines, lies not only in the tactical and strategic use of data, but also in the strategy to monetize data. Dianchun Li provides, in Chapter 7, insightful strategies for the market in the Pearl River Delta region.

Notes

1 David L. Rogers, *The Digital Transformation Playbook: Rethink Your Business for the Digital Age* (New York: Columbia Business School, 2016), p. 7.
2 Jason Clampet, "The Fifties Are the New Target Demographic for Travel Brands," *SKIFT MEGATRENDS 2017: Megatrends Defining Travel in 2017*, January 2017, p. 14.
3 Travelers who not only tend to integrate their business and personal life styles but also take along family members are beginning to be referred to as "bleisure" travelers.

4 Association of Corporate Travel Executives (ACTE), "Meet the Modern Business Traveller: Insights into the Lives of today's Corporate Travelers," *American Express*, Global Business Travel Survey, October 2016.
5 "The Future of Commerce Has Arrived," Understanding the New Asian Consumer, *Accenture*, 2016, p. 6.
6 "Packages Need to Be More Dynamic," Pamela Whitby, editor of *EyeForTravel*, reported in *Tnooz Reports*, February 28, 2017.
7 "Banking Shaped by the Customer: Intuitive, Intelligent, Individual," Accenture, *2015 North America Consumer Digital Banking Survey*, 2015, p. 13.
8 Jeff Gothelf and Josh Seiden, *Sense & Respond: How Successful Organizations Listen to Customers and Create New Products Continuously* (Boston: MA, Harvard Business Review Press, 2017).
9 Yeoh Siew Hoon, "Low-Cost Carriers Are Changing Asia," *Travel Weekly*, July 17, 2016.
10 "Vietnam Airlines 2017 Outlook: Slower Growth and Smaller Profits as Competition Intensifies," *Centre for Aviation, CAPA*, January 12, 2017.

2 Platform-based and networked businesses

New forms of collaboration

If airlines are to take an outside-in approach to re-design their products and services, then it would help to spend some time exploring how some new businesses, as well as some conventional businesses, are raising the bar to deal with changing customer expectations discussed in the previous chapter. Although all kinds of service business sectors– banks, airlines, hotels, car-rental companies, insurance companies, for example – have been trying to optimize their customers' experience for a very long time, the steps taken have been at an incremental level. Such a situation had been acceptable in a marketplace that changed slowly. Now, in a much more dynamic and increasingly unpredictable marketplace, the changes need to be much more fundamental in creating value while facilitating the exchange between producers and consumers. To create new value for both buyers and sellers, new businesses established in the sharing economies relating to products, services, and knowledge – Airbnb, BlaBlaCar, Facebook, Uber, and YouTube, for example – have been leveraging platforms and scalable networks. Within the dramatically changing business landscape, now the traditional businesses, such as GE, Haier, IBM, and Mercedes, have begun to pivot their business models in the direction of platform-based and networked businesses with an eye toward new forms of collaboration. They think differently about value and value creation. Consider how Facebook, Google, and Uber operate and now how traditional companies, such as GE and IBM, are beginning to pivot their business models. The focus is now on how to enable consumers to create and consume value; build businesses around networks, consumer databases, analytics, and connected technologies; accelerate the sharing of knowledge via networks; transition from product to digital strategies; focus more on culture, design, and talent strategy; and initiate data-driven creativity and innovation. For some imaginative scenarios of not just digitization, but radical digitization, in the airline industry, read Stefan Jenzowsky's contribution to Chapter 7. If you are interested in how airports, particularly regional airports can digitize their business by developing platforms, see Parm Sidhu's contribution to Chapter 7.

This chapter begins with some insights on the macroeconomic shift in businesses from the industrial era to the digital era and then follows with some perspectives for airlines on both opportunities and dilemmas when it comes to adapting to the high customer service and experience bar set by businesses such as Amazon and Apple.

The macroeconomic shift: industrial era to digital era

The structure of most business is shifting in fundamental ways, as shown in the information contained in Figure 2.1. Start with the first area in this figure, the focus of a business. It is changing from the firm looking internally at its own operations to looking externally at the potential opportunities to work with networks. Even within internal operations, managers are looking at how and where capital should be allocated as opposed to how the conventional operations can be made more efficient. This means moving from the use of conventional business rules to challenging assumptions, learning from experiments, and adapting to the changing business environment.

One clear insight from new businesses is that they are asset-light, and the assets that they do have are intangible. The shift from physical to digital assets is coupled with a migration from physical technologies to digital technologies. This change from being asset-heavy to asset-light, and the deployment of digital technologies, along with an orientation to work with external partners, has led to a significant reduction in marginal costs and the achievement of not only economies of scale but also economies of scope. Moreover, developing a willingness to share data rather than own data within the ecosystems has enabled the new platform-based and networked businesses to extend the boundaries of their businesses rather than rely on organic growth.

In the digital era, capital has been moving from traditional businesses to the new platform-based and networked businesses. Uber reportedly has increased its market capitalization from $40 billion to $60 billion. Reports indicate that even though Uber has not been making any profit, it has managed to continuously raise capital, and at higher valuations. Traditional businesses have not been able to achieve such success. For example, the market capitalization of Hertz,

Industrial Era	Digital Era
• **Focus**	• **Focus**
– Firm-Centricity	– Network-Centricity
– Internal	– External
– Operations	– Capital Allocation
– Conventional Business Rules	– Challenging, Learning, Adapting
• **Asset: Physical, Tangible**	• **Asset: Digital, Intangible**
• **Technology: Physical**	• **Technology: Digital**
• **Marginal Costs: High**	• **Marginal Costs: Low**
• **Orientation**	• **Orientation**
– Products for Customers	– Experience for Customers
– Economies of Scale	– Economies of Scope
– Returns on Internal Assets	– Returns on Ecosystem Assets
– Slow Organic Growth	– Fast Network-Driven Growth
– Growing the Core Business	– Extending the Core Business
– Owning Data	– Sharing Data

Figure 2.1 Technology-driven macroeconomic shifts

the car-rental company with global operations, is only $7.8 billion. Compare this to Uber's market capitalization. And Uber has no cars, whereas Hertz has 350,000 cars.[1] Uber is reported to be losing money on every ride, even though it is achieving large volumes.[2] Although the business has benefited from the network effects – more customers and more drivers – Uber has faced some barriers. Did Uber raise so much money because it needed to invest in new technology to set up in different countries, because it lost so much during its early period or to expand into new markets, or because of some combination of reasons? The answer would appear to be that capital seems to be flowing toward platform-based enterprises because of their demonstrated growth, global scalability, and huge addressable markets. This is in sharp contrast to the single-digit growth horizon, slowing penetration, and asset-heavy profile of their legacy competitors. It is also interesting to note that Uber has been able to raise capital not only without showing profits, but also while facing significant challenges resulting from regulations and politics. Finally, it is also noteworthy that Uber and other new businesses have had access not only to capital, but also to exceptionally talented employees. New ideas about creating and delivering value to both customers and businesses, coupled with new technologies, have provided almost instant access to capital and talent, which further led to the generation of new ideas. Moreover, the cycle is continuing.

Observing the success of new businesses, many traditional businesses have begun to pivot their business models, starting with decisions on where to invest their funds from an allocation point of view. Most traditional businesses know that they get relatively low margins from their traditional operations. As a result, they have been thinking about getting much higher margins from investing in new technologies, such as the cloud, discussed below. One only needs to see how the allocation schemes have been changing for not only traditional businesses – such as GE, Haier, IBM, and Mercedes – but also relatively new companies, such as Amazon, Cisco, Google, and Microsoft. Are there any insights for the larger traditional airlines? Should a large global airline invest in non-conventional business areas and then lease out its newly acquired capabilities to other airlines? Should a major airline continue to invest so heavily in maintenance, repair, and overhaul (MRO), for example, when the returns may be minute compared to investments in other areas, such as information and analytics or even platforms? Not only are the margins higher, but investments in new technology will help the airline making the investment to stay competitive.

Figure 2.1 shows that a new type of business develops a focus that is external, based around a network, and with decisions centered on (1) how to allocate capital as opposed to increasing the efficiency of internal operations and (2) how to enable other businesses to produce and sell its products and services. The business is built around digital capabilities, as opposed to physical technologies. The new businesses are motivated by the value of economies of scope, returns on the assets deployed within the ecosystem, lower marginal costs, and fast network-driven growth. Moreover, the ability to co-create value through members in the ecosystem and customers themselves, as well as through the deployment of big data and analytics, enables new businesses to extend their boundaries. Managers need to develop a co-creator mind-set to create value in new areas.

In terms of strategy, new businesses are allocating more resources to the deployment of information rather than conventional products. IBM was one of the first ones to do so when it sold its personal-computer division to Lenovo and made investments in information-related businesses such as Bluemix and SoftLayer (cloud infrastructure) and Watson (cognitive technologies). Similarly, Nike, which initially invested heavily in the production of shoes, has recently been investing in sensors, transmitters, and receivers to monitor the physical activity of people wearing the shoes. Sensors and transmitters are embedded in the shoes, and receivers are embedded in the Nike+Sportband.

Customers can be important co-creators of value, given the increasing interest in user-generated content, exemplified by Square. Square is an organization for facilitating payments between a buyer and seller anywhere. Square developed user-generated videos showing the experience of different users with its payment service. Coca-Cola, with its "Share a Coke" campaign, strengthened its brand's bond with users. Through an invitation – *Share a Coke with (insert name)* – the company was asking a user to have his or her name shown on a can. The availability of digital technology facilitated the development of user-generated content.

Platforms

New, powerful businesses – Airbnb, Alibaba, Amazon, Facebook, Tencent, and Uber – are based on business platforms that connect sellers and buyers (as well as the resources of different sellers) more efficiently and effectively. These new business models work with frameworks that monetize networks that enable the creation and exchange of value. In their book *Platform Revolution*, Geoffrey Parker, Marshall Van Alstyne, and Sangeet Paul Choudary explain the difference between a traditional business and a new type of business with the terms "pipeline" and "platform." In a pipeline, a traditional business produces its products using its own resources and functions and markets the product through the pipeline with the producer at one end and the buyer at the other end. Examples of such businesses are GE and Wal-Mart. In the context of a platform, a business produces and markets the product using the resources and functions of other businesses operating with the platform. Moreover, using platforms, value is "co-created" through the connections enabled by platforms.[3] Value is not just co-created, it is enhanced by the organizations within the platform network. Examples of platforms are Airbnb, Amazon, eBay, Facebook, Uber, and YouTube. Let us not forget about how apps have added value to smartphones.

In their book *Modern Monopolies*, Alex Moazed and Nicholas Johnson provide four functions of platforms. First, a platform needs to create a place where buyers and sellers can come together. Second, the platform needs to have efficient and effective ways to connect the right buyer with the right seller. Third, the platform needs to make available the infrastructure to facilitate the transactions, again in efficient and effective ways. Finally, the platform needs to have guidelines relating to behavior of the participants.[4] Platform businesses create value by deploying technologies to enable different groups to exchange products and services. Platform businesses do not make products in the traditional sense. They connect the people who make them and the groups who need to acquire them. eBay and Priceline.com are early examples. eBay was simply a web site that enabled sellers of all kinds of products (worldwide and some hard-to-find items) to put all kinds of information about their products on the company's web site. Then it enabled all kinds of buyers worldwide to access these products, evaluate them, and purchase them. The point was that, regardless of the product and its condition, there was a buyer somewhere willing to evaluate it and undergo the arbitrage. With Priceline.com, the business model was to help travelers obtain discounted airline tickets, hotel rooms, and rental cars. Priceline.com did not provide the airline service or the hotel accommodation itself. It simply facilitated the transaction between a buyer and a seller. The interesting twist was for a buyer to "name his own price" for the service requested – an airline seat or a hotel room, for example. The buyer would provide the city pair for air travel and the general location for hotel accommodations. The seller would identify the exact itinerary or the hotel location after the purchase. Cancellation was generally not possible. Priceline.com earned its money from the difference between the price named by a buyer and the price charged by the seller.

Platform-based businesses are technology-driven and focused on innovation from the outside in to create new value for consumers and for businesses. They are changing the ways business is conducted. It is not the availability of a vast quantity of products and services that can be acquired from a business like Amazon. The fundamental asset is the platform that enables the sale of these products and services. Platform businesses are facilitated by such technology services as the cloud (Amazon's Amazon Web Services, Microsoft's Azure Web Services, and Alibaba's AliCloud), and these services enable the Internet of Things (IoT) to operate in almost real time. In his book *Platform Scale*, Sangeet Paul Choudary describes how platform-based business models work: software empowers the effective integration of tangible and intangible assets so that buyers and sellers can make intelligent decisions.[5] Using technology, platforms facilitate transactions but do not control the behavior of the users of the platform. Obviously, the platform features need to be such that they attract users, and there need to be rules for their operations. In *Modern Monopolies*, Alex Moazed and Nicholas Johnson distinguish between "exchange" platforms and "maker" platforms. Exchange platforms provide value by facilitating an exchange between a buyer and a seller. Maker platforms generate value by helping producers create complementary products and distribute them to a large number of people.[6]

In *The Digital Transformation Playbook*, David Rogers elaborates on how a business can leverage customer networks by using technologies (platforms and information) to compete more effectively – for example, by not just making better products and services but also innovating through the experimentation process.[7]

New, powerful businesses, such as Airbnb, are not only fulfilling a demand for alternative accommodations, but also prompting existing hotel chains to realign their strategies. In order to stay competitive, hotel business Accor acquired One-finestay, for example, an organization that has more than 2,000 properties in major cities around the world. See Figure 6.1 in Chapter 6.

Leaving aside the speed aspect, these platforms also enable global reach, not to mention scalability. In *Sense and Respond*, Jeff Gothelf and Josh Seiden illustrate how platform businesses can obtain global geographic reach at an incredible speed and achieve scale almost instantly. They explain, for example, how one could compare the market capitalization and employment numbers for new and traditional businesses.[8] According to various web sites, as of December 2016, Facebook and GE had similar market capitalizations, around $300 billion. Yet, Facebook had only about 17,000 employees, compared to about 295,000 at GE. Similarly, Alibaba and Wal-Mart had about the same market capitalization (around $200 billion). Yet, Alibaba had only about 36,000 employees, compared to about 2.3 million at Wal-Mart. See Table 2.1. Although new businesses still have employees, (a) there are only a few, and (b) they are more like partners than employees in the traditional sense, a difference that gives them a feeling of ownership.

In his book *Narrative and Numbers*, experienced investor Aswath Damodaran provides significant insights as to how some of these highly visible platform businesses were able to obtain incredibly high valuations. The high valuations were based more on the power and the compelling nature of their stories than on the financial numbers and their projections. According to Damodaran, it was the narrative that added substance to the numbers at the time of public offerings of high-flyer businesses such as Facebook and Uber.[9]

In ten years, Airbnb scaled its operations to well over 100 countries, offering well over half a million properties, and diverted a substantial portion of customers from the conventional hospitality sector. The amazing characteristic of Airbnb is that it does not develop, own, license, franchise, or manage any hospitality-related properties. Alibaba, based in China, offers an incredible amount of products for sale on its platform without manufacturing them. Facebook offers entertainment services (looking at photos and videos, listening to music) without producing any original content.[10] The situation is similar with Uber, which neither owns vehicles nor has drivers. Clearly, conventional businesses (traditional hotels and taxis) that own their assets and have their own employees must compete for visibility with

Table 2.1 Market capitalization and number of employees at selected new and traditional businesses

	Facebook	*Wal-Mart*	*GE*	*Alibaba*
Market Capitalization	$300 billion	$200 billion	$315 billion	$220 billion
Employees	17,000	2.3 million	295,000	36,000

Source: Various web sites (Data as of December 2016)

the new platform businesses that have neither any physical assets nor employees to work with these assets.

Another way of looking at platforms is to describe them as "network orchestrators," a term used by Libert, Beck, and Wind. The *network orchestrators* create and deliver value through connectivity, compared to *asset builders* that deliver value through the deployment of physical assets, *service providers* that deliver value through the deployment of skilled people, or *technology creators* that deliver value through ideas. In a detailed study, of 1,351 businesses, the researchers found that only 1 percent of the businesses could be classified as *network orchestrators*. These researchers provide examples of each of the four types as Wal-Mart as an asset builder, JPMorgan Chase as a service provider, Microsoft as a technology creator, and Uber as a network orchestrator.[11]

Platforms are given many different names, but the concept is simply to create markets: to connect buyers with sellers. Some, for example, call them "multisided platforms" – businesses that create value in two markets by identifying and reducing transaction cost.[12] Although it makes sense to consider network effects to mean that adding more customers would attract other customers, it is also important to consider customers on different sides of the market who interact through the platform. Consider three quite different examples.

In the case of the platform OpenTable, while more diners on one side attract other diners, more restaurants on the other side also attract more restaurants, which, in turn, attract more diners and which, in turn, attract more restaurants. In a second example, Couchsurfing is a networked accommodation platform-based business that operates in a relatively simple way. Users go through the verification and create an account. Members can then use the couches of other members at different locations to rest and sleep without exchanging any money. Whereas in previous times the process worked among friends and relatives, now the process works among strangers. According to an interview with Jennifer Billock, the CEO of Couchsurfing, the business is not just an accommodation platform but rather a social network in which users of the service have a primary goal of meeting new people and making friends and a secondary goal of obtaining accommodations.[13]

Peer-to-peer currency exchange would be a third example of a platform. Relating to currency exchanges, in *The Sharing Economy*, Arun Sundararajan suggests using the terms "bitcoin" and "Bitcoin" in the following way: refer to the lowercased word "bitcoin" as a currency and the uppercased word "Bitcoin" as a platform, technology, or an ecosystem.[14] In this peer-to-peer currency exchange, transactions are conducted directly between users and do not involve any intermediaries. The transactions are verified within the network and recorded in a distributed ledger, known as *blockchain*, which uses bitcoin as units in an account. In this context, the currency is called a "virtual currency" or "digital currency," and consumers can use bitcoins to access products and services from vendors and merchants, as well as to access other currencies. Typically, merchants pay fees of 2–3 percent to credit-card companies. The use of bitcoins, however, requires fees that are much less than those charged by credit-card companies. In some cases, the fee could be zero.

Network effects

What is a multisided platform business? In *Matchmakers*, David Evans and Richard Schmalensee provide an extremely understandable answer. For example, a shopping mall is a business designed to connect selected types of shoppers and retailers. The shopping mall developer selects the location and the layout of the mall to meet the needs of specific kinds of shoppers and retailers.[15] Evans and Schmalensee provide another easy to understand example of a multisided platform, OpenTable, discussed above. This business provides a system through which diners can make reservations at restaurants. Restaurants can use OpenTable's system to manage their reservations – place table availability online, make changes for cancelled reservations, fill up empty tables, and, in some cases develop relationships with selected customers. On the diner side, diners can make reservations online at different restaurants and receive points for making reservations. Restaurants, reportedly, pay a small fee for each reservation made and a monthly fee for using the system.[16]

The network effects mentioned above refer to the benefits, for example, of some producers connecting with other producers and some consumers connecting with other consumers to increase the value of products being produced or consumed. Platform providers can monetize the use of their platforms by asking for some parts of the additional value created for buyers and sellers with the platform. Suppose there was a platform that enabled airline and hotels and car-rental companies to network on the platform. The hotel could learn from the airline about when the passenger might be checking in at the hotel. Assuming that it is very early in the morning, the hotel could make a room available for an early check-in. Similarly, a car-rental company could find out from an airline the exact time of arrival of the passenger and send a driver to provide the rental car right at the curbside. The platform provider could monetize its services in the form of transaction fees for providing the information or fees based on the additional value provided to producers or users. Again, the concept is to co-create value and then share the co-created value. In *Platform Revolution*, Parker, Van Alstyne, and Choudary provide detailed descriptions of different monetization options.[17]

Technologies

The World Economic Forum's Global Agenda Council on the Future of Software and Society conducted a survey of 800 executives to determine the timing and impact (positive and negative) of game-changing technologies. The results were published in a September 2015 report, *Deep Shift – Technology, Tipping Points and Social Impact*, and are summarized in a book by Klaus Schwab, founder and executive chairman of the World Economic Forum.[18] The report presents 23 technologies having a significant impact. Four technologies listed are data, the IoT, cloud computing, and artificial intelligence/augmented reality (AI/AR). These four technologies are briefly discussed below.

Data

Three aspects of data have been evolving significantly during the past 10 years: the availability of the quantity of data, the complexity of the data, and the technologies available to synthesize the data. In the case of air travel, the quantity of data available relates both to consumers looking for travel services and to airlines offering travel services. It is the availability of this deluge of information that can enable airlines to undertake much more effective segmentation processes with respect to buying behavior, tracking the behavior of travelers across their life cycles, and monitoring the experience at critical digital touchpoints. On the buyer side, there is now much more information on the availability of services long before the purchase decisions are made, and the information is available through the channel selected by the buyer. Buyers are accessing the information digitally, which means that they are leaving locators (bread crumbs) for airlines to analyze the information accessed by consumers. In addition, since different information is available to different groups within an airline through different channels, technology is now available to help the airline gather, integrate, and synthesize this information across functions after the noise has been filtered out. As discussed throughout this book, emerging technologies have the potential to change the customer experience dramatically, whether the customer is shopping for airline services or being processed at airports. Self-service, for example, is one area – searching for flights, checking in at airports and dropping off bags, and, in some cases, obtaining electronic visas. Emerging technologies, such as self-driving vehicles, voice-engaging concierges, and biometrics (empowered by artificial intelligence (AI) and the Internet of Things (IoT)) will take customer service to new heights. Technology is available not only to help businesses deliver customized products and services more effectively but also to help them receive feedback and then make changes to products and services in real time through engagement and interaction.

Relating to data, there is increasing concern about security and privacy in terms of businesses misusing the data collected. On the other hand, the more data that is collected, the better and more personalized services a business can provide. These challenges and opportunities raise some questions about what consumers, businesses, and governments should do. How can consumers demand transparency from businesses, for example?

The Internet of Things (IOT)

The Internet of Things (IoT) is the framework in which devices interconnect with a capability to share information through the Internet. Consider the new value delivered by Nest Labs, the developers of sensor-driven home automation products: thermostats, smoke detectors, and security systems. Although such automation systems are not new, users now get extra value because they are Wi-Fi-enabled, they have self-learning capability, and they work in tandem. Consider Nest Labs' Nest Learning Thermostat, which optimizes the heating and cooling of spaces not just to conserve energy but also to meet individual users' preferences based on algorithms. The company also offers Nest Protect, an advanced smoke and carbon monoxide detector with multi-colored lights and motion-detector as well as voice-activated features. Moreover, the Nest Protect system is able to communicate with the Nest Learning Thermostat, providing even more value to users.

Consider also the role of IoT in the development of "smart cars" and medical devices. For cars, consider the value being added by Apple's CarPlay and Google's Android Auto. Apple's CarPlay system enables a car's radio to be a display and act as a controller for the iPhone. Android Auto allows mobile devices to work in cars through the dashboard's head unit. The system offers drivers significant control over mapping, navigation, web searches, telephony, SMS, and music through voice-controlled operations. In the retail sector, consider the use of beacon technology to enhance the shopping experience. In some circles, the IoT is now beginning to be called the Internet of Everything. Some analysts claim that we are transitioning from the "Information Age" to the "Intelligence Age," in which behaviors are analyzed and predicted and recommendations are personalized through the use of the IoT.

Cloud computing

The cloud allows users to have access, through the Internet, to large quantities of data and services that are stored centrally in the cloud (Amazon Web Services, for example).

Cloud computing, also referred to as Internet-based computing, are businesses where powerful technology businesses such as Amazon, Google, and Microsoft lease out time for the use of their computer networks, data centers, storage space, and applications. The providers of cloud computing also help users manage data and conduct analyses. The new element is machine learning, through which computers can make interpretations based on the use of "smart data." Some of the data used may belong to the user, while other data may belong to the company renting the use of the technology. Moving to the cloud can not only help businesses avoid the use of legacy technologies and save costs, but also lead to agility in the decision-making process for the user.

Businesses have lots of data. The challenge relates to what to do with the data businesses have already, let alone the new data that they can get. The cloud creates value from the data that a business has, and combines with the data the business might need to add, through the deployment of a new generation of apps. Consider the data generated in the IoT environment. A self-driving car has hundreds of central processing systems embedded in it. Presumably, most of the computations are done "on the ground," within the vehicle, so that real-time actions can be taken. There could also be some computations done in the cloud if the urgency is less and the need for additional data is high. Within the aviation sector, consider the thousands of sensors embedded in a modern aircraft. Think about the data they are generating while flying. How is that data being and going to be analyzed?

Large technology companies providing cloud computing services also have access to smaller machine learning companies, and experienced data scientists are on staff to make sense of the data. The breadth and depth of cloud computing services is helping traditional businesses take advantage of innovation that is being enabled by IoT, as well as digital technologies such as AI and AR, as discussed below. This type of transformation is enabling businesses to become much more nimble in searching for ways to become more effective – not just producing the right product or service but developing it and marketing it at a lower cost and in a timely manner – via an app, for example.

The idea of moving to the cloud is not just about getting access to apps that can produce more effective ways to share data, both internally and externally. It is possible for a business to move its entire data center to the cloud. The data storage capacity needed by a major global airline is enormous, given the millions of passengers transported. Add to that the capacity needed for the collection of data on the experience of each passenger and in real time and during various phases of the passenger's journey. A passenger flying around on an airline is continuously connected to the airline's data center, providing and receiving data. Moreover, the data transmitted is not just transactional. It could be videos showing the configuration of the premium cabins, for example. Then there is the vast quantity of information generated during a disruption from each passenger by the minute, from the staff, the airport, the partners, and so forth. Consider the amount of information generated during a disruption, when there are a number of colleagues flying from different cities to meet up for a meeting. These situations make the case for scale and platforms.

There is the issue of cybersecurity, the security of the data sitting in the cloud and the disruptions it would cause. The threat obviously relates to the location of the data and the value of the data. So does that mean that some critical data should reside at two places, with some in the airline's data center and some in the cloud?

Artificial intelligence (AI) and augmented reality (AR)

Artificial intelligence (AI) is enabling the collection and integration of data from very different sources to enable people to make intelligent decisions, do the right thing, do it right, and do it in almost real time. For businesses, AI is enabling the workforce to be much more collaborative. This technology can actually be used to transform the employees by giving them access to data and other employees throughout the entire organization, and possibly even partners. The technology is enabling the use of business analytics to develop business and customer intelligence. Artificially intelligent personal assistants– Apple's Siri, Google's Now, and Amazon's Alexa – can lead to the value-adding synthesization and utilization of an enormous amount of data residing in the cloud. For example, Amazon Echo is a device that listens to all speech and responds to the name "Alexa." It is a voice-activated personal assistant that answers a broad spectrum of questions, plays music, and provides real-time information relating to weather, traffic, and so forth. Machines with natural language–processing capability have already led to the introduction of robotic butlers in hotels and robotic baggage carts at airports, for example. While artificial assistants are already providing useful responses to everyday inquiries, advanced versions are being developed that deploy AI to learn speech patterns and incorporate predictive technologies. One only needs to consider the progress that has already been made with the development of autonomous ground vehicles.

In the last 10 years, AI has advanced significantly, with greater understanding of deep learning, natural language processing, cognitive computing, and computer vision (also referred to as "machine vision"). Consider computer vision, for example, an area that relates to how computers can gain high-level comprehension and analyze information from digital images. This area of technology can facilitate the development of machines that can take over the tasks performed by humans. Self-driving vehicles, as discussed by Jim Peters in Chapter 7, could help transport bags, with curbside pickup and with drop-off at the check-in area. The technology for machine learning, including the development of self-learning robotics, will soon be able to respond to "unbounded conversations."

AI is also beginning to push the frontiers of biometric verification. AI-enabled systems can identify the location of a person, verify the identity of the person, and know and understand the area surrounding the person. This information can help airlines, airports, car-rental business, and hotels provide navigational assistance and contextual-based services. It is the provision of these services, facilitated by digital technologies, that creates the integration of the physical and the digital worlds. Imagine vehicles located near aircraft that can take deplaning passengers to their destinations based on whether they are going to stay in the arriving city, transfer to other planes, or go to car-rental locations at or near airports. Initially the design process could involve three separate types of vehicles driven by humans, but eventually automated vehicles could provide such ground services. To see the feasibility of such a scenario, one only needs to see the progress Amazon has already made in processing the handling in its warehouses of ordered products. Domino's Pizza is experimenting with three different types of robots, those that can take orders, those that can make the pizzas, and those that can deliver the pizzas.

As with some other businesses, AI and machine learning have the potential to reinvent the travel business: web searches for airlines and self-driving vehicles for airports, for example. It is possible that, not too long from now, most travelers will be using speech recognition: talking to and engaging with machines. People are already using Amazon's Alexa and Google's Home. Soon, AI will enable machines to interact with people not only based on the full information provided but also when the information provided is incomplete.

Augmented reality (AR) adds further value for businesses and consumers. Augmented-reality glasses (with lenses, cameras, sensors, and screens) can take digital content and imagery and locate it in the view of users anywhere in the world. The glasses can have access to the information available in the cloud. These glasses are not just for travelers to enhance their travel experience. They are also for airlines to take care of their business. One employee at one location can look at what is happening at a different location and work with the staff to help find a solution to a problem, quickly. Consider the value of these tools in maintenance, especially at small locations with few facilities.

Voice-controlled interfaces, robotics, and augmented reality will improve, just as the capabilities of the Internet have increased. The new technologies are not only getting more affordable but also have much more user-friendly interfaces. Robotics can already see, hear, sense, and react to situations. Some technologists are predicting that not only will voice-controlled interfaces proliferate but also the communication environment will expand to include "gesture, touch, and sight." On another front, start-ups have already been building apps to make the evaluation and purchase of products and services much more effective. However, some technologists see that it will be possible for consumers to build their own apps by deploying their own voices. Consumers will be able to change these apps easily and frequently, given the ease of undertaking "programming" aspects.

Human resources

Most business sectors, including aviation, are in the midst of a fundamental change, led by digital technology. Digitization relates, however, not just to technology but also to people, as well as to cultures. Technology is simply an enabler, and in some cases possibly even a driver. However, the outcomes are achieved successfully, namely the solutions created, depend on people. One could ask who these people are. They are consumers, employees, and partners, and soon all three are going to be digital. Digital millennials, for example, are not just consumers but also employees and in many cases partners. Virgin America is a case in point. It was based in Silicon Valley, had tech-savvy customers, high-tech products, and tech-savvy employees.

Although it appears that many traditional companies want to become software businesses to capitalize on the innovations taking place outside of their businesses, the task is not easy, as it requires many developers and the resources the developers would need in turn. The human resources required will also most likely call for a change in the organizational style, from one based on command-and-control to one in which employees are contributors and empowered stakeholders.

Many businesses are also attempting to become data-driven. However, being data-driven also means welcoming input in the decision-making process at all levels and in all areas. Employees are not just helping customers, they are also helping other employees at all levels as well as partners. The involvement of people will become even more important when the IoT takes off. Consequently, it is really people who are driving change, with technology as just an enabler. Unfortunately, at some businesses, including a few airlines, people are inhibiting the use of technology. For example, when an employee leaves the business, there should not need to be a struggle to find a solution to his or her leaving. There are other employees in the same company and others around the world, including partners, to help and produce operational agility. Based on insights from pioneering businesses, it appears that if strategies, processes, and systems are becoming digital, then the employees need to get a digital orientation too. Businesses must ask whether their employees are even comfortable with the use of data and different kinds of analytics, let alone comfortable with the use of people analytics that enable people to be connected.

Implications for airlines

Tectonic shifts are taking place in consumer behavior, as shown in the previous chapter and in technology as discussed in this chapter. Interestingly, some changes in consumer behavior have been the result of changes in technology. Can existing business models meet the needs of consumers? Can airlines develop and implement digitally networked business models that would provide the value sought by emerging consumers? Which organizations within the ecosystems would an airline need to collaborate with? Presumably, at the beginning the partners would be different suppliers of travel service – airports, hotels, car-rental companies, and information-rich technology businesses. What assets would be needed, both tangible and intangible? Tangible assets would presumably be airplanes, trains, and autos, as well as properties to provide accommodations. How about the intangible assets – the data, the software, the analytics? The next step is the challenge, visualizing how the assets would be integrated within the ecosystem to create value. How would value be not just created but shared, based on contribution? How would the airline operate within the network? Would it be willing to simply acquire, insure, crew, fuel, fly, and maintain the airplanes? Would it be willing to let the information-loaded partners (say Google or Facebook) develop the marketing package and a GDS make the reservations? Who would create the platform, a global airline or a technology organization? Who would manage the platform? How would value be measured and tracked? How would it be delivered? How would the rewards be shared?

The next step would be to analyze scalability and global reach, presumably facilitated by the Internet and digital technologies. The development of a platform can facilitate integration across alliance partners, as well as integration between members of the travel chain – airports, hotels, car-rentals, and so forth. A platform can help with the analysis of new ways to optimize the supply and demand value chains to create mutual value for the buyers and sellers. As discussed above with reference to Amazon, the focus should not be on products; it should be on platforms on which products are produced and sold. More focus is needed on digital assets and less on physical assets, as well as the benefits and costs of both types of assets, with the full consideration of economies of scale and economies of scope, such as global reach. The capacity of a typical legacy data center at an airline is limited, even for the data that is being collected right now. Therefore, moving to the cloud makes sense even now. It certainly will be necessary when the volume of data increases and there is a need to use predictive analytics to adapt to the hyper-competitive environment.

What will differentiate one airline from another, aside from its geographic scope and perhaps degree of localization, is the collection, synthesis, and deployment of information. The strategy needs to be developed based on information.

Forward-thinking airlines recognize that they should not necessarily be concerned with which of their conventional competitors – other airlines – have information on customers. They should be concerned with *whoever* has information on their actual and potential customers. It could be Amazon, Expedia, Facebook, Google, or Twitter. That raises the question of who has the responsibility for information. It may be the chief information officer (CIO); however, there are many aspects to information – its collection, integration, synthesis, intelligence, and use for product or service development and marketing. Therefore, is the right person perhaps the chief digital officer (CDO), or the chief transformation officer (CTO)?

Some airlines have begun to work with small (even start-up) businesses to drive innovation: Lufthansa through its Innovation Lab, jetBlue through its Technology Ventures Group, and Ryanair through its Ryan Labs. These concepts are sound, assuming that large airlines can work with start-ups in light of the silo and hierarchical organizational structures that exist at most airlines. Large, newer-generation technology companies have been following a similar strategy for some time. Microsoft, for example, reportedly works with a concept called "creative realism," in which start-ups can have some flexibility in terms of working in unconventional ways to push the boundaries of businesses.[19] The newer-generation large technology businesses recognize that the following characteristics of start-ups contribute to their success.

- They seem to have a passion for whatever they are doing.
- They seem to be truly focused on finding solutions to problems.
- They are agility-driven with respect, for example, to changing direction and business goals and pivoting their business models. They are flexible because they are also rigorous and focused.
- They are very data-driven, deploying insightful analytics, and they believe in failing fast.
- They believe in the collaborative approach, particularly with technology.

Now a number of leading traditional businesses are trying to behave like start-ups, exemplified by the likes of GE and IBM. Although airlines themselves are not trying to behave like start-ups, some are teaming up with start-ups to extend their businesses. A few airlines are beginning to invest in start-ups to get fresh ideas on the business side as well as the technology side to watch how the technology evolves to look beyond the horizon. British Airways, for example, launched UnGrounded, an innovation lab, in 2013, and more recently in its new organization called Hangar 51. The linkages can either help an airline integrate the initiatives of the start-up in its own operations or pre-empt the development of a competitive force. Some start-ups have been in the area of search or aspects of developing the content of what is being offered. Airlines have been supporting the start-ups that have presented them with new ideas – for example, artificial intelligence tools for travel, specifically business travel. AccorHotels got lots of coverage when it acquired Onefinestay, for example, an accommodation-related start-up.

AccorHotels has been investing in digital distribution to extend its business from simply accommodations.

Here is an example of an interesting start-up. DistancesBetween.com is a platform through which travelers can make bookings to fulfill their multi-modal needs. Bookings can be made on the standard forms of transportation: air, rail, bus, and taxi. This platform is being introduced in India, a huge country with millions of kilometers of roads in various stages of development. The platform facilitates door-to-door travel by presenting timetables and maps in simple formats and bringing some transparency into the total fares. Revenues will presumably come from commissions as well as advertisements. Although covering the last mile may not be difficult in regions such as North America and Europe, it can be quite a challenge in most parts of India, where there are even major questions involving trains and buses. How many places does a consumer need to go in order to comparison shop for and book the various legs of his or her trip? Some current travel booking sites do not even have the names of some remote places. In a recent article, reporter Martin Cowen provides one example of a passenger wanting to travel from Haridwar, in Uttarakhand, India, to Rameshwaram, Tamil Nadu, India.[20] The web site DistancesBetween.com provides, for a search made on April 24, 2017, for travel on May 2, 2017, six possible itineraries, ranging in price from 1,974 to 7,610 rupees. The cheapest option takes 53 hours and 15 minutes, involving a 17-minute walk at the origin, two train rides, and a rickshaw from the second train station to the destination, a distance of one kilometer, that would take seven minutes. The most expensive option would involve a taxi at the origin to Delhi Airport with a flight to Chennai Airport and a taxi to the final destination. The total trip time would be 13 hours.

Think about another start-up, Recharge, a mobile app that enables a user to book a luxury hotel room for use by the minute. The offer provides services in two major cities at this time, San Francisco and New York City. This is an example of an innovative app that is ideal for flexible-length stays. It is reported that room rates can vary from $0.66 per minute to $3.00 per minute. Think about the rooms that are vacant during many hours of the day after the guest has checked out. Great for business travelers and great for businesses.

If airlines were to move out of their conventional businesses, they could face some regulatory challenges, just as Uber and Airbnb had to deal with governmental concerns about safety and taxes. Since these new businesses do not fit into the normal regulatory schemes, governments have struggled to find ways to control and accommodate them. Leaving aside the idea of airlines getting into new businesses such as platforms and networks, some airlines are still concerned about conventional types of questions – for example, about their entry into conventional businesses relating to the deployment of advanced airplanes coming in (Airbus A350s, Boeing 787s, Airbus A321neoLRs, and Boeing 737 MAXs) that could open up new markets, given the economics and payload-range capabilities of new airplanes. The important point is still that an airline needs to develop its core products and services – its network and its schedules – but then strengthen the core products by leveraging the products and services offered by partners within the ecosystem, including start-ups.

Merging the development of physical and digital products and working within the ecosystem calls for a major shift in the planning process for airlines. It means basically reinventing the airline business from the viewpoint of not just optimizing the use of conventional airline business physical assets, such as fleet, but also deploying digital technologies and strategies to extract digital value out of these assets. This duality requires, in turn, two key criteria for evaluating technology: (1) strategies that an airline can initiate and that are actionable immediately, to provide additional value to customers and to break down the silo system, and (2) strategies that can be developed for the near future, say one to three years, to enable cooperation within the ecosystem.

Would working within the ecosystem require the deployment of a platform to add much value for producers and consumers? If so, who would develop the platform, an airline or an outside technology business? The airline business is complicated. It is capital-intensive, given the cost of airplanes. It is information-intensive, given the need for vast quantities of information to flow among vast functions outside of an airline and between various departments within an airline. Consider also the regulatory aspects, given that airlines cannot fly to any destination in any country without government approvals. Next, the security-related challenges keep changing. Since most airlines do work within the three global alliance systems, is it possible for a platform to emerge that could use technology to gather information on the travel needs of consumers and enable the development of schedules that synchronize demand and supply more efficiently in some sectors, well beyond the coordination performed within the joint ventures within the alliances? The platform could even enable airlines that are members in different alliances. The platform would enhance the network value by adding not only suppliers of different travel services (airlines, trains, cruise ships, taxis, and so on), but also information-rich companies such as Facebook, data-driven insights from companies such as Google, and companies with advanced network, fleet, and schedule–planning systems such as Sabre. The platform would enable an airline to shift from being the seller of basic products, such as a seat from airport A to airport B, to becoming the provider of solutions to mobility problems.

Merging physical assets, such as airplanes and maintenance facilities, and the digital assets, such as information, networks, and relationships, is an enormous challenge. Because whereas physical assets decrease in value through usage, intangible assets such as digital assets do not. In fact, their value may even increase. It is the use of digital technologies that enable these assets to be created and used to produce scalability. Although the benefits of using intangible assets are clear, the challenge is to manage these assets. Take, for example, two aspects of intangible assets: information and customers. Information has a lot of value, but different participants in the network hold different types and quantities of information. Information could be shared if it were to be treated like a currency that could be traded. The second aspect relates to the co-creation by customers of the content and value of products, as well as services and the related communications through social media. In many businesses, the value of tangible assets is decreasing in light of the money that is tied up. In the auto industry, expensive physical assets exist in the form of extensive plants. The auto sector now faces competition from self-driving cars. Traditional, capital-intensive car-rental companies are facing competition from the likes of Uber and BlaBlaCar. Similarly, large amounts of capital are tied up in hotel buildings, and the hotel sector is now facing competition from different types of rental properties.

Could airlines with large amounts of capital tied up in airplanes and hangars similarly face competition from new, asset-light platform businesses? If the answer is yes, then the first priority is to optimize the current business model for producing and selling an airline's core products: its network and schedules. This is the subject of the next chapter.

Takeaways

• The main characteristic of new businesses such as Airbnb, Amazon, Facebook, and Uber is that their focus is not on products but on platforms, on which solutions are produced and sold, and on digital assets, not physical assets, with benefits relating to costs with respect to economies of scale and global reach.

• A business can leverage customer networks by using technologies (platforms and information) to compete more effectively by not just making better products and services but also innovating through the experimentation process.

• Large airlines are beginning to work with small businesses (even start-ups) to drive innovation. Although the concepts are sound, the challenge for large airlines is to be able to work with start-ups given their silo and hierarchical organizational structures.

• New businesses such as Airbnb are not only fulfilling a demand for alternative accommodations but also prompting existing hotel chains to realign their strategies.

• Developing value is not an easy task in businesses that are asset-heavy, such as airlines. Uber, an asset-light business, found a way, but what are the possibilities for airlines? Identifying and delivering value for customers is one pillar of the recommended approach, and maximizing the utilization of an airline's expensive physical assets is another pillar. The optimization process must deal with both – referred to throughout the book as "mutual value."

• The connected consumer is not a challenge for a business; it is an asset.

• Most business sectors, including aviation, are in the midst of a fundamental change, led by digital technology. However, digitization relates not just to technology but also to people, as well as cultures. In network and revenue management, for example, human and intelligent technology are working together to help businesses make better and faster decisions.

• Technology is available not only to help businesses deliver customized products and services more effectively but also to help them receive feedback and then make changes to products and services in real time through engagement and interaction.

- Platforms can facilitate the synergistic integration within the ecosystem and achieve scalability within the supply and demand chains. Data needs to be collected, but, even more important, it needs to be shared, and that means it needs to be treated like currency.
- Automation is a sound strategy, but it has to be developed and implemented intelligently with artificial intelligence.

Notes

1 Barry Libert, Megan Beck, and Jerry Wind, *The Network Imperative: How to Survive and Grow in the Age of Digital Business Models* (Boston, MA: Harvard Business Review Press, 2016), p. 4.
2 Gary Leff, "Uber's Confidential Financials Revealed. They Lose Money on Every Ride But Make It Up on Volume," *VIEW from the WING*, January 17, 2017.
3 Geoffrey G. Parker, Marshall W. Van Alstyne, and Sangeet Paul Choudary, *Platform Revolution: How Networked Markets Are Transforming the Economy and How to Make Them Work for You* (New York: W.W. Norton, 2016), pp. 3 and 6.
4 Alex Moazed and Nicholas L. Johnson, *Modern Monopolies: What It Takes to Dominate the 21st-Century Economy* (New York: St. Martin's Press, 2016), p. 126.
5 Sangeet Paul Choudary, *Platform Scale: How a New Breed of Startups Is Building Large Empires With Minimum Investment* (Platform Thinking Labs Pte. Ltd., 2015), pp. 17–18.
6 Moazed and Johnson, p. 41.
7 David L. Rogers, *The Digital Transformation Playbook: Rethink Your Business for the Digital Age* (New York: Columbia Business School, 2016).
8 Jeff Gothelf and Josh Seiden, *Sense & Respond: How Successful Organizations Listen to Customers and Create New Products Continuously* (Boston, MA: Harvard Business Review Press, 2017), p. 96.
9 Aswath Damodaran, *Narrative and Numbers: The Value of Stories in Business* (New York: Columbia University Press, 2017), front book jacket flap.
10 Parker, Van Alystyne, and Choudary, p. 3.
11 Libert, Beck, and Wind, pp. 13–14.
12 David S. Evans and Richard Schmalensee, *Matchmakers: The New Economics of Multisided Platforms* (Boston, MA: Harvard Business Review Press, 2016).
13 Arun Sundararajan, *The Sharing Economy: The End of Employment and the Rise of Crowd-Based Capitalism* (Cambridge, MA: The MIT Press, 2016), pp. 38–9.
14 Ibid., p. 87.
15 Evans and Schmalensee, pp. 17–18.
16 Ibid., pp. 9–12.
17 Parker, Van Alystyne, and Choudary, Chapter 6.
18 Klaus Schwab, *The Fourth Industrial Revolution* (Geneva, Switzerland: World Economic Forum, 2016), pp. 121–72.
19 Shameen Prashantham and George S. Yip, "Microsoft Starts UP," *strategy + business, PwC, strategy&*, Spring 2017, pp. 10–12.
20 Martin Cowen, "Startup Pitch – DistancesBetween Tackles India's Door-to-Door Dilemma," *tnooz.com*, April 24, 2017, https://www.tnooz.com/article/startup-pitch-distancesbetween-tackles-indias-door-to-door-dilemma/

3 Innovating and evolving airline network planning

Should an airline, regardless of size and type of operation, work within a platform framework discussed in Chapter 2 to meet the changing expectations and behaviors of consumers discussed in Chapter 1? Furthermore, should an airline develop digital strategies deploying digital technologies, including information and analytics, not only to adapt to the dramatically changing expectations of older and newer generations of consumers, but also to defend against the potential entry of new and powerful digital intermediaries? Based on the transformations occurring within leading traditional businesses, it appears that the ideal situation would be to establish a bimodal management structure. Examples include the likes of GE and IBM in the US, Mercedes and Siemens in Germany, Haier in China, and Metro Trans in Australia, discussed in Chapter 7. Within this structure, one organizational part of an airline would continue to optimize its operations using the existing conventional systems and processes. Simultaneously, a second part of the company's organization would develop and implement new digital strategies to explore new frontiers in value, both for customers and for the business. In *Lead and Disrupt*, Charles O'Reilly III and Michael Tushman give an excellent example of how to run a bimodal business that they call "ambidexterity" capability.[1]

This chapter and the next chapter focus on the organizational part of the airline that would be optimizing the existing business model within the context of investments, costs, and revenues, as well as making the business much more nimble.

Current and evolving systems

Making the network and schedule–planning processes much more nimble, robust, and proactive calls for simplification, as well as the minimization of constraints. Although some constraints, such as infrastructure in general and airport slots in particular, are external, others, such as the undertaking of different functional processes in a sequence mode (crew scheduling, maintenance planning, and fleet assignment, for instance) as opposed to in a parallel and an integrated mode, are internal. As for complexities, one only needs to look at the substantial overlap in the composition of the fleet of a major European or American airline. These airlines have multiple types of airplanes with similar capacity, range, and performance attributes. It is quite common for a major airline to have not only the Airbus and the Boeing narrow-body aircraft, but also many different versions of each – for example, the Airbus A319, A320, and A321 models and the Boeing 737–700, 800, and 900 models. Similarly, a major airline can fly a number of versions of the Airbus A330 and at the same time different versions of the Boeing 777. Undoubtedly, these multiple types of narrow-body and wide-body aircraft do provide network and schedule planners the ability to match capacity to demand more closely, but the additional costs relating to crew scheduling, maintenance, and ground operations are phenomenal, not to mention the additional tasks of managing complexity and dealing with irregular operations, when the backup airplanes do not match the size and range of the airplane to be replaced.

On the revenue-management side (discussed in the next chapter), major airlines typically have a couple of dozen fare buckets that are managed in each flight, for each of the hundreds of itineraries associated with each flight, and for all itineraries for every day of the year in advance. Dealing with these complexities relating to revenue management on a daily basis is a monumental challenge in its own right, but the challenge reaches an incredible level when the impact of revenue management is considered within the network and schedule–planning analyses. It is such constraints and complexities that make the network and schedule–planning process consume a year. Although it is true that minor changes are often made during the year to account for seasonality and the day-of-week variation, the overall cycle time is still generally one year. Moreover, while the network and schedule–planning function is the heart and soul of planning the airline product, other vital components of commercial and operations planning functions add their own constraints and complexities. Consequently, within the broader context of planning, some managers are wondering whether they might bring about a seismic change to accelerate business performance. The concepts presented in this chapter can support such a change.

Given the diversity of airlines, there is no one answer to the question of what is the ideal level of transformation to accelerate business performance. For some airlines, transformation can be at an incremental and operational level; for others, it can be at an innovative and at a disruptive level. To help different airlines based in different regions, at different stages of development, and with different levels of skills, each airline could think about a technology-capability diagram that shows what it can achieve with what technology and with what level of human skills and internal interactive collaboration. The beginning of a platform, from one perspective, is highlighted in Figure 3.1, where there are basically four interacting components of technology that can enable an airline to undertake transformation at four levels. Each layer of technology and capability can enable an airline to introduce enhancements in airline productivity (reduced decision-making and planning-cycle times, for example) and customer satisfaction (relating to products, experience, and personalization, for example).

If the final goal for an airline is to become a digital business, then even the team that is optimizing the conventional business model needs to think about the long-term deployment of a platform. Figure 3.1 provides an outline of a technology framework that would eventually become part of the platform business.

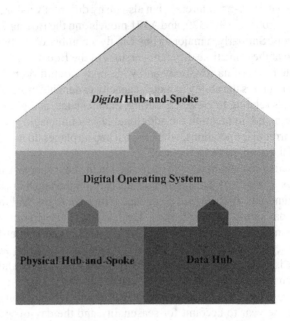

Figure 3.1 Transformation technology components

For airlines in general, the most basic level of transformation is to optimize their *physical* hubs (the lower left-hand component of Figure 3.1) with respect to their network, fleet, schedules, and alliance partnerships. Even this calls for the design of a network based on integrated input from all sub-functions, with optimizations based at an enterprise level, rather than at each functional level. In addition, revenue management, discussed in the next chapter, not only needs to be integrated within different commercial sub-functions within its own space, but also plays an important role in the design of the physical hub. Most important, however, the development and operation of the physical hub must work very closely with the finance department to get information in the form of one version of the data truth, at an extremely "granular" level, and in almost real time, right until each flight physically takes off. This aspect, shown in Figure 3.3, will be discussed shortly. For now, the main point is that optimizations need to be made at the corporate level, not at the sub-functional or even at the functional level.

The second transformational component, shown in Figure 3.1, represents a *data* hub that enables an airline to integrate its corporate data along with varying types of analytics to achieve excellence at the operational level. It is with a data hub that an airline can evaluate many more scenarios much more quickly, than is currently possible using existing disparate data and relatively unsophisticated analytics. The analytics currently in use provide, at best, information about what happened and why – with respect to financial performance and the drivers of financial performance. However, there are analytics that can provide information on what could

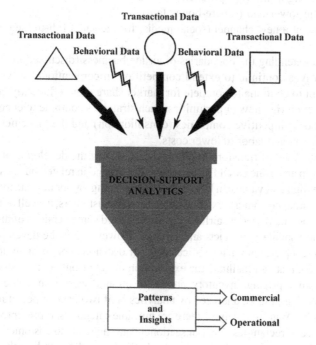

Figure 3.2 Digital hub-and-spoke system

happen to the financial performance under different scenarios of sharing codes and what should be the prices of various code-shared seats. This aspect will also be discussed shortly within the context of Figure 3.2. From an integrated point of view, however, although it is important to identify optimal flights to be code-shared from an airline's perspective, it is even more important to focus on the needs of connecting passengers and their actual origins and destinations (O&Ds). The data hub can obtain such information from different *listening centers* relating to social media communications, coupled with the deployment of mobile-based analytics.

The third transformational component is the development of a *digital* hub, shown at the top of Figure 3.1. This component would not just facilitate, but force cross-functional integration to create new value for the airline *and* its customers at a customer-service level and not just at the operational level. It would provide 360-degree views of customers and their trips that would enable an airline to create personal relationships with its customers. Obviously, the object is to grow and sustain the bottom line. However, the goal is not just to extend the current core business in conventional ways, such as the following:

- Flying to new destinations
- Bringing in a new strategic alliance partner (to extend the network in a regulatory constrained environment)

- Introducing a different product, either at the higher end (a first-class suite) or at the lower end (a bare-bones fare)
- Looking at a new channel (social media, for the sale of distressed inventory)

Rather than extending the boundaries of airline business (discussed in Chapter 6), these initiatives continue to extend competition in conventional ways and lead management to continue to compete for market share more efficiently. Moreover, rather than exploring new opportunities, such strategies continue to encourage the acquisition of competitive companies (consolidation) and the placement of pressure on vendors and labor to lower costs.

The fourth level of transformation, the beginning of the development of a platform, can help an airline extend its boundary and expand in related businesses where margins are high and value can be enhanced for existing and/or new customers: new value for existing customers, existing value for new customers, as well as new value for new customers. Recently, airlines clearly explored some versions of these strategies in selling ancillary products and services. However, it is the development of a *digital* hub, coupled with a sophisticated set of decision-support analytics (shown in Figure 3.2), that can facilitate the exploration of new frontiers in customer value such as dynamic pricing, inventory, and redemption, discussed in the next chapter. The data coming in to be analyzed by analytics is of two basic types: transactional and behavioral. Within each type, there are multiple categories, represented by triangles, circles, and rectangles. The transactional data can relate to customers, partners, employees, operations, vendors, and so forth. Similarly, data can be behavioral and relate to passengers – for example, their behavior while searching for information on a web site or making a selection of a particular price-service option or even a brand. The sophisticated analytics organize the random data into meaningful patterns and insights that are further divided into user groups, such as those in the operational function or in the commercial function. The digital hub, using the patterns and insights developed by analytics, can enable an airline to provide an enhanced customer experience and, ultimately, more complete solutions for customers' mobility needs, both leading to an increase in profitability. After all, it is the availability of relevant information on customers and the value being offered, as well as analyses of interactions with customers in real time, that will help bring about a significant reduction in decision-making times and an increase in conversion rates.

This fourth transformational component comes from the availability of (1) a digital operating system that is essentially a combination of the two systems below it – namely, the physical hub and the data hub – and (2) an open-access platform. A digital operating system would enable an airline to rebuild its business from the ground up to capture new frontiers in value for customers (in terms of enhanced experience and personalization, for example) and for the airline (in terms of profitability and growth, for example). Clearly, travelers want solutions to their mobility problems at a fair value, and businesses want higher productivity and better financial performance.

This fourth transformational component can be part of an open-access platform in which different partners can bring in value through apps, data, and analytics and receive value through the willingness of consumers to pay higher prices to meet their personal mobility needs. The transformation of businesses enabled by open-access platforms has overturned many core views of competition among many different business sectors and challenged conventional management wisdom. Insights from other businesses show that technology (for example, cloud-based customer technologies and computing services leveraged by an open-access platform) has enabled integrated and data-driven solutions that have added more value, not just in incremental improvements to existing products and services, but in new and better ways of meeting customers' needs while generating higher profits.

The disruptive era is calling for all businesses to re-think their business models to generate new value for customers to meet needs they have not even considered. This call for action is more than a call for the acquisition of more technology. It is about disruptive thinking and not about constraints. It is about investments in enabling technology but coupled with changes in operations and processes to develop strategies to identify and fill customers' unmet needs. And it is about reorganizing dramatically the marketing and sales functions to become analytically driven and, in turn, become agile and proactive.

Conventional planning-module limitations

Although airline network and schedule–planning processes have always been complex, the degree of complexity has increased due to the expansion of various categories of low-cost carriers, the expansion of the newer-generation network airlines, and consumers' ability to undertake effective comparison shopping to evaluate different aspects of an airline's schedule. On the other hand, while complexity has been increasing, airline schedulers have felt an increasing need to be nimbler and more proactive in planning their competitive responses to the changes in the marketplace. Although recognizing the importance of an airline's network is not a new insight, what is different now is the value of new types of network and schedule–planning modules and the integration capability to not only optimize an airline's network but also produce

- a planning platform that is much more agile and proactive,
- a reduction in the planning-cycle time,
- a much more robust schedule to accommodate the changes necessary during the day of operation, and
- an improvement in internal communications to generate feedback that can influence the evolution of the schedule.

As an example of one limitation of conventional planning perspectives, consider the network extension possibilities facing a network planner out of high-population cities in India (other than Delhi and Mumbai), say, Hyderabad, Bangalore, Chennai, and Kolkata. These are major cities with growing populations and with increasing levels of disposable income. From an opportunity perspective, consider just two comparisons. First, compare the low number of long-haul international destinations served out of these cities relative to other large cities around the world – Atlanta, Hong Kong, and Madrid – for example, and the number of international destinations they serve. Second, while it is true that these big cities have relatively small O&D passenger traffic levels, consider how the three carriers based in the Persian Gulf developed their gigantic global networks even with tiny population bases and extremely low O&D passenger traffic levels. Older-generation conventional network and schedule–planning models cannot identify the long-haul routes from these potential hubs and show their plausible profitability.

Consider the difficult decisions some carriers have had to make in recent years using the older-generation network planning models.

- Emirates made a recent decision to fly an A380 nonstop between Dubai and Auckland with about 490 seats, including about 15 in first-class suites and about 75 in business class with pod configurations. Reportedly, the aircraft also offers shower spas in the front and a lounge in the back. Passengers on this flight, around 17 hours northbound, can connect with a number of destinations in Europe taking another six to seven hours. Given that Emirates serves multiple airports in the UK (in London, Manchester, and Birmingham, for example), passengers can start the journey from one airport and return to a different airport. Could the older-generation systems predict how many passengers would consider the nonstop flight time to be so long that they would prefer to take a connecting flight?
- United Airlines, which had been previously serving Beijing and Shanghai, recently decided to provide nonstop service from San Francisco to Xi'an, Chengdu, and Hangzhou. In addition, United decided to increase the frequency of its service to Shanghai from San Francisco. Could the older-generation systems evaluate the impact on traffic from diversions and stimulation aspects, let alone the network effects of United's total nonstop flights to China from the US, almost 100 a day?
- Singapore Airlines made two network decisions recently using the older-generation models. One involved having Scoot, a wholly-owned subsidiary, provide four flights a week from Singapore to Athens, in a Boeing 787-8 with about 330 seats, including about 20 in a premium cabin. This ultra-long-haul flight for Scoot is planned to connect with the services provided by Singapore Airlines and its other subsidiary, Tigerair. Next, Singapore Airlines decided to replace its nonstop service between Moscow and Houston with a new service between Manchester and Houston. Older-generation systems are constrained into making decisions of the optimization at the enterprise level, having taken into consideration the positive and negative impact from all functions while working with consistent assumptions.

The inability of conventional planning systems to adequately take into consideration the changing nature of competition is serious. In the US domestic markets, for example, low-cost carriers have entered the high-density markets dominated by the major carriers. Spirit, for example, has entered the markets dominated by

American, Delta, and United. As a result, the legacy carriers have begun to intro-duce new low fares. Delta introduced its basic fares to enable it to compete more effectively. However, as of the beginning of 2017, the jury is still out on the long-term commercial viability of these fares. Similar situations exist in other parts of the world. Consider the route Mumbai-Delhi (BOM-DEL), where low-cost carriers such as IndiGo, GoAir, SpiceJet and Vistara began to carry more traffic than the legacy carriers (Air India and Jet Airways). Since the middle of 2014, patterns have shifted and the traffic carried by the legacy carriers has been increasing, due in part to the introduction of lower fares, enabled, in turn, by the lower price of fuel. Again, conventional network- and schedule–planning systems do not have the capability to analyze numerous options quickly and consistently and select the optimal path. The conventional systems can provide limited insights, but even those come at a great expense from the viewpoint of time consumed, not to mention the lack of knowledge about the optimality of the final strategy adopted.

An example of the limitations of conventional planning systems is their inability to enable network planners to determine comprehensively the financial impact of analyzing emerging aircraft options. Think about the role that the Boe-ing 787 has played in the re-design of networks of airlines such as All Nippon Airways in offering nonstop service in secondary markets and service in new markets. All Nippon, having received more than fifty 787s by the end of 2016, started to consider offering service in such diverse markets as Tokyo, Phnom Penh, and Mexico City. And it is not the recent drop in the price of fuel but, hopefully, the economic performance of the new long-haul aircraft that has led Singapore Airlines' plan to re-start its nonstop service between Singapore and New York. Similarly, the availability of advanced single-aisle aircraft such as the Airbus A321neoLR and the Boeing MAX can enable an airline's network-planners – for example, at jetBlue, WestJet, and Norwegian Air Shuttle – to think about nonstop transatlantic services. Think about the role that an A321neoLR or a potential replacement for the Boeing 757 could play in the development of direct services between major cities in China and smaller cities in Europe or smaller cities in China and major cities in Europe. Lower-cost airline Norwegian (which has ordered 100 Boeing MAX aircraft) has announced its decision to fly between secondary cities across the North Atlantic. The conventional network- and schedule–planning systems, however, do not have the capability to analyze these options to optimize financial performance at the enterprise level, let alone perform rapidly dynamic iterations.

Now sophisticated and integrated fleet-management and network-management systems are becoming available to help an airline such as Norwegian experiment with different city pairs, leveraging the operating cost structure of a Boeing MAX that shows seat-mile costs to be even lower than for a Boeing 787. At the same time, these advanced and integrated planning systems can help traditional airlines compete more effectively with the potentially powerful low-cost airlines expand-ing their intercontinental operations. These traditional airlines can evaluate more comprehensively their lower-cost subsidiaries – Air Canada with Rouge, Lufthansa with Eurowings, Singapore with Scoot, and Qantas with Jetstar. These systems can also add much value for traditional airlines that want to use a different strategy than a low-cost subsidiary – for example, through the addition of more seats on existing flights. Think about even more options for an airline such as British Airways. Is the decision to start Level, a lower-cost subsidiary, to fly across the Atlantic better than a strategy to re-network Aer Lingus or add more seats to existing aircraft and fly from secondary hubs – London and Dublin? Whereas conventional planning systems have had limited capability, newer systems can enable network planners to evaluate each option within the context of an airline's entire service offering and at an enterprise level as opposed to a functional level.

New modules and integrative planning

While the existing network planning systems are becoming more sophisticated incrementally in their capability, there are also new planning modules that can now be integrated into existing systems to analyze increasingly complex challenges and new opportunities. Consider the aviation industry in India, for example. The government is now encouraging airlines, under its Regional Connectivity Scheme, to offer affordable air-travel services in markets outside of the main urban areas. So, how should an airline like IndiGo, which has been growing very rapidly, re-design its network that has concentrated mostly on domestic markets and those around just four cities, Bangalore, Delhi, Kolkata, and Mumbai? One answer is to use sophisticated models that are, for example, logit-based and that can forecast to a much higher degree of accuracy while integrating with the existing module to forecast profitability and new code-sharing and slot utilization modules.

The new modules in the network- and schedule–planning suite help to address complexity. For example, first, airlines have developed a broad spectrum of alliances in such areas as operations, joint ventures, and equity. Second, within the network and scheduling perspective, on every flight an airline now competes not just on price and schedule but also on the service delivered by the brand as well as ancillary revenue generated by context-based offers that enhance the customer's experience. Third, some airlines have created the potential for cannibalization from their airlines-within-airlines – Eurowings within Lufthansa, Jetstar within Qantas, Scoot within Singapore, and Rouge within Air Canada. To deal with these complexities, new modules and their integration with existing modules can not only provide step changes for the network- and schedule-planning groups but also help the revenue-management groups to maximize profits. This is discussed in the next chapter.

Although airlines have had inter-line marketing agreements and even code-shared flights for a very long time, the complexity has increased for at least four reasons. First, there is an increase in the number of partners within each of the three global alliances – oneworld, SkyTeam, and Star Alliance. Second is the development of joint ventures within each major global alliance. Third is the willingness and acceptance of an airline to work, at the same time, with partners in other global alliances. Fourth, airlines are now changing their memberships in alliances with a greater speed. This increasingly complex and dynamic nature of the marketplace now calls for much more agility. For example, the process of identifying the optimal set of code-shared flights has become far more complex, given the increase in the number of partners at the strategic, equity, and inter-line levels, and an increase in the number of flights. Yet, airlines cannot increase the number of flight digits from more than the conventional number of four digits. Consequently, given the limited number of slots available at key airports, the decision on which flights to code-share becomes critical. Until now, this element of network- and schedule-planning has been undertaken either manually or with the use of fairly rudimentary analytic systems. However, sophisticated slot and code-share evaluation and management systems are now available to help airlines achieve optimization at the enterprise level while working with multiple strategic and inter-line partners. Although these slot and code-share evaluation systems are sophisticated in their own right, they also enable network and schedule planners to conduct analyses through the use of integrated systems. Moreover, as already mentioned, the slot-evaluation module can provide valuable information to revenue management that already contains data on yields. More importantly, slot evaluation and management systems enable airlines to not only optimize their currently planned schedules but also facilitate the trading of new slots through a network of parties.

Examples of comprehensive, dynamic, and integrated planning

Vietnam Airlines

Suppose Vietnam Airlines were to consider service to and from the US, say in the Ho Chi Minh City–Los Angeles market (SGN-LAX), a market that currently does not have nonstop service. The market-evaluation process undoubtedly would start with the network planner looking at the size of the market using data published by a number of organizations, such as OAG. The planner might see the size of the market with a number such as over 200,000 bookings in 2015 (using connecting services). Following could be the steps taken by the planner using a conventional system and some new modules discussed above.

- Most airlines have scheduling systems to start the process, shown in Figure 3.3, with the circle "Market and Route Forecasts."
- What is new is that the information on the selected market can now be fed into a Slot Evaluator and then into a module for analyzing code-shares with alliance and non-alliance partners. Would there be a need for slots in Los Angeles and, if so, how would those slots be obtained, and at what cost? Similarly, which carrier(s) within the SkyTeam alliance would Vietnam Airlines share its flights in Los Angeles with – Delta and/or Aeromexico? And with which carrier(s) in Ho Chi Minh City –Air France, for example?

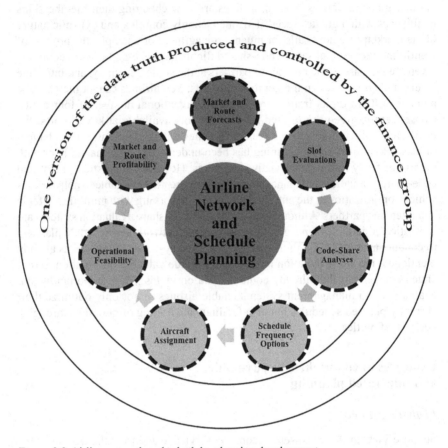

Figure 3.3 Airline network and schedule–planning development

Alternatively, would it be economically viable to code-share with an airline in a different alliance? The output from these three sub-systems can then be fed into the next module, Schedule and Frequency Options, which would produce an initial recommendation for frequency (from two to seven times a week) and the proposed departure and arrival times.

- Information is then entered into the Aircraft Assignment module to select the optimal aircraft for the route, to match capacity with the forecasted demand.
- The proposed schedule is then fed into a module to determine the Operational Feasibility from the perspectives of crews, ground operations, and maintenance at both ends of the segment.
- Information on the operationally viable schedule can then be fed into the Market and Route Profitability module, which analyzes revenues and costs to forecast profits. The profitability module itself has many other sub-systems to provide input on detailed costs (fuel, labor, aircraft, etc.) and detailed revenues based on demand, market shares, fares, and so forth.

The final output may or may not be acceptable, leading to several iterations. For each iteration, the planner should be able to ask for the use of *real-cost* data at a much more detailed and granular level from the finance department. Typically, flight profitability forecasts have been made using average costs in multiple areas. Take, for instance, costs of operating a flight at a congested and slot-controlled airport. Whereas using average costs for evaluating a flight under consideration may be adequate for the first go-around, further iterations may require real-cost data based on the details of the planned operations. What would be the cost of the specific slot used for the flight? What are the costs likely to be invoiced by the ground-operations vendor for handling the flight at an unusual departure or arrival time? How likely would a planned landing time close to the beginning of a night curfew disrupt the operation, and what would be the consequential cost? Knowing costs at granular levels will provide meaningful insights into the profitability of new flights. Moreover, such levels of detail would also enable planners to make effective adjustments after operations begin – changes to departure time, frequency, code-shares, crew pairings and crew rotations, and so forth – very quickly, not months later. Crew constraints, particularly with respect to crew pairing and crew rotation, have always been difficult. Now with improvements in optimization techniques, including computation power and speed, it is possible to perform simultaneous optimization processes.

Although this description is very simplistic, it does highlight a few key points.

- Sophisticated systems are needed for newer-generation activities, such as slots and code-shares, that integrate with scheduling and revenue-management systems. Although the challenges and opportunities relating to slots and code-shares are not new, what is new is the need to analyze quickly and comprehensively the best options, given the existence of different categories of alliance partners. As mentioned, think about Delta, which has an equity stake in Virgin Atlantic flying across the Atlantic and is in a strategic alliance with Air France in SkyTeam. What would be the best option to route a particular passenger from Atlanta to Delhi, with a connection in Amsterdam (on KLM), or with a connection in Paris (on Air France), or with a connection in London (on Virgin Atlantic)? What would be the criteria: trip duration, code-share fares, or some other criterion? How about competition from other airlines, such as Lufthansa via Frankfurt, British Airways via London, Turkish via Istanbul, or Qatar via Doha?
- The process is iterative, using linked systems: existing and new. Although airline network and schedule planners take input from and provide input to all functions within an airline, the input is often fragmented and untimely for different departments working with a different set of assumptions. For example, operations may show that the desired schedule calls for additional crew, and the costs would be prohibitive unless the fleet assignment planner were to select a different aircraft, one that may not match capacity and demand optimally.
- Iterations involve different time frames: long-term, medium-term, and short-term. The long-term framework might look, for example, not just at current

slots and partners but also at potential partners. It may also pay less attention to such factors as operational feasibility, facility requirements, passenger connectivity, and seasonal variations, factors that would be much more relevant within the medium-term perspective. The short-term framework would take into consideration day-of-the-week considerations and special events, not to mention potential competitive actions and reactions.

- Data considerations are basically threefold. First, the finance department should be the primary source of data on costs and revenues, because of the finance department's ability to (a) go down to a much more granular level, (b) receive and provide data that is robust, and (c) provide data in almost real time. Second, the information on the schedule should provide input data to all other planning systems, starting, of course, with the publication of the schedule itself. And all departments should have real-time access to all changes in the schedule. Third, there needs to be a single source for data relating to the industry – data on time zones and airports, for example.

- If the final results show, in the above example, that the proposed market (SGN-LAX) is not feasible, then the systems can allow the analysis to be conducted easily, but consistently, on another market – say, Ho Chi Minh–San Francisco (SGN-SFO). Although the O&D data would show that this is a smaller market than SGN-LAX, the advanced features in the planning systems could produce different results depending on factors as the level of competition and potential partners for code-shared flights. It is also possible that, while neither market may make sense, the two markets together might show financial viability. There is also the possibility to analyze a third market – for example, Ho Chi Minh–Washington, Dulles (SGN-IAD), individually or in combination with one or both of the other two markets.

Alitalia, Air Berlin, and Jet Airways

Consider the lack of integrated network planning by various members within the group in which Etihad Airways purchased equity stakes, particularly the three struggling airlines Alitalia, Air Berlin, and Jet Airways. Other members in the group included Air Seychelles, Air Serbia, Darwin, and Virgin Australia. If the key members (Alitalia, Air Berlin, and Jet) had planned their network in an integrated manner using systems to provide traffic feed to provide optimizations at the enterprise level, the results would have been quite different than what actually happened. The concept made sense, as it would have enabled Etihad – the smallest of the three new Persian Gulf–based airlines, operating to and from an airport with a small amount of O&D traffic – to very quickly become a global player, and it would have strengthened the other players from the joint traffic feed. However, the task of integration turned out, presumably, to be far more complex than envisioned. For example, many routes out of Europe to the Asia-Pacific region required a double connection in the case of traffic feed coming from Air Berlin or Alitalia because of the relatively thin O&D traffic base to and from Abu Dhabi. Computing the value of a double connection to different kinds of passengers is an enormously difficult task for conventional planning systems. Integration with Alitalia was also supposed to have taken into consideration the positive aspect of the opening of Linate Airport in Milan, a more convenient airport for long-haul flights – a development that did not fully materialize. In addition, from a competitive point of view, Alitalia underestimated its role to add incremental traffic to Etihad, again, presumably, due to increasing competition from LCCs, particularly easyJet and Ryanair.

Similarly, the integration of Jet Airways' network did not produce optimal results, presumably due to its inability to optimize the combined network at the enterprise level. One obvious option would have been for Jet Airways to use sophisticated systems to decide the ideal place for a European hub: Amsterdam, Brussels, or Düsseldorf. How should Jet have resolved its partnership issues? What would the systems have suggested, partnership with Air France-KLM, or Delta, or Virgin Atlantic? And in the case of Air Berlin, based on reports in the press, Air Berlin did not provide the envisioned benefits from network integration, based presumably on the use of constrained conventional network planning systems. Now Air Berlin has been looking at the optimal strategy for downsizing its network. Would conventional planning answer the question of whether to locate a hub in Berlin versus Düsseldorf? How about the decision relating to the wet lease of a large fleet of aircraft to Lufthansa, and the re-alignment of the relationship with Etihad on one side and TUI on the other side? These decisions could easily have been made earlier with the use of integrated models producing optimizations at the enterprise level.

Norwegian Air Shuttle

The conventional wisdom used to be that low-cost airlines will not succeed in long-haul intercontinental markets. Jetstar, a division of Qantas, has been operating international services for more than ten years. Now, Norwegian and Scoot, a division of Singapore Airlines, have been expanding their network with Scoot flying nonstop between Singapore and Athens. In fact, Norwegian is taking the concept two steps further. First, in July 2017 it introduced the advanced narrow-body aircraft (the Boeing 737 MAX 8) across the Atlantic from Ireland to a number of smaller cities in the eastern United States. Second, Norwegian, which had already been flying exceptionally long-haul routes as a low-cost carrier (Copenhagen–Los Angeles, Stockholm-Bangkok, and Oslo-Bangkok) announced it would fly nonstop between London and Singapore (almost 11,000 kilometers) starting in September 2017 with a Boeing 787-9 configured with 344 seats in two classes.

Norwegian is expanding its network very fast within Europe, between Europe and Asia, and between Europe and North America. Figure 3.4 shows the existing and planned routes outside of Europe. This route map does not even include Norwegian's plans for routes to be operated between various cities in Europe and the announced services to Buenos Aires as well as other cities in South America, to and from Buenos Aires with as many as ten Boeing 737s based there. Norwegian could also start services to South Africa with the Boeing 787s.

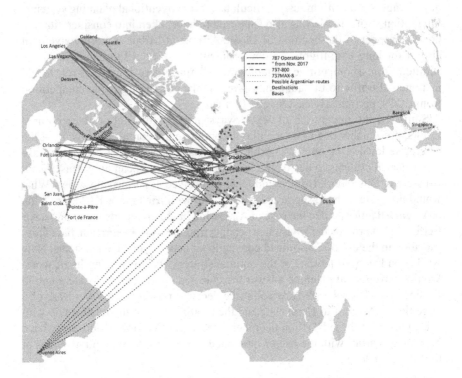

Figure 3.4 Services offered and announced by Norwegian Air Shuttle and its subsidiaries

Source: Map drawn by Aviation Strategy Ltd., UK, with the map drawn using an equidistant map projection based on London

It is unlikely that the conventional disjointed network-planning systems will enable Norwegian to evaluate different scenarios with agility, let alone with analyses conducted on an integrated cross-functional basis. Moreover, the achievement of accurate analyses of profitability of individual flights on their own, as well as their real contribution of the system-wide operations, would require the use of one version of the data truth produced and controlled by the finance group, as shown in Figure 3.3. The network-planning exercises had always been a challenge, but the degree of complexity has been increasing quickly. Consider the challenges faced in the past by long-haul low-cost airlines, such as those that Oasis Hong Kong Airlines experienced in 2006 (on its Hong Kong–London and Hong Kong–Vancouver services) and those that AirAsia X experienced in 2012 (on its Kuala Lumpur–Europe services). Now, the complexity has been increasing – for example, by the addition of services by new long-haul low-cost carriers such as Eurowings (Cologne-Bangkok) and French Blue (Paris–La Réunion) as well as the expansion of services provided by the three major carriers based in the Persian Gulf. There are also new factors in the profitability equation – for example, the lower price of fuel, the superior economic performance of such aircraft as the Boeing 787, the much higher margins from the sale of ancillary products and services, and the potential opportunity to inter-line with full-service airlines. Deployment of advanced network planning systems has a much greater chance of predicting the long-term economic viability of long-haul operations of lower-cost airlines. Moreover, these planning systems can enable an airline to conduct analyses with agility and to implement services on a trial-and-error basis.

What's next?

The availability of new and integrated network planning systems discussed above can enable airlines, particularly those willing to develop virtual operations, to develop much more integrated operations within alliances. They can help an airline adapt quickly to the increasingly challenging but opportune marketplace with optimizations made (a) around an airline's equity partners and (b) at the enterprise level as opposed to the functional level. These new systems can take into consideration the potential impact of such drivers as revenue per customer (not revenue per seat) for each connection, not to mention other considerations, such as the development of the brand and customer loyalty.

   However, if the goal is to become much more nimble by reducing the planning cycle time, then there are two other steps. One is mentioned in this chapter – namely, the initiative to develop a digital operating system enabling the planning team to work with consistent commercial and operational data (transactional and behavioral) and customer journey analytics. Digital operating systems can help answer "what and if" questions much more accurately and quickly, enabling agility and robustness. An alternative approach might be to work with truly dynamic network, fleet, and schedule development models. For example, instead of developing fixed schedules and variable fares, an airline could work with variable schedules and fixed fares, described by Dietmar Kirchner in Chapter 7 as "Turning the Airline Operating Model Downside UP."

Takeaways

* As indicated in the beginning of this chapter, it is possible for an airline to work within a platform framework for the reasons, and along the lines, discussed in the previous chapter. Given the nature of the airline business (the development of the network, fleet, and schedule being the heart and soul of this business), one plausible starting point is the development of a digital operating system that itself would call for a data hub and a digital hub-and-spoke system. In addition, there would be a need, based on insights coming from other businesses, for an airline to consider working within a bimodal organizational structure.
* Within such a structure, one group would focus on optimizing the existing business model while a second group explored the value of digital strategies. Under this scenario, even the group in charge of optimizing the conventional

physical hub-and-spoke system would need to use the new-generation planning systems. The dynamics of the marketplace in which the airline industry operates, have been changing rapidly, making the legacy network planning systems inadequate. New systems are available that not only enable network and schedule planners to optimize the current business model at the enterprise level, but also achieve results with agility and results that are more robust. Specifically, the analyses no longer need to be:

- ○ performed on a piecemeal and sequential basis due to technological limitations of the legacy systems,
- ○ conducted manually on small subsets due to the sheer volume of options, and
- ○ adjusted manually to comply with constraints such as airport slots, noise restrictions, maintenance requirements and crew assignments, not to mention day-of-week schedule changes to allow for peaks and troughs.

- Deploying increasingly sophisticated individual airline network and scheduling components has the potential to produce incremental benefits in costs and/or revenues even in the context of a physical hub-and-spoke system. However, the new integrated systems, including new modules such as slot and code-share evaluation, will lead to more organizational agility to identify and analyze a wide array of products very quickly and consistently. However, although the theory discussed in this chapter seems sound, in the end, it is all about execution: does the design fulfill the promise, how is transition managed, and can people and the organization fly the faster system?
- On the other hand, an airline's resulting network strategy, identified on the basis of truly integrated cross-functional input, will lay the foundation for the airline to develop the market with respect to strategic decisions in other areas, such as products, partners (alliance or equity), distribution, and revenue management, the subject of the next chapter.

Note

1 Charles A. O'Reilly III and Michael L. Tushman, *Lead and Disrupt: How to Solve the Innovator's Dilemma* (Stanford, CA: Stanford University Press, 2016).

4   Re-thinking revenue management

In the last chapter it was suggested that before an airline decides to take some initiative in digitizing, the executive team should consider newer-generation processes to optimize the conventional airline business model, starting with the development of network, fleet, and schedules. The use of the newer-generation thinking will reduce operating costs and generate more revenues, but, even more important, it will lead to the development of systems and processes that result in much greater agility and robustness in the overall planning process. A similar argument applies to the second important airline function, revenue management.

Although airlines clearly have made significant progress in managing their revenues, there is still room for growth. Just as the switch from leg-based systems to O&D-based systems was a game changer, there is now a potential opportunity for another game changer, given the asymmetry in information. An airline has a lot of information on its products, but relatively little on its passengers. Conversely, passengers have access to a lot of information on an airline and relatively little on its products. Therefore, if an airline were to respond to consumers' requests based on information on competitive prices and seat availability as well as consumers' revealed preferences, the result would be a higher conversion rate, not to mention a reduction in frustration on the part of the customer.

Historical perspective

The yield-management system was pioneered in the mid-1970s by British Airways (then British Overseas Airways Corporation) with the introduction of "Early Bird Fares." The concept took off in the early 1980s, after American Airlines used it to make smarter decisions about prices and inventory to compete with tour operators and low-cost low-fare airlines, respectively. Later, attempts were made to simplify the fare structure and levels. Back in the early 1990s, American attempted, for example, to introduce a "Value Pricing" initiative containing just four booking classes: first class, regular economy class, and two categories of advance purchase economy class, 7 days and 14 days. The objective, presumably, was to simplify fares for consumers and to eliminate discounts for corporations. On the inventory side, to maximize revenues, airlines began to switch from the use of leg-based systems to O&D-based systems. As for pricing, different categories of airlines (low-fare, full-service, and, recently, hybrid airlines) have been experimenting with different fare structures based around the travel restriction-flexibility dimension and targeted segments that are either price or schedule sensitive.

Within the two basic parts of the revenue-management system, pricing and inventory, pricing has remained fairly static relative to inventory control. And with respect to inventory, although it is controlled dynamically, the changes are made manually. Consequently, the degree to which changes can be made dynamically has been limited due to the need to conduct the operations manually. Think about the numbers for a minute. If a large airline has 5,000 flights a day, and there are 30,000 itineraries per day associated with these flights, and bookings are taken for each itinerary up to 330 days in advance, how many flights can be monitored manually, even by a team of planners? Ironically, there are advanced revenue-management systems that will suggest movements in inventory automatically. However, in practice, analysts tend to override the suggestions made by the automated system, even though analysts can monitor only a few flights and take into account only a few implications.

Analysts principally do not trust the automated systems. They do not have enough confidence in the recommendations presented, for two primary reasons. The first reason relates to the latency of the data used. The second reason is that the system provides recommendations without an explanation. Consequently, there is no transparency. Moreover, even when revenue-management analysts do make changes dynamically (but manually), they are internally focused. They do not have full knowledge of what is happening in the marketplace, particularly with respect to actions of competitors and many aspects of the shopping activity. Manual decisions may be acceptable for a small airline, such as a low-cost carrier, if it has limited connecting traffic. For a large airline, however, analysts need to use systems that are contextually sensitive. Such systems are now being developed, systems that utilize sophisticated machine learning algorithms to model consumer choice. As for the confidence of analysts, they can even enter their own preferred key performance indicators (KPIs) and then let the system make recommendations within the selected KPI framework.

Existing systems and process challenges

On the airline side

Switching from leg-based systems to O&D-based systems involved a lot of work, relating, for example, to such needs as forecasting demand and performing revenue planning on customers' itineraries as opposed to individual flights. Important considerations emerged relating to factors such as analyses of connections: online, inter-line within alliance partnerships, and inter-line outside of alliance partnerships. There were also significant staff challenges relating to staff capabilities within the revenue-management function, not to mention the need for some new KPIs – for example, the total level of revenue at the network level, including from code-shared flights, as opposed to the level of yield and load factors. These considerations required the staff to make decisions on

- overbooking strategies to protect seats for the higher-fare passengers who tend to book late while minimizing denied boarding compensation,
- bid pricing – a threshold price for a booking class when demand exceeds supply and the booking fare must be at or above the bid price to obtain a seat – a task that becomes even more complex when, for example, a situation involves both an operating airline and a marketing airline,
- forecasting demand for the true O&D of the customer when travel involves a destination on an alliance partner (that is, demand for services on both the operating carrier and the marketing carrier),
- determining seat price for both the operating and the marketing carrier, and
- forecasting the number of redeemable seats by loyal customers now that loyalty benefits are becoming based on revenue generated rather than miles flown.

Up until now, the reservations booking designator (RBD), also known as the "booking class," has served as (a) a criterion for customer segmentation to manage fares with respect to inventory pricing, rules, availability, and control and (b) a mode of distribution via the GDS. Although this type of segmentation process worked reasonably well in the past, it has become a challenge with changes in customer purchases calling for a different customer-centric process. Examples of pricing and rules have related to information on the degree of advance purchase and length of stay. However, the price within a booking class is generally fairly static during the day, even though availability can fluctuate. Consequently, the term "dynamic pricing," going forward, is likely to be based on the attributes of a customer, or, at least, the attributes of a trip, as discussed below, as a customer may or may not provide a comprehensive list of attributes.

How about challenges relating to the fact that whereas some airlines may consider that they have vast quantities of data, the data are limited from the viewpoint of a traveler's whole journey? Think about the massive quantities of complex data captured and stored by a broad group of travel suppliers (airlines, hotels, cruise lines, car-rental companies, and rail and ferry lines) and intermediaries (online travel agencies and GDSs). Most suppliers of travel services recognize that with the use of analytics, the data captured by the supplier group can be converted into information on customers' preferences and purchase and consumption behaviors and patterns. Suppliers can then use the information to create products, provide better customer service and a seamless experience, and generate high-margin revenues through targeted but contextually-based offers. It is this line of thinking that would lead to the development of a platform to develop services that meet the dramatically changed expectations and behaviors of consumers. Even at a much more basic level, suppliers can use this data to make their web sites much more consumer-friendly and more effective at acquiring customers, not to mention, making the business more agile. However, the challenges relating to data are complex:

- First, it is necessary to make sure that the relevant data is collected in the first place (data from web surfing, shopping, booking and ticketing, checking in, user-generated travel reviews).
- Second, relevant systems are needed to (a) accept different types of data coming in (from social media, email, and so forth) and (b) to clean the data.
- Third, it is necessary to establish a location for the data that has been cleaned.
- Fourth, in an ideal situation, it would be helpful if the travel suppliers were willing to share the data. This challenge may be the most difficult to overcome, as at some businesses (for example, airlines), different functions within the same company do not want to share data.
- Finally, the data needs to be generated in real time.

On the customer side

When it comes to buying airline tickets, customer frustration often relates to the time spent on shopping, the rapid change in the availability of a fare, and, in recent years, the fact that the price paid may not end up being the final price, as charges may be added for ancillary products and services that were not necessarily clear at the time the reservation was made. Most consumers cannot understand the airline industry's revenue-management process. Having become frustrated with airlines' attempts to find different ways of optimizing revenue, consumers have also been looking at ways to "reverse engineer" the revenue-management process and find ways of optimizing their booking processes. Some consumers have, for example, begun to use the services of technology companies that help consumers determine the ideal time to make a booking in order to obtain the lowest fare. Some consumers have begun to purchase insurance to obtain a refund if an airline reduces the fare between the time of the booking and the time of travel. Some consumers have begun to buy insurance in case of cancellation of a non-refundable fare by weighing the cost of the insurance against the service fees involved for making changes to the reservation.

Step-changing options: opportunities and challenges

Revenue-management-system designers have been improving the systems and processes, keeping in mind the following six assumptions.

- Consumers now have much more information while they are shopping, and consumers' shopping and booking patterns are changing.
- Consumers are looking for, to varying degrees, personalized services with a focus on their experience throughout the journey.
- Airlines like to offer the right content to the right customer through the right channel at different stages of the trip, shown in Figure 4.1.

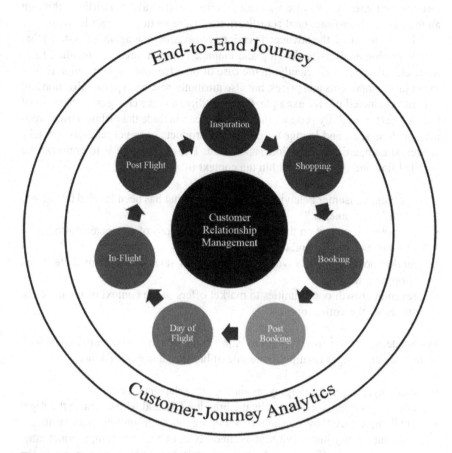

Figure 4.1 Customer relationship management throughout the journey

• Airlines want to maintain, if not increase, profit margins from the sale of ancillary products and services.
• The CEO's office needs to see the ramifications of various decisions by various heads of different functions to ensure optimizations at an enterprise level, including the impact on the back-office functions.
• Airlines, being under pressure on profit margins, need to eliminate, or at least reduce, yield leakage.

Technology (data, analytics, algorithms, and computing power) is now available to help airlines optimize from three perspectives. First is the optimization relating to the process, integrating all elements – not just prices and inventory, but also ancillaries, channels, and a broad spectrum of code-shares. Second is the provision of agility to speed up the decision-making process. The third perspective is to enable revenue-management decisions that generate both (a) value for customers, through customer-centric offers and simplicity, and (b) value for airlines, through an increase in inter-functional coordination and a reduction in yield leakage.

Take, for instance, the advanced versions of revenue-management systems that enable pricing analysts to develop and manage branded fares and bundled fares more effectively and efficiently. In the case of branded fares, optimization relates to not just components and prices, but also attributes related to personalization and experience, including, for example, the flexibility to make changes. In the case of bundled fares, ancillary products and services can include the airline's own products, such as seats and lounge access, or the products of travel partners – hotels, car-rental companies, cruise lines, and so on. The opportunity is to optimize the branded fare and the bundle within the context of:

- evolving consumer behavior – for example, what has been labeled by Google as "micro-moments,"
- the potential impact on the heightening expectations of connected customers – for example, on-demand customer experience,
- market positioning relative to competition for sales based on attribute-based shopping, and
- revenue growth opportunities to market offers in the context of the different stages of the entire journey.

System designers are also working to improve the systems even more to deal with three more challenges relating to the sale of branded and bundled fares:

- challenges faced by employees during irregular operations
- challenges relating to who sells the branded fare and who operates the flight
- challenges faced by consumers shopping on their mobile phones to get information not just about seat availability but about location, product attributes, and rules (for example, baggage rules), based on their status in the frequent flyer program

Customer segmentation and personalization

One key decision-making criterion in the revenue-management process has been segmentation. In the past, segmentation was handled with the development of booking classes, which, in turn, were controlled by such aspects as the booking time prior to departure and the conventional elements of trip purpose. In recent times, attention has focused on customer-based segmentation. However, given the complexity of customer-based segmentation, technologists are exploring segmentation criteria based on the purpose of the trip, which, in turn, is based on "revealed preferences." A "revealed preference" parameter could relate to the brand of the airline, such as one of the three Persian Gulf–based airlines, or a preferred airport for making a connection based on the type of trip, such as a fast connection through Helsinki versus a leisurely connection through Dubai or Doha. Another example of a "revealed preference" parameter is going to Abu Dhabi for shopping or going to

Keflavík International Airport in Iceland, where the locally-based airline may allow a stopover without an additional charge. The trip purpose envisioned goes beyond the conventional attributes (business, leisure, and VFR). For example, is the business trip a day-return or a trip requiring one or more nights' stay? Will it include a personal component at the beginning or the end? Trip-based segmentation can work whether the customer is anonymous or identifiable. And answering requests based on trip segmentation can also take into account compliance with corporate policies and rules, discussed in Chapter 1, to obtain higher conversion rates.

Subsequently, a personalization aspect can also enter into the trip-based framework. The personalization step, enhancing the trip level, can be facilitated significantly by leveraging artificial intelligence and machine learning spheres. Moreover, personalization can be achieved in real time and on a contextual basis, by making offers based on location and personal preference. It can also include such parameters as customer value, including lifetime value, and status in the loyalty program. However, for airlines to deliver products and services that are even more personalized calls for deeper knowledge of customer preferences and shopping behavior by distribution channel. Such knowledge requires data and analytics relating to each stage of a customer's journey, from inspiration to post travel, shown in Figure 4.1, so that an airline can display targeted and relevant content, based on implicit and explicit information. This task is particularly complex if the airline does not know who the customer is on the web site (anonymous). Even if the customer is known (identified after the customer has logged on with his or her known identity), the customer may not have stated his or her preferences for that particular trip. For a discussion on the role that loyalty programs have played in the development of richer data sets and stronger analytics capability, see Evert de Boer's contribution to Chapter 7.

Consequently, it makes more sense to start the personalization process at the trip level than at an individual level. Imagine a person saying, "I want to take my family on a vacation for three days in San Francisco." There could be many personal variations, not just by the day but also by direction. Since the customer is concerned with not only all components of the entire air journey but the entire trip (hotel, car-rental, etc.), there would be a need for coordination, leading to a need to collect and share data. The question then is not who would or should collect the data but also whether the different parties would be willing to share the data. Eventually this process would take place, and the organization could easily be one that already has lots of data – Facebook, Google, a GDS, or some combination of these. It is true that customers would need to give permission for data to be collected and shared, but newer generations are more likely to provide data, especially if the organizations collecting the data are global brands such as Google and Facebook. For further information on segmentation by purpose of trip, see B. Vinod's contribution to Chapter 7.

The key point is that if airlines do not take care of the entire trip, someone else will, by working through a platform-based business as discussed in Chapter 2. Airlines claim that they have lots of data – contained in the loyalty program, for example. But unfortunately that data tends to be used only when it comes to travelers in the highest level of loyalty – to provide ground transportation, a meet-and-greet service, and escort service throughout the airport. Some hotels are doing the same thing for their top-tier guests. A hotel can send out a car to the airport to pick up an extremely high-status incoming passenger. The driver can even advise the concierge at the hotel to come out just as the passenger is arriving at the entrance and the customer can be met, greeted, and escorted to the room, where the customer can fill in the registration form. In fact, since a hotel already knows all the data of a top-tier customer, there should be no need for a registration form. Who will scale such processes to meet the needs of travelers in tiers lower than the very top – will it be travel suppliers, or will it be the new digital distributors?

Pricing and fare management

Conventional revenue-management systems for pricing and inventory control are not appropriate any longer. In the Internet era, consumers are seeking transparency with respect to schedules and prices that are competitive, and social media can have an impact on travel preferences through user-generated content, such as customer reviews. Consequently, with relatively static prices, analysis of historical booking patterns and information on ticketing, while useful, is not sufficient.

Although prices can be, and have been, changed virtually within hours, during the day they tend to be relatively static in the context of dynamic pricing. A low-cost low-fare airline could have, say, three fares, with variation in each one based on an advance-booking period – 7 days, 14 days, or 21 days, for example. If one booking class is closed, does the analyst look at the prices for the next booking class and make changes? On pricing, just as with inventory (discussed above), analysts make decisions for each product based on the market, itinerary, ancillaries, and so forth. Although systems are now becoming available to make recommendations on pricing, analysts appear to be reluctant to accept decisions made by systems, just as in the case of inventory control. In fact, they do not even allow the system to make decisions within a price range, say from $300 to $400. Allowing the systems to make such decisions could add much value for conducting simulation studies to measure the impact of different pricing decisions.

Undoubtedly, although the concept of dynamic pricing is appealing, its application is quite complex. First, it might be helpful to discuss a misperception. Analysts point to the millions of fares filed daily either by an airline being proactive or by it responding to the fares filed by one or more competitors. This process is not dynamic pricing in the true sense of the concept, in which an airline develops a capability to evaluate the marketplace and offer the optimal fare to a customer, based on an airline's own revenue-management practices, its inventory, and its competitiveness in the market relative to the fare. The fare offered to a customer may well be very different than the fare filed. Within this context, dynamic pricing would be tied very closely to dynamic availability. Dynamic pricing should not be confused with personalized pricing, which means offering a fare based on an individual consumer's profile and travel behavior – current and past, not to mention information on price elasticity.

Let us now turn to the complexity of dynamic pricing as envisioned in the industry in the current environment. First, the analyst must consider dynamic pricing and dynamic inventory simultaneously, a consideration that requires information on competitive tactics: selling fares, the status of RBD availability, and a forecast of the expected ticket price. Consider flights from Dallas to New York, from Dallas–Fort Worth Airport in the case of American and from Dallas's Love Field in the case of Southwest. Let us say American is offering a fare of $274 and Southwest a fare of $199. Should American reduce its fare, or should Southwest increase its fare? Who has a better product, and from whose point of view, passengers' or the airlines'? How do different customers view the product: service through DFW versus through Love Field? Monitoring competitive fares needs to go further than the examination of the fares filed with the Airline Tariff Publishing Company (ATPCO). There is a need to explore the dynamics of the marketplace: actual fares, discounts offered, and seat availability, as well as the quality of the selling airline's product and services. There continues to be a gap between the prices offered by one airline and the prices of its competitors, not the fares filed. It would be a giant step just obtaining the critical information and acting on it. GDSs are clearly one source of information on shopping and purchase trends in the marketplace at any given point in time.

Second, optimization of revenue management based on the use of dynamic pricing and dynamic inventory requires estimates of the attractiveness of each itinerary offered based on revealed preferences and the modeling of customer choice, customer journey, shopping, booking, and so forth. At the very least, dynamic pricing needs to ensure that within each booking class the selling price (ticketed fare) is higher than the bid price. And, if the identity of the customer is known, the dynamic pricing system can adjust the offer based on some aspects of personalization – at the trip-segmented level or at the customer-segmented level – by changing the components within a bundle and/or the price of the bundle itself. Dynamic pricing also plays an important role in the allocation of inventory for different categories of code-share partners, within and outside of an alliance or joint venture, using seats in different categories such as hard blocks, soft blocks, and free-sell. In the last category, the marketing code-share partner continues to sell and report until a message is received by the operating code-share partner to stop further sales. A further decision is needed if the operating code-share airline decides to work with a bid price exchange system instead of the free-sell approach. For further information on dynamic pricing, see B. Vinod's contribution to Chapter 7.

Adding to the complexity of pricing is the fact that dynamic pricing is needed not just in the area of maximizing revenues within the context of revenue management. In some cases, the objective could be to maximize yield. Think about markets in which capacity is restricted or an airport where slots are restricted: for example, London Heathrow. In such cases, the objective may well be to increase the yield of passengers on capacity-restricted flights. Other examples of not maximizing revenue within the context of revenue management might be some promotional reasons, such as service on new routes or new service on code-shared flights with new partners.

As for fare management, A/B testing can significantly facilitate the exploration of different strategies. Should an airline offer different prices or simply different components relating to a fare, such as no change fees or free baggage? Although this technique is not new, new technology can instill greater confidence in the validation process and provide more agility. Additionally, responding to customer requests based on revealed preferences can lead to higher conversion rates and reduce the level of frustration for the customer. However, providing an optimized response to a request will require comprehensive analysis based on not only the deployment of preference-driven programs, customer-choice models, and A/B testing techniques, but also sophisticated ways of deploying dynamic pricing and dynamic availability. Within each parameter, there is a need to drill deep. For example, if the dynamic pricing option is selected, there is then a need for further input in such areas as an estimate of the willingness to pay (derived from the deployment of A/B testing) for the bundle to be created for the offer.

What will happen with requests where consumers can provide detailed information on their preference? Take, for example, a request for an itinerary between New York's JFK and Singapore Airport (JFK-SIN). The web site of online travel agency Expedia showed about three dozen airlines offering services (December 5, 2016, JFK-SIN and December 13, 2016, SIN-JFK) involving one- or two-stop flights and fares between $807 and $6,226. The shopper was given the capability to rank the available itineraries by price, trip duration, time of departure, or time of arrival. Although there were four rank-ordering possibilities, a shopper could select only one of the four criteria at a time. Technology now allows the inclusion of more parameters and also the ability to weight the importance of each parameter to suit an individual passenger's needs. Examples of additional parameters are the importance of the connecting airport and the refundability or non-refundability of the fare. Moreover, it is now possible to let the customer develop the bundle based on the components desired by the customer and the weight assigned by the customer to each consideration.

These capabilities can play an important role in the development and implementation of travel packages within the framework of subscriptions by airlines and third parties, as well as in different tactics for airlines to re-purchase sold tickets and for customers to sell back purchased tickets that they do not need. In fact, some start-ups are already developing sophisticated apps that will open up a secondary market for the re-purchase and re-sale of airline tickets. The successful apps will undoubtedly establish a framework that creates a win-win situation for sellers, buyers, transaction facilitators, and the airlines.

Algorithms are now becoming available for generating the best set of itineraries in response to a shopping request – outbound and inbound with considerations of fares and fare conditions – to meet customers' needs and maximize conversion rates. Ultimately, the offer-management process, particularly involving online activity, could be a step-changing process if it harnesses the power of artificial intelligence and its role in the development of machine-driven natural language recognition, understanding, and translation (concepts mentioned in Chapter 6). These aspects of artificial intelligence, which can be accessed through cloud computing services, are accelerating the further development of "chatbots." How would revenue be managed when consumers start to use their digital assistants (empowered by artificial intelligence) to make bookings? As this chapter has shown, it is now possible to (a) broaden the scope of parameters, (b) accelerate response time, and (c) internalize more marketplace feedback. However, although the technology is here, the question relates to execution and the ability of those responsible to manage revenue. There is now the potential for machine learning and AI to make deeper sense of the information in the three points above and to identify the implications for network management discussed in Chapter 3 and revenue management in this chapter.

The customer experience

Experience is part of revenue management in a direct and an indirect way. From the direct relationship side, the experience element affects the sale of high-margin ancillary services. From the indirect relationship side, experience is now part of the product, which, in turn, is an integral component of revenue management. However, the context of experience is very broad, as travel experience encompasses the entire journey. If a customer books other components of travel through an airline (hotel and car-rental, for example), then customers expect the selling airline to make contingency planning seamless. If the airline flight is delayed or cancelled, then, according to customers, it is the airline that needs to offer alternative and viable options to the customers for all components of air travel. Is an airline a customer-service business or a business that flies aircraft and sells seats between airports? If it is a customer-service business, then a certain level of commitment requires the provision of solutions. From a customer's perspective, experience involves more than just experience on the airplane. It also involves what happens at the airport as well as during shopping.

Companies such as Google and Airbnb are trying to have more control of a travel customer's end-to-end relationship using the digital space. Recently, both Google and Airbnb launched new travel products, Google Trips and Airbnb Trips. Google not only has information on what travel consumers are looking for, but also is in a position to work with appropriate partners to deliver the product as well as the experience. In the case of Airbnb, although the initial product features of Trips relate to "Experiences, Prices, and Homes," the company reportedly is expanding into other areas of travel, such as the enablement of bookings for travel services and destination activities via an app. The leisure segment of travel consumers, in particular, finds the booking process complex and frustrating. Consequently, the processes being explored by the new digital intermediaries deal with not only the booking part of travel, but also the experience part. As such, the new digital intermediaries are likely to use artificial intelligence to become total travel solution providers.

Although becoming a business that handles all aspects of travel – services as well as experience – is a major challenge, it is also an opportunity to sell ancillary products and services. The key is to deploy a platform to launch a digital hub.

Ryanair has reported that it wants to be the "Amazon of Air Travel." British Airways has launched a travel port, "British Airways Holidays." Swiss International Air Lines has launched its "Swiss Holidays" travel portal. JetBlue has launched its "JetBlue Getaways" travel portal. These portals enable consumers to book major parts of their travel (airline, hotel, car-rental, and so forth) and provide some means to customize the trip. The idea, of course, is to create digital retailing opportunities for the airline and experience for customers who are becoming more and more connected. However, new products such as Airbnb's Trips are planning to deal with destination-related options, recommendations, and experiences. For airlines to take a deep dive in this area, it will take significant effort to work with a very broad spectrum of partners to achieve the twin goals: revenue for them and experience for customers.

The question then is, can an airline think of itself as something more than an airline? Could a commercial airline think of itself as a *travel-service* provider, with a focus on solutions and experience strategies? If an airline was to think along these dimensions – integrated service and seamless experience at all touchpoints – then various levels of personalization can begin to be considered. These considerations will affect the brand and ancillary revenue, two essential components of revenue management. A few airlines have begun to think along these lines. JetBlue, for example, is reportedly checking in its passengers automatically 24 hours prior to departure. A passenger receives an email with the information that he or she has been checked in – with a seat assigned, assuming that the airline knows the passenger's preference – along with a boarding pass. However, an airline could also think about a fundamentally new way for managing its revenue, one that is in the interest of both the customer and the airline and works well from the viewpoints of simplicity, rationale, and transparency. For a thought-provoking concept in this area, see Dietmar Kirchner's contribution to Chapter 7.

Takeaways

- Although revenue management has evolved significantly in the past four decades, there is still considerable potential. Improvements can be achieved given the availability of much more comprehensive and real-time data, analytics for harnessing customer and business intelligence, and enabling technologies to work with information of elasticities at the individual or trip level (to the degree possible) and the informational gap between the fares offered by one airline and its competitors, not the fares filed.
- Revenue management needs to work around three basic dimensions: prices, inventory, and time. From this perspective, both price and inventory must be managed in real time. As such, the information used cannot be old.
- Dynamic pricing should not be confused with personalized pricing. The current process in which millions of fares filed daily either by an airline's being proactive or by its responding to the fares filed by one or more competitors does not represent dynamic pricing. Dynamic pricing is a process in which an airline develops a capability to evaluate the marketplace and

offer the optimal fare to a customer, based on an airline's own revenue-management practices, its inventory, and its competitiveness in the market relative to the fare. The fare offered to a customer may well be very different from the fare filed. Personalized pricing means offering a fare based on an individual consumer's profile and travel behavior – past, current, and expected in the future.

- Segmentation based on the purpose of the trip, incorporating revealed preference, is a better driver of revenue management for making offers to targeted consumers, whether their identity is known or whether they are anonymous. The rationale is that a typical consumer has multiple profiles based on the context of the trip.

- As for fare management, the process can now be facilitated significantly with A/B testing using new technology that instills greater confidence in the validation process and provides more agility. Additionally, responding to customer requests based on revealed preferences can increase conversion rates and reduce customer frustration.

- The customer experience can affect the sale of high-margin ancillary services. But the customer experience is now also part of revenue management in an indirect way: it is part of the product, which, in turn, is an integral component of revenue management.

5   Re-designing services for a next-generation customer experience

In light of the changing expectations and behaviors of consumers discussed in Chapter 1, most businesses are taking steps to improve their customers' experience. Within the airline industry, the forward-thinking airlines are exploring the three domains shown in Figure 5.1 for improving passengers' experience: passenger trends, discussed in Chapter 1; platform-based businesses, discussed in Chapter 2; and data and analytics, discussed throughout the book. However, becoming obsessed with customers' experience requires a new way of looking at the business. It requires not only imagination, but also a design focus, a subject discussed in this chapter. The reason it requires some imagination is that one cannot just think about incremental changes to the current business models. Imagining a very new business model requires more than just new technologies and an analysis of new processes and new tools. It requires a vision such as Peter Thiel discussed in his book *Zero to One*. As he said, many companies develop products or services that take "the world from 1 to *n*, adding more of something familiar." However, what is needed is for a business to develop and create something new that would take the world "from 0 to 1."[1] The starting point for such a vision could be for the staff to work with an outside-in focus, meaning with insights from other forward-thinking businesses, some new (Airbnb, Alibaba, Amazon, Facebook, Uber) and some old (GE, Mercedes-Benz cars and Westpac bank), that are taking the transformation journey. As for the focus on design, the planning team needs to work with agreed-upon assumptions and with staff in all functions speaking the same language.

As for imagination, consider three new businesses: Uber, Airbnb, and Alibaba. Uber thought about alternative ways to provide personal ground transportation, and Airbnb alternative types of personalized short-term accommodations, leveraging the transformational power within the digital space. What is Alibaba doing? It is helping small businesses solve their problems. How? It is equipping sellers with the necessary tools and analytics for them to elaborate on their value propositions. Alibaba even makes investments in small businesses at terms better than other lending institutions. How about the vision of Uber to help drivers acquire cars as well as to insure them? How about the vision of Airbnb working with hosts to provide insurance to take care of potential damages to their properties? These are not only platforms; they are smart platforms that select carefully the sellers and buyers to work with and the app developers.

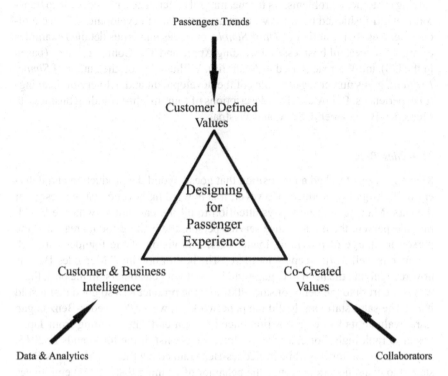

Figure 5.1 Forces creating a need to change and innovate

What is the transformational power of digitization in the airline industry? Think about the opportunities that can be created by leveraging the platform-based ecosystems to re-define and re-invent the airline business. This chapter focuses on some aspects relating to re-defining the customer experience and customer expectations, and the next chapter looks at some aspects relating to platforms and digitization. In the case of the second point, it is the technology-empowered platform-based ecosystems that will enable the creation of value. Just think about what self-driving cars are going to do for ground transportation. Consider even further the potential impact of self-driving cars on short-haul air travel with respect to both O&D traffic and traffic connecting to longer-haul flights.

Multi-industry insights

If airlines draw only three insights from other successful businesses, they should be (1) simplicity, (2) a focus on solving customers' problems, and (3) the delivery of meaningful experiences. As for simplicity, it should be considered not only from the perspective of customers but also from the perspective of the business itself, including, of course, the employees. As for customers' problems, the focus needs to be not only on customers but also on the problems faced by employees in solving customers' problems. As for meaningful experiences, it is possible to transform an old-fashioned business without using the latest developments in technology. Ken Segall, the author of *Think Simple*, provides numerous detailed examples of highly successful businesses, including Apple and The Container Store (based in the US) and Westpac (based in Australia). William Taylor, the author of *Simply Brilliant*, gives numerous examples of the development and delivery of meaningful experiences. Below are short descriptions of four insight-providing businesses: Mercedes-Benz, Uber, USAA, and Westpac.

Mercedes-Benz

Mercedes-Benz has had a proposition that goes beyond the production and delivery of high-quality products. However, it is now going beyond just the design of the cars. Management now pays attention to all the encounters with the brand: the salesperson, the maintenance service person, the waiting room areas, and the person in charge of providing loaner cars. The vision of the founder, Gottlieb Daimler, is well worth keeping in mind: "The best or nothing." Mercedes-Benz is now recognizing the need to engage and interact with customers. In the past, there was some truth to the belief of sales staff that the product was so good that it sold itself. The sales staff simply did the paperwork. However, Mercedes-Benz began to re-evaluate its value proposition once the high-end autos coming from Japan began to rank high. For example, on Interbrand's list of the top brands in 2015, Toyota ranked number 6 while Mercedes-Benz ranked number 12. Mercedes-Benz started to examine and influence the behavior of its more than 20,000 employees in the US.[2] Partly as a result of the initiatives taken in the list of Interbrand's top brands, in 2016 the rankings changed to number 5 for Toyota and number 9 for Mercedes-Benz.

Uber

Uber started by looking at the problems of both employees and customers. In many cities, to operate a taxi, drivers had to obtain "medallions," a lengthy and costly process. These costs were transferred to customers. In addition, because the supply of medallions was limited, it affected demand. In some cases, customers had trouble obtaining taxis, especially during peak times or during inclement weather. Then there were occasions when the driver did not know the address of the destination. On the customer side, customers did not know what the fare would be or whether they would be driven to the destination in the most direct way. Uber simplified the process for both drivers and customers. The customer simply installs an app on his or her mobile device and provides information about the credit-card to be billed. Once installed, the app can be used to request a ride by entering only the destination info. The customer receives notification of the time the driver will arrive at the pick-up location, information about the driver (name, photo, and a review score), the car (make and license number), and the fare. The driver is notified of the location of the destination through a built-in GPS system. Upon arrival at the destination, the customer simply leaves the vehicle, and the credit-card is automatically charged the quoted fare. The customer then receives an email with the information on the fare charged and the route taken by the driver. The customer can also provide a review of the driver. The rides can be shared, and the customer can request different types of cars. Customers can rate the driver via the surveys provided after the rides. Presumably, there is security, as drivers are screened and the vehicle is tracked. Drivers get the benefit of flexible work hours and fast payment. In general, fares tend to be lower than those charged by conventional taxis. Uber does not own any cars, nor does it have any drivers. It simply is an intermediary with software that connects drivers with users. It certainly is having an impact on existing taxi companies.

Uber is an example of not only a compelling value proposition, but also a simplification of the business. Uber did not invest money in the traditional form of marketing and advertising; it relied instead on word-of-mouth as well as social media. Word-of-mouth is an extremely effective method of promotion for businesses that offer truly compelling value propositions. In the case of Uber, the company is diverting traffic from existing companies, as well as stimulating demand. The company is also diversifying, starting with ride pooling and going on to offering delivery services in other areas. The key part of the distinguishing value proposition is the customer experience that simplifies the taxi service. Uber does have competition, since the system can be copied. However, while the company's strategy for rapid growth has not pre-empted competition, it has kept the newcomers to a minimum. The network effects, discussed in Chapter 2, certainly apply: the more cars, the less waiting time for users; the more users, the more cars. Consider one more aspect of the network. If a user has an Uber app and uses it in one city, she is likely to use the same app and Uber in a different city. Which will be the company that successfully develops the self-driving car – Uber or Google?[3]

USAA

USAA, a large insurance company that provides financial services to military personnel and their families, is an example of how a business can provide its customers with a meaningful experience. William Taylor, in his book *Simply Brilliant*, looks at USAA in detail. USAA's value proposition is basically through the delivery of a meaningful experience, one created and delivered by motivated employees. They focus on the development of culture and brand to deliver such a service. However, according to Taylor, the business's culture is the platform that sustains the brand. USAA's product line includes home and auto insurance, credit-cards, mortgages, and some banking services. Business is conducted solely via phone and the Internet, with no physical branches. The customer base comprises active and retired military personnel and their families. It is a large base with specific needs. Specifically, USAA's value proposition is "accessibility, responsiveness, and on-the-spot problem solving skills." It truly focuses on its frontline employee-training programs, which emphasize not just the technical skills relating to the products, but also skill at interacting with customers through text message and online chat. USAA employees are trained to look at each customer as though he or she is a soldier in the field. Some employees even do a training simulation in which they engage with and respond to the real-time and situation-based needs of customers who are deployed overseas (think of the need to transfer funds via mobile phone or via text message). A significant percentage of USAA employees themselves are military spouses or ex-military.[4]

Westpac

Westpac, possibly the oldest company in Australia, wanted to launch a brand, Bank of Melbourne, by identifying and focusing on a special niche, rather than trying to be all things to all people. (For example, the bank has a focus on "home financing, starting or growing a business, and preparing for retirement.") Every branch of this bank was designed to create an environment that promoted personal and productive conversations and face-to-face interactions, rather than an environment that promoted efficient transactions enabled by technology. The goal, presumably, was "to solve problems and offer advice." It is interesting to note that the bank managers preferred to recruit staff from the local community rather than other banks. Even the call center was staffed by locals.[5] Westpac simplified the home-lending process, reducing the time it took to obtain a mortgage to less than 60 minutes and a "top-off" to 10 minutes. (A top-off is an additional loan after the initial mortgage for renovation or other purposes.) It is interesting to note that according to the old processes, the time for top-offs used to be longer than the time for processing the original mortgages.[6] Typically, products offered by banks, in general, have been associated with confusion (including confusion over fees and rates), inflexibility, and high charges. Westpac clearly wanted to differentiate its image from this stereotype.

Re-defining value and designing for it

Before defining value, let alone re-defining it or designing for it, an airline's first question should be about its customer base, both now and in the future. Does the airline want to address the specific needs of specific segments, or does it want to serve all kinds of customers? Considerations for the development of value propositions go far beyond the buying-selling transaction. Considerations also include, for example, working with selected customer bases to get customers to promote an airline's products and services, and that involves social collaboration and user-generated content. Such considerations generate network effects: more users lead to more input into the content being generated, which leads to even more users, and that makes the product and the service more valuable. Think about Waze, a very large GPS-based and community-based traffic and navigation app. It helps drivers select the best route (with turn-by-turn information) based on real-time input from other drivers.[7] Assuming that customer bases, current and future, have been selected, how do airlines determine the value to be provided to these segments?

Let us start with the basic products. Airlines have invested huge amounts of money in aircraft, maintenance facilities, airport facilities, and other operational systems, including skilled employees. Using these physical assets, they create valuable products for customers: safe and reliable scheduled services in selected markets by themselves or through memberships in alliances. These services are provided by different categories of airlines with different price-service options. Traditionally, different segments of consumers have used different criteria for evaluating an airline's traditional product, a seat from A to B. Such criteria include schedules, frequency, fares, loyalty awards, and so forth. In recent times, based partly on their experiences in other business sectors, consumers are beginning to look for digital features surrounding the physical features that enhance the experiential aspects within the services provided by airlines. The question then turns to the role of digitization from the viewpoint of experiential aspects of airline service – specifically, how airlines can deliver new kinds of value to their customers and receive more value from the physical assets they offer. In other words, can digitization, in fact, help an airline increase the value created for customers and partners from physical assets? This question leads to both a challenge and an opportunity relating to the use of physical assets. Can software be added to the hardware, including sensors, algorithms, information, and analytics, to increase the value of the physical assets? Let us not forget networks. Although networks are not physical assets in the sense of aircraft and maintenance facilities, airlines have invested huge amounts of money to acquire and maintain these assets.

In the new environment, an airline must change its focus from managing physical assets to managing for value, both for customers and the airline, and from the use both of existing physical assets and of digital assets. It is a given that customers want physical assets. However, customers are now increasingly connecting those physical assets with the customer experience they are looking for – one that is seamless and consistent. The point is to find out how physical assets can be deployed to provide more value in the form of experience. That means working within the travel chain with other members that also have physical assets, say, airports, to design for the end-to-end experience and its delivery on a consistent basis.

The starting point is a solid understanding of customer needs discussed throughout the book. When an airline wants to create new value for selected segments through digitization, it needs insights from other business sectors, and it needs a design process that enables the airline to continuously adapt to the changing needs of customers. The design process described below takes into consideration not only key performance indicators and controls, but also loyalty and brand. However, the two key factors affecting the design are (1) the need to change the operational mind-set for flying between A and B safely, efficiently, and effectively and (2) the need to extend the executive team's outlook from short term to long term. With respect to the first factor, most airlines' focus continues to be on the efficiency of operations and the delivery of physical products rather than the effectiveness of operations and the delivery of outcomes. With respect to the second factor, the focus continues to be on the short term – in some cases, financial performance in the next quarter to, at least, meet the expectations of the financial sector. In some ways it is ironic in that this might be a good time to invest in digitization – at least, for the airlines that have finally begun to generate reasonable amounts of profits, having consolidated, implemented controls over capacity, gained some power over pricing, developed powerful joint ventures within the alliance framework, and monetized the loyalty programs.

Consider some examples of insights on failures and successes in other business sectors. The failure of some companies that stuck to their product-based models and the success of companies that focused on the development of platforms are well illustrated by Moazed and Johnson in their insightful research on the development of mobile devices. Specifically they show how Nokia and Research in Motion (RIM) failed, while Apple and Android became successful. Both Nokia and RIM (with its BlackBerry phone) continued work with their limited proprietary operating systems, Symbian and the BlackBerry OS, respectively. On the other hand, both Apple (in 2007 for its iPhone using the iOS) and Google (in 2008 for its Android) developed software platforms through which third-party developers could and did develop an incredible number of apps that consumers valued. Both Apple and Google foresaw the convergence of hardware and software. On the other hand, Nokia and RIM continued to promote product features.

BlackBerry continued to promote, for example, its QWERTY keyboard and longer battery life. Apple, on the other hand, recognized the value to consumers of its platform, which included iOS, iTunes, and the App Store. Similarly, Google introduced Google Search and the Android (and later the Android Market and the Google Play Store).[8] Moreover, Google's operating system, Android, was an open system that allowed anyone to develop apps. Subsequently, Google even launched the Open Handset Alliance (OHA), a large group of technology and mobile companies, to accelerate innovation to improve user experience for consumers. Initially, Apple's operating system was also proprietary, but it changed after Apple introduced its App Store, which led all kinds of developers to develop apps for the iPhone.

Next, consider the value generated and delivered by the connected car. Using the technology embedded in the car, auto manufacturers are generating enormous value created within the ecosystem (representing different business sectors – sensors, remote diagnostics, infotainment, cloud-based data) through innovation. The car-sharing ecosystem even includes some insurance companies, which offer new pricing systems such as prices based on the detailed type of driving, facilitated by the use of sensors and data analytics. Uber, using mobile devices to connect drivers to customers, is now extending its core business by developing UberEATS and UberHEALTH. UberEATS is a platform for ordering and delivering meals. Using a mobile device, a user can go online, view a menu from a nearby participating restaurant, place an order for a meal, and then pay for the meal using the mobile device or a credit or debit card that is on file. The meal can be delivered by courier. UberHEALTH is an on-demand healthcare system. Qualified nurses using Uber can provide on-demand medical services, such as flu vaccinations.

Within the hospitality sector, two leading hotels recently announced marketing campaigns that provide added benefits to customers booking directly. Consider

Hilton Hotels, for example, and its eye-catching marketing campaign, "Stop Clicking Around," that informs potential customers that the hotel will offer the lowest price anywhere, as well as free Wi-Fi, for booking directly with the hotel. Members in its loyalty program, "Hilton Honors," are promised, in addition to loyalty points, exclusive discounts if they book directly through the hotel's web site, or its HHonors app, or its call center, or its preferred corporate travel partners, or its approved travel agents. As for personalization, members can choose their rooms from a digital floor plan and be able to use a "digital key" through the HHonors app on a smartphone. The idea is to make shopping easier, through the best online prices, to get customers to book directly with the hotel rather than go through a third party.

The Marriott chain of hotels introduced a similar marketing campaign, "It Pays to Book Direct," for customers interested in its portfolio: Marriott Hotels, JW Marriott, The Ritz-Carlton, Courtyard by Marriott, Residence Inn by Marriott, and a number of other properties. As with Hilton, the clear message is that members in its loyalty program who book directly with the hotel acquire the lowest rates for the properties in Marriott's portfolio. In its campaign, Marriott even offered a "best rate guarantee" feature, under which a member, finding a lower rate within 24 hours of booking directly with the hotel, could get the hotel to match the rate and receive a 25 percent discount. Examples of personalization include, via the Marriott Mobile app, digital check-in and checkout as well as an alert when a room is available for check-in.

Mapping the experience

How do customers perceive the experience provided by an airline? The answer is often very different from the one held by the employees who designed the services. Why the gap? Let us start with consumers' desires for simplification relating to both the price and value proposition. There is a large gap between the thinking of airlines and consumers. In *Simplify*, Richard Koch and Greg Lockwood provide an excellent analysis of the differences between simplification based on price and on value proposition. They provide examples from different business sectors and different time frames: General Motors, Apple, Uber, Airbnb.[9] Should an airline simplify its pricing structure, simplify its value proposition, or do both? In the case of Airbnb, its distinctive value proposition relates to both the renter and the host and is in the experience space. The local host can be in the accommodation business quickly with a global reach while offering a local experience. The renter can specify the exact type of accommodations and amenities needed and glance through reviews. Simplification refers to the ability of the hosts to advertise and the guests to get the accommodations. Both hosts and guests can write and read reviews.

As for experience, it consists of many impressions, some of which are not under the airline's control. This is extremely valid in the airline business, which is dependent on the services provided by other members in the travel chain, such as airports, air traffic control, and security agencies. In addition, the airline business is at the mercy of the weather. Even more damaging are the impressions, whether positive or negative, that customers bring before even experiencing the service provided by an airline. In any case, customers are not the same, and even a given customer can be very different on different days and in different situations. Think about a customer whose bag was misplaced even though the cabin service was great. How about the passenger who was held up in the security line and missed the flight? Or the one who was held up in customs, after deplaning an international flight, and missed a connecting flight in a domestic market?

Passengers' frustrations generally do not relate to their on-board experience, but they start with the planning and purchasing processes. First, they may have difficulty in getting relevant and transparent information. Then there is the aspect of variable pricing, a situation that ordinary consumers are not able to comprehend. Then there are the fees for baggage and changes to reservations, and finally delays. These frustrations do not even include those related to passenger processing at airports, long lines and the uncertainty of the time needed for not just for checking in but for getting through security.[10] Consequently, since customer experience and interaction are not just at a single touchpoint, it is necessary for an airline to design for customer experience across product lines and across channels. The delivery and measurement of meaningful and consistent customer experience – end-to-end – must become a strategic priority for the design team, because it will lead to a competitive advantage and sustainability of customer loyalty. It is easy to see why investments in customer experience are not often strategic priorities. There is the difficulty of quantifying business value and measuring return on investments in this area. However, there is evidence of the value of creating and managing the customer experience even within the airline industry. One just needs to look at the history of Singapore Airlines, a business that has made money consistently and with high margins.

How do airlines close the gap between what employees perceive they are delivering and what customers perceive they are receiving? Jim Kalbach suggests an extremely useful way for transforming the design and service processes by mapping the experience and getting rigorous customer-focused and employee-focused visualizations of it, given that images are more useful than text. It is particularly useful for services that are complex and where the systems required to deliver the services are also complex. The key elements are an outside-in perspective and identifications with employees and customers. This mapping process can help airlines identify not only challenges, but also opportunities to make improvements. The key point is that expressing concepts visually is more difficult than writing them down. The problem with large airlines is that often one function does not understand in detail what another function is doing relative to the need for looking at a customer's end-to-end journey. Obviously, no one wants to create or deliver a bad experience. The problem is what an airline thinks it is delivering vs. what its customers think they are receiving. The service designed often does not represent reality. In some recent cases, there is even too much focus on what technology can do instead of what is being delivered. Such gaps point to the need for an outside-in perspective. In the case of many airlines, the focus seems to be inside-out while satisfying internal constraints relating to systems, processes, regulations, and employees. The often-discussed problem relating to silos continues, with little integration among functions and up and down within each function. Data often resides in so many different places and so many different formats that it is difficult to analyze when attempting to produce what Jim Kalbach calls "value alignment": when the value envisioned and the value delivered are the same. Because the value created and the value delivered depend on input and output from different functions, there needs to be total integration and optimization within an integrated framework. Visualization is a good way to see the experience from a customer's perspective.[11]

Next, the design team needs to focus on competition, not from other airlines but from indirect competitors: the digital intermediaries. These information- and analytics-armed businesses, such as Airbnb and Google, are beginning to understand consumers and their desires in much more detail than airlines. Airbnb is reported to be looking into offering airline services. Google is already offering services in both hotel and airline reservations but is reportedly looking into the use of voice-based travel services. The indirect competitors are looking at both the direct value and the indirect value to consumers who are ever more connected. It is not just that consumers want to be connected to find more products more easily, but that they want to find each other more quickly. The new competitors are taking into consideration the availability of information in the cloud, coupled with the use of new and sophisticated apps, and, of course, through totally re-designed web sites.

Then there is the issue of how to design products and services to build trust, which will build loyalty. The key is to design the delivery of the end-to-end service from a customer's perspective, instead of from the perspective of the airline's internally organized functions and processes. This might call for the organization of assets in a different framework, not only the assets of the airline, but also the assets of partners: other airlines, as well as other members in the value chain. The key point to keep in mind is that consumers not only have smart devices, but also have access to high-speed Internet almost everywhere and a vast number of low-cost or free apps. On the other hand, airlines now also have access to low-cost computing based on the data and systems available in the cloud. Consequently, it should now be easier to create value for customers and businesses at the same time.

Should the design team be split? One thought is to have two groups: one group explores the current situation, while the other looks at the future. What values will consumers look for in the future? In *Value Proposition Design*, Alex Osterwalder, Yves Pigneur, Greg Bernarda, and Alan Smith explain in simple terms not only how to design a product or service for value but also how to test and deliver the value to customers.[12] Even from the current perspective, the task is not easy, because it calls for the gathering and synthesizing of data on, and visualization and agreement among the team members regarding, the value that targeted customers are currently seeking. The process is an iterative one, one that evolves over time. Even the design process for the current values is quite complicated, because it involves an analysis of targeted segments of customers and the value propositions sought by each segment, the resources required, the different functions that would need to be involved to develop and offer such values, and the returns. In fact, the challenge starts with the assumption that the team has some background in design thinking. The next challenge is the development of profiles of the segments selected and their pain points, as well as the laying over of the value maps showing the relief provided by the value propositions. To relieve the pain points, should the product features be physical or digital? As mentioned, many times the problem is not with what has been designed but with what is being delivered. Next, the challenge is that the contexts of the selected customers change, and that requires knowledge on how the customer profiles are generated. Obviously one could start with data. Then there is the issue of engaging with customers based on observations and interviews. How does an airline get the voice of the customer and receive feedback?

While one design group is exploring value propositions along with product features (physical and digital) based on the current situation, the other one needs to be looking at what is coming in the future: a bimodal design team. The conventional design group is already saddled with challenges listed above. In some ways, the design group exploring new frontiers in value – the digital group – has less of a challenge in that it is not constrained by the need to operate the current business model. On the other hand, the digital group will have a different challenge: the need to prove the benefits of what they are proposing and to support their assumptions about the location of customer values. On top of that, there is the challenge for leadership to integrate the conclusions of both groups. Although the two groups need to work independently, at some point, they will need to have discussions regarding transitions.

Managing customer loyalty and the brand

As mentioned numerous times, a critical success factor for designing a next-generation airline customer experience is the existence of cross-functional integration. Consider two functions: loyalty and brand management. What are the roles and relevance of loyalty and brand management in the era of digital marketing? Some say that the role of brands is diminishing in the era of social media, while others say it can become more important if managed properly, especially when engaging with younger consumers. The fundamental question relates to the development and communication of the value proposition, its relevance and appeal to the consumer, and its difference from competitive products and services in the digital landscape. Does the airline's brand address the expectations of a segment of consumers while adapting to the changing behavior of the consumers within the segment? As new intermediaries enter the marketplace, how will the airline control how its brand is communicated? In developing a value proposition, what does a particular airline know about the consumers it serves that its competitors do not know? Does an airline even know the behavior of its customers, let alone know it better than its competitors do? The data is there, but do marketers know how to extract insights from the data? Does the planning group understand how the customer is receiving the experience versus how it is supposed to be delivered? What are the standards around which the brand should be developed and promises delivered? How about the metrics for measuring the acceptance and the performance of the brand? Are the different functions integrated that relate to the brand: pricing, operations, customer service, loyalty? (Lack of integration is one thing, but rivalry is another. Think about the tension between loyalty and revenue management.) What are the best ways to get feedback from customers? How does the group developing the brand deal with the issues of transparency and integrity? It is relatively easy to say that brands should engage with consumers in a significant way. However, how does one measure whether the engagement is taking place?

Major airlines in the US have been transforming their loyalty programs both in terms of how loyalty is rewarded as well as in terms of monetization. With respect to the first point, credit is being given not just on the amount of miles flown, but on the amount of money spent. Second, even though the initial objective of the loyalty programs was to make passengers become loyal, airlines now have been generating enormous amounts of revenue from two new sources. With respect to the second point, airlines have aggressively been promoting the development and sale of co-branded credit-cards with banks. The credit-card companies, such as American Express, Barclays, MasterCard, and VISA, pay substantial amounts of money to buy the miles to make their credit-cards attractive to consumers who are willing to pay higher annual fees to have access to airline miles. Moreover, airlines have also been selling miles to third parties, such as hotels and other retailers, as well as airline partners. Delta is reportedly selling enough miles to partners to generate an estimated value of $3 billion.[13] It is reported that American is expected to increase its pre-tax income by more than $1.5 billion in the next couple of years through its agreements with multiple major credit-card companies (Barclaycard US, Citi, and MasterCard).[14]

Managing service and experience during disruptions

Disruptions in operations, referred to as irregular operations (IROPS), have an enormous impact on both the operating costs of an airline and the airline customers' experience. Typical problems relate to inclement weather, aircraft maintenance issues, constrained infrastructure relating to the capacity of the airports and air traffic systems, and breakdowns of computer systems.

In addition, there are two other serious problems. First, delays at one location are magnified and cause delays at multiple other locations due to the "knock-on effects." Ira Gershkoff provides an illustration of how a major disruption in Central Europe can affect airline operations and passengers at many airports not only throughout Europe but also throughout North America, South America, Africa, Asia, and Australasia.[15] Second, some functions that are major challenges in the first place – for example, crew pairing and crew rotations, as pointed out in Chapter 3 – become even more critical during disruptions. One estimate of costs of disruptions at the industry level is 8 percent of the total revenue, or about $60 billion, on a global basis.[16] Researchers also point out that there are additional costs, such as the lost productivity of passengers who are delayed and the impact on related businesses, such as the hospitality sector.

Although airline systems operations groups have done well with the resources available, they can now manage much better given the ability to manage aircraft and data more efficiently. Let us start with the aircraft itself. Certain types of inclement weather (for example, lightning) will not allow employees to work on ramps, which may force aircraft to wait for lengthy periods before docking to gates. Technology is now being used in a terminal in Miami to guide an aircraft down toward the gate and help it dock itself so that it can be connected to a jet bridge that is operated by a staff member in the jet bridge.[17]

By integrating data, airlines can manage disruption problems much better with respect to cost efficiency and their passengers' experience. For example, an airline can use technology to identify and implement much more cost-effective ways to re-balance aircraft and crew rotations as well as passenger itineraries. Or it can use more comprehensive metrics to evaluate different options and select the best contextually-based solution.[18] Consider the latter. The issue is not just the time required to re-accommodate passengers and re-route aircraft and re-assign crews but also (a) the optimization process involving all three considerations simultaneously and (b) the quality of the re-accommodations offered to passengers and costs related to re-storing aircraft and crews. Data and analytics are enabling airlines to be much more proactive in handling IROPS – for example, with respect to predicting outcomes, integrating with other internal functions, and communicating much better not only with customers but also with other members in the travel chain, such as hotels. The internal communications relate both to different groups within an airline as well as other members in the travel chain, specifically airports, to identify and offer better outcomes.

Technology can also offer options for stranded customers to serve themselves (digital options for self-service at different touchpoints) as opposed to waiting in lines at the airport: proactive customer care. However, self-service solutions should be limited. For example, a passenger should not be able to re-book herself on a competitor's flight. A more efficient solution would be to complement the self-service solution capability with the establishment of dedicated connection centers at airports with trained and empowered airline and airport staff and sufficient facilities, such as vehicles, to quickly transport passengers and baggage to various gates.

Customers' expectations are rising. If passengers are being re-routed, they expect to receive timely information regarding all the options on their mobile devices. The existence of and the power of social media, coupled with the online and real-time information held by customers, cannot be underestimated if customers' expectations are not satisfied. Customers want visibility and solutions, and if they are not provided with both, an airline's brand will suffer, as evidenced in recent years. This requirement calls for airlines to be proactive. On the other hand, an airline can use social media proactively and positively to alert passengers.

Problems get more complicated when customers' needs conflict with airlines' needs. For example, an airline will only re-accommodate most of its passengers on its own flights or those of its alliance partners. Only top-tier passengers will be accommodated on competitors' flights. Since capacity is limited on the flights that are still operating, how will the decision be made as to who gets re-accommodated from the list of passengers affected by a disrupted flight? Presumably, passengers in the top-tier program have priority. Do all passengers know this information? How is each passenger on the disrupted flight going to get re-accommodated? Does every passenger have this information at the time of booking? What are the rules anyway? Can passengers purchase "upgrades" on the priority list? What if two passengers have the same tier status and have paid the same fare but there is only one seat available? What are the criteria and parameters embedded in passenger service systems (PSSs) and departure control systems (DCSs)? How much control does the staff have in systems control centers (SCCs)? Does every employee handling the situation have the right to overrule the embedded parameters? Where do the Customer Experience Department and the Loyalty Department staff of an airline fit? How does the airline factor in the revenue derived from ancillary revenue sales in the re-accommodation process? For example, what if a passenger purchased the right to sit in an aisle seat but an aisle seat is not available on the aircraft on which the passenger is being re-accommodated? Answers to these questions need to be incorporated at the design stage of the customer experience, and databases, internal and external, need to be integrated.

Takeaways

- Customers decide what is value to them. Airlines can learn to observe how their customers assign value to their products and services, learn how to measure value, and find out ways to get feedback as to whether the airlines are providing the right value.
- Three major reasons for an airline to re-design its services around the customer's experience are passenger trends, big data and analytics, and platform-based collaboration.
- The three most important values that airlines can learn from other successful businesses are simplicity, a focus on solving customers' problems, and the delivery of meaningful experiences.
- Adding digital features does increase value for customers. For airlines, the question is what to digitize and how to digitize it.
- The focus must change from managing physical assets to managing for value, both for customers and for the airline, and from the use of both existing physical assets and digital assets.
- Value can be created by working with different partners in the traditional and non-traditional value chains, different channels, different technologies, and different talents.
- The role of brands is not diminishing in the era of social media, and it can become more important if managed properly, especially when engaging with younger consumers.
- Disruptions represent a major cost item, estimated to be about 8 percent of the industry's revenue base, and they have an enormous impact on the services received by customers.

- Advancing technology for managing information and cross-functional integration will reduce both the costs of disruptions and lead to a substantial improvement in customer service.
- Connection centers should be established at airports with trained and empowered airline and airport staff as well as sufficient facilities, such as vehicles, to transport passengers and baggage quickly to various gates.

Notes

1 Peter Thiel (with Blake Masters), *Zero to One: Notes on Startups, or How to Build the Future* (New York: Crown Publishing Group, 2014), Preface.
2 Joseph A. Michelli, *Driven to Delight: Delivering World-Class Customer Experience the Mercedes-Benz Way* (New York: McGraw Hill, 2016).
3 Richard Koch and Greg Lockwood, *Simplify: How the Best Businesses in the World Succeed* (London: Piatkus, 2016), pp. 60–6.
4 William C. Taylor, *Simply Brilliant: How Great Organizations Do Ordinary Things in Extraordinary Ways!* (New York: Portfolio/Penguin, 2016), pp. 149–54.
5 Ken Segall, *Think Simple: How Smart Leaders Defeat Complexity* (New York: Portfolio/Penguin, 2014).
6 Ibid., pp. 73, 121–2, 135–9.
7 Waze was acquired by Google in 2013.
8 Alex Moazed and Nicholas L. Johnson, *Modern Monopolies: What It Takes to Dominate the 21st-Century Economy* (New York: St. Martin's Press, 2016), pp. 1–15.
9 Koch and Lockwood, *Simplify*.
10 Thomas A. Stewart and Patricia O'Connell, "The Art of Customer Delight," *strategy + business*, Spring 2017, pp. 24–8.
11 Jim Kalbach, *Mapping Experiences: A Complete Guide to Creating Value Through Journeys, Blueprints & Diagrams* (Sebastopol, CA: O'Reilly Media, 2016), p. xiv.
12 Alex Osterwalder, Yves Pigneur, Greg Bernarda, and Alan Smith, *Value Proposition Design* (Hoboken, NJ: Wiley & Sons, 2014).
13 "America's Golden Eggs," *Airline Weekly*, August 1, 2016, p. 1.
14 "American: Creating Returns for Stakeholders," *Aviation Strategy*, November 2016, pp. 11–15.
15 Ira Gershkoff, "Shaping the Future of Airline Disruption Management (IROPS)," *T2RL-Amadeus*, 2016, pp. 6–7.
16 Ibid., p. 4.
17 Ibid., p. 17.
18 Ira Gershkoff, "Airline Disruption Management: Whitepaper," *T2RL-Amadeus*, September 2016.

6   Re-thinking the airline business for the digital era

The preface to the book laid out some challenges – compelling forces for disruption – and some opportunities for creating a 21st century airline by connecting the dots at four different levels. Connecting the dots at the first level relates to events taking place globally.

- Given the pace of global economic development, the increase in people's desire to travel, and the spread of suppliers and locations in the supply chain, it is more important than ever for airlines to extend their network reach, at a pace that has never been seen before. However, the reach of the network should be extended in more than the conventional sense of adding more O&D points on the map, even in the sense of profitable growth in an airline's scope of business. Consideration should also be given not just to new cities, countries, or services, but also to monetization of data, allocation of capital, or value creation via new business models.
- Not only will extending the network affect demand and vice versa, but the demand will be coming from many travelers who are new in the global travel marketplace. This stimulation in demand will most likely be enhanced by new forms of price-service options that would have been inconceivable in years past.
- Digital technologies that have led to global connectivity will enable unprecedented flexibility. Consequently, planning horizons within the airline industry need to be re-defined. In the future, what will be the value of two seasonal schedule changes, planned six months in advance? Alternatively, what will be the value of looking at competition that may change from day to day when it begins to change within the same day? How can an airline respond to the needs of its customers when it looks at its products in the context of days and hours but customers look at their needs in the context of micro-moments? This also raises the question of whether the potential of offering near-total flexibility raises or diminishes the need for the brand to stand for something in the minds of both consumers and associates.
- Technologies are enabling point-to-point travel solutions using existing physical transportation systems, and in the not-too-distant future, those solutions may make use of new types of physical transportation systems: autonomous vehicles.

To provide solutions to the challenges and opportunities raised above, dots will need to be connected at the next level to develop platform-based businesses. It is the platform-based businesses that will reduce costs, enhance revenues, and make the businesses much more nimble, enabling them to conduct experiments to identify the optimal value propositions that produce value for both customers and airlines.

- Platforms can produce the scalability needed for the "network reach" that is currently constrained by the existence of silos within companies throughout the airline industry.
- As discussed in Chapter 3, multiple departments – from planning to operations to marketing – that need to be involved in considering even a single route addition make it impossible to cost-effectively address the network reach needs at a global level.
- Enormous amounts of white space continue to exist between the various functional silos in airline organizations, leading to not creation of value but, in some cases, destruction of value.
- Moreover, white spaces lead to latency problems, which, in turn, reduce the ability of an airline to respond to competitive opportunities and to address value-degenerating losses to consumers. This situation stifles innovation. Latency also prevents the capitalization of great ideas injected from the outside into value propositions for making money and providing desirable experiences.

At the next level, dots must be connected to coordinate more effectively within the travel value chain to offer better solutions to customers.

- Clearly, a chain is only as strong as the weakest link. In the past, the weakest link in the airline business has been shopping. It is amazing what airlines have been able to do for customers in other areas, such as providing boarding passes on mobile phones and the depth and breadth of in-flight entertainment services. Yet, even when shopping for relatively simple trips, the experience does not come anywhere close to the one offered by leading retailers such as Amazon, with its "one click shopping" value proposition, or the ease with which Uber makes it possible for a customer to hail, ride, pay for, and rate a journey.
- The greatest problem within the travel chain appears to be not about getting more personalized offers or creating new types of end-to-end solutions. Although these are important, the *most* important issue to customers appears to be obtaining fundamental information in a way that is easy to consume (relating to the choices/options), making it easy to purchase and use the service. Although it is relatively easy to fly after purchasing a ticket, all the other services that one might need during travel are not so easy. Consider, for example, the high fees most airlines charge to make a change to a reservation.

- Perhaps it is time to re-visit the inherent conflict between (a) maximizing conversion and extracting every conceivable increment of ancillary revenue from consumers and (b) building revenue and customer equity by taking the friction out of the purchase process. Although it is clearly unreasonable to ask management to walk away from the profits when revenues are growing, one must recognize that this is also an opportunity for this industry to evolve rapidly, when industry after industry is witnessing the flow of capital and the growth in valuations with the development of new business models.
- Within the airline industry, there is the challenge of buying basic transportation in the context of micro-moments. Compare this situation with that of Google, which can focus on this aspect and make all the other parts of what Google is responsible for easy, given that micro-moments are a natural extension of Google's product. The experience of Google, Amazon, and other businesses also demonstrates how market leverage can grow when the value in the data can be put to work. In other words, fulfilling micro-moments is a lot easier when a business has mega-data.

At the next level, the dots can be connected for an airline to be linked with other connectors (organizations in the social networking arena, for example) to extend the travel chain and work within the framework of a platform. Consider the hundreds of millions of people who communicate with each other constantly through global social networks, not just Facebook, but also the likes of WeChat and WhatsApp. Yet, most airlines have a very limited social network presence. Some have virtually none. Imagine how much information airlines could get by developing a platform that provides access to the voice of the customer through social media networks.

An airline's platform does not need to start out big. It can extend its reach slowly. One just needs to see the progress made by Amazon, a business that started with a relatively simple platform enabling customers to buy virtually any book at a low price and receive it quickly. It is true that a customer might have gotten the book faster by going to a store, but most stores carried a much smaller inventory, to optimize the value of their limited spaces. Consider that starting point for a platform and its evolution to the current time, when almost any product can be purchased through the Amazon platform. The key for a business considering becoming a platform is not that it has to be big and profitable from the start. It can start small if it can demonstrate that it can scale. Moreover, as it grows, it can also be less than profitable, as long as it can attract sufficient capital to keep growing until profitability is achieved.

Platforms

Based on the success of some new and some relatively new businesses (for example, Airbnb, Alibaba, Amazon, Facebook, Uber), it is clear that traditional businesses should consider adopting the platform framework to build, for example, scalability. Chapter 2 provided some background on the role of platform-based and networked businesses. The financial community is clearly recognizing the value of platform-based businesses, given that capital is flowing toward those enterprises because of their demonstrated growth, global scalability, and huge addressable markets. This is in sharp contrast to the single-digit growth horizon, slower market penetration, and asset-heavy characteristic of many legacy competitors. However, if an airline were seriously to start thinking about developing a platform-based business and work in the digital environment, it might be helpful to think about its four critical aspects: developing a digital mind-set, leveraging digital technologies, identifying and implementing digital strategies, and creating a digital workplace.

A digital mind-set

The digital mind-set calls for the recognition of a number of fundamental changes. First, it is necessary to accept that we now have sharing economies, in which new businesses are capitalizing on the use of assets that have been underutilized in conventional business settings. Consider BlaBlaCar, Uber, and Waze within the ground transportation framework. Second, the mind-set should be willing to adapt to the existence of information-empowered consumers, mobile devices with sophisticated apps, and the availability of services through the cloud. Third, the mind-set should be willing to work within an open-source environment that enables talented third-party developers from around the world to build applications without having to be concerned about licensing issues; a larger community of developers means better self-support. Third-party contributors add value as well as receive value from their participation in platforms.

Within the digital environment, management must also be willing to leave conventional wisdom aside and work in three other spaces from a new perspective. First, there is a need to re-examine customers, competitors, and partners. Second, there is a need to re-visit technological capabilities with an eye toward (a) improving operations and profitability with agility and (b) improving the customer experience with various levels of personalization. Third, there is a need to explore new frontiers in value with a focus on (a) outcomes, not products and services, and (b) simplification of the business with respect to pricing, value proposition, trip planning, and trip monitoring. It is a digital environment.

Building a platform that simply connects buyers with sellers is, however, not sufficient. It is necessary, but it also needs to improve the relationship between buyers and sellers, possibly even create new markets. The goal should be to conduct a trade that is more than just an exchange of products or services. The starting point is a platform that creates a framework where not only do buyers and sellers connect, but the right type of buyers and the right type of sellers show up. Ideally, there is some quality control. Airbnb, for example, has a rating system for both the guests and the hosts. So the platform's value is actually enhanced by the quality of the interaction between buyers and sellers or traders. In other words, the value of a platform is not just based on reducing transaction costs. How about reducing the hassles, if not eliminating them? It is also about the capability of the platform to enable the exchange of information in situations where there is information

VeryChic

Travel Keys   25hours Hotels

Rixos Hotels   Availpro

Potel & Chabot   AccorHotels   Banyan Tree

onefinestay   FRHI

Oasis and
Square Break   Huazhu
John Paul

Figure 6.1 AccorHotels' actual and announced partnerships

asymmetry, in which one side has more information than the other side. Think about the value eBay added for buyers and sellers in the secondhand market. Amazon not only sold books at a lower price than traditional bookstores but provided a platform for shoppers to read reviews. Think about the digital transformation that AccorHotels is undertaking to bring about changes in its distribution and services. The chain is expanding at an enormous speed to capitalize on the growth within the travel industry. Figure 6.1 shows some actual acquisitions and some announced partners. With respect to distribution, the chain is enabling a large group of independent hotels to distribute their products on the AccorHotels.com platform alongside its own group of brands. The hotels that can participate in the distribution platform are selected on the basis of certain criteria, including guest reviews, and, once selected, they are given a number of valuable digital tools. The platform offers its services in an open marketplace around the world, from France to Brazil to Australia. As for diversification within its own group, think about the acquisition of onefinestay, a UK-based company that enables the owners of distinctive and upmarket homes to rent out their properties when not using them. As of the beginning of 2017, the number of properties in the portfolio is estimated to be approaching 3,000.

Digital technologies

New businesses such as Airbnb, Amazon, and Uber have been disrupting traditional businesses by leveraging new technologies: data, analytics, software, sensors, and machine learning to create new value through business intelligence for smartness, agility, and scalability, by connecting buyers and sellers as well as resources. These businesses use platforms that center around networks, particularly digital networks. These platforms have enabled businesses such Airbnb, Facebook, Google, and Uber to grow fast through scalability, collaboration with different organizations within ecosystems, and deployment of digital technologies to extend businesses horizontally. New technologies have made connections within the ecosystems more efficient and more effective in ways that add more value for buyers and sellers of products and services. The connections enable buyers and sellers to capitalize on alternate market opportunities while enhancing the buying experience. As an example, businesses are using the cloud for scalability and SaaS (software as a service) for efficiency. Technology costs may in fact be coming down due to the increase in the capabilities of the cloud and mobile technologies. The key requirement is the willingness to (1) use data, (2) share data, and (3) protect data within the ecosystem. Consumers must feel sure that the data they provide to a business will not be abused, not just by that one business but also within the ecosystem.

In the case of airlines, merging consumer technology will enable an airline to offer new and creative ways to improve customer service and the customer experience. However, consumer technologies can do much more than just reduce the needs for some basic functions, such as the printing of boarding passes. The connected and biometric devices (for example, smartphones and beacons) can not only utilize relevant data but also produce relevant data. Moreover, the merging of augmented reality and digital technology can enhance the customer experience. Looking ahead a little, cognitive capabilities can provide quick but holistic solutions to complicated mobility problems based on the breadth and depth of the knowledge of the problem of the user and the capabilities of different parts of the service provider, not to mention the capabilities within the travel supply chain. Cognitive technology will undoubtedly be embedded into smart devices, mobile as well as IoT, and be part of the social media domain, resulting in the capability to deliver personalized responses in an interactive framework.

Whereas digital solutions worked within the framework of structured and transactional data, cognitive solutions add the "tone and emotional" state of the person looking for a solution. Think about a frustrated passenger looking for a solution to a problem. Cognitive capability can respond to the tone and emotional aspects of the frustration and need for type and timing of the solution. Furthermore, cognitive capability can address the need for scale. Think about the ability to find solutions for all 200 passengers on a cancelled flight, not just those in the top tier. Moreover, the cognitive capability has an even higher value if it is included in an open platform, enabling others to innovate in various aspects of mobility. It is the emergence of innovative third parties, particularly the start-ups working in the areas of artificial intelligence, machine learning, and robotics.

According to experts at IBM, cognitive systems can "sense, reason, and learn." With these incredible capabilities, all travelers should be able to find solutions to their mobility problems rapidly, on a personalized basis, and within an interactive framework that provide them with a continuous string of options. We are just beginning to see the value of voice as a new platform of choice. Amazon's

Alexa, Apple's Siri, and Google's Now are already becoming voice-controlled assistants of choice for everyday activities. Although the voice-related capability of these assistants to perform tasks is already remarkable, currently they have a limited understanding of natural language, which makes for some inconsistency in users' experience. A second challenge is that although the number of devices that are voice-controlled is increasing, it can be difficult for users to interact with the different devices in a consistent way. A third challenge relates to what happens when two or more voice-activated devices are in the proximity of each other.

These challenges will no doubt soon be resolved, resulting in the capability of cognitive technologies to provide personalized solutions to mobility problems, leading to higher margins and an increase in brand loyalty. Moreover, cognitive technologies with embedded artificial intelligence capabilities can enable the combination of consumer intelligence and business intelligence to produce personalized services and experience throughout the shopping and travel process. In addition, artificial intelligence that helps interpret consumer intelligence and business intelligence can enable an airline to understand the travel behavior patterns of targeted consumers and offer personalized solutions in real time to their complex requests. The solutions offered will be context- and situation-based and few in number, to simplify the decision-making process of the consumer. Think about how many apps a person can have on a single mobile device and how many informational aspects can be added on to each app. Cognitive capabilities will reduce stress, not increase it.

Digital strategies

The object of digital strategies is to make consumers' lives easier within the context of their own individual environments, as well as to find ways to stimulate prevailing customers and find new customers. Consider a digital strategy developed by Mercedes and administrated through Mercedes-provided IDs to enrich a customer's experience. Mercedes offers its customers a web site through an app called Mercedes Me – a digital product to help consumers engage with the company through the Mercedes platform. It collects information about a customer's car and places it in an app on the customer's mobile device. When questions arise – for example, relating to the operation of the car – the user can see a how-to video or speak with an agent. It is also possible to glance through the service records, schedule maintenance, or review the payments made (in the case of a lease, for example) though the app. It also enables the user to have access to music and travel-related information.

Mercedes is trying to digitize, to the extent possible, the entire value chain. The starting point is to look at digitization from the customers' viewpoints (relating to safety, information, comfort, and entertainment) to make their lives easier. All these aspects relate to some form of connectivity: connectivity with the vehicle, connectivity with the environment, connectivity among the vehicles, and so forth. The information needed can relate to real-time traffic, or an urgency related to a maintenance issue. Within the company, digitization relates to design, development, production, sales, maintenance, and customer engagement. The term used at Mercedes is "Industrie 4" to describe the digitization process. The idea, however, is to optimize within the context of the value chain, encompassing employees, vendors, partners, customers, and so forth, through the program called "DigitalLife@Daimler," with a focus on one aspect: how to make customers' lives easier.

Customers' desires for cars, and now mobility services, are changing around the world. Are now the C, E, and S classes of cars sufficient to meet the demand of the marketplace? Alternatively, even if the models have sufficient variety, with different product features relating to safety, comfort, and entertainment, what other elements are needed to satisfy customers' needs? Given that sophisticated cars now have software that encompasses millions of lines of code, especially the autonomous cars, auto companies are already becoming service companies, relying on the use of software capabilities. If a customer does not pay for all the available software options at the time of purchase, additional software can easily be purchased and activated later. Consequently, digitization is transforming automakers into not just mobility providers but, more specifically, networked mobility providers. Now the digitization process relates to both internal operations (computer-added design options, and augmented reality devices, and electric power plants, and digital showrooms) and engagement with customers. On the external side, it is about autonomous driving and communication with other cars, the manufacturer, and other drivers. In addition, given the trends relating to ride-sharing, connected car mobility, and connectivity with social media, auto manufacturers are partnering with the platform-based ride businesses. It is reported that Uber will be purchasing its self-driving cars from Daimler, and GM has announced that it will work with Lyft.

The key aspect of digital strategies is to go beyond making customers' lives easier. It is to build relationships with customers. In the past, auto manufacturers did not really engage with customers after the car had been purchased or leased. Now they are thinking about all kinds of services that they can provide: help in finding a parking place, help in paying for parking, help with car-riding services to and from airports, easier and lower-cost financial services for buying and renting cars, concierge services for drivers, and physical geographic locations for information and help. They are learning from the outside-in perspective. Think about Apple, which had the iPod and iTunes – a mutually beneficial value-adding system that generated money for Apple and a great experience for customers. Then there are Apple Stores, which not only sell products but also provide stylish places for customers to seek information and help.

What might be some insights for airlines? If an auto manufacturer is thinking about becoming a provider of personal mobility, what about an airline? What can airlines do that is similar to iTunes?

Prior to the late 1960s, air travel was not available to the masses. However, to the extent it was available to the public, it did provide full service to passengers, refundable tickets, no change fees, inter-line travel, free meals, free bags, and more. Of course, there was variation based on the class of service, first class versus economy class. Although low-cost scheduled services in intercontinental operations are associated with airlines such as Laker Airways (in the late 1970s), airlines such as Loftleiðir offered low-price air travel between the US and Europe via Iceland in the 1960s. The services were attractive to the younger generation as well as other price-conscious travelers. Initially the main feature of the LCCs was simplicity – think about the services offered by Southwest. Even Southwest later added some complexity by flying into high-density markets, introducing fairly sophisticated revenue-management processes, and selling through indirect channels. Others – for example, easyJet and Azul – added more complexity too by adding more types of airplanes. JetBlue even added a premium cabin, as part of its Mint service.

As for digitization, in some ways it is not new to the airline industry. On the customer side, consider the introduction of e-tickets, online reservations, bar-coded baggage, on-board Wi-Fi, kiosks for self-check-in. On the operations side, consider fly-by-wire systems, engine maintenance sensing and monitoring systems, flight management, and flight crew electronic flight bags. Although airlines have certainly been digitizing many processes for many years and even transforming some areas of the airline business, the question now relates to the potential for far-reaching digitization of the airline business – for example, the establishment of virtual airlines. A few airlines are, however, exploring some new areas into which they can extend their current digitization business practices. What are some new areas into which airlines can extend their business? Let us begin with the low-cost sector, in which independent airlines, such as Norwegian, now offer services across the North Atlantic and into Asia. Keith McMullan and James Halstead provide an insightful analysis, in Chapter 7, of the opportunity for long-haul low-cost airlines and their potential threat to the traditional full-service airlines.

Here is a relatively simple example of a scenario in which an airline could add a digital feature to a physical product. Low-cost low-fare airlines are already offering services in international markets in most parts of the world. See Figure 6.2. For example, passengers can take WestJet from Honolulu to New York. From New York, passengers can take Norwegian to fly to Europe and on to cities in Asia. From cities in Asia, AirAsia and AirAsia X offer services to Australia as well as back to Honolulu. There are other airlines that can provide services in other markets, such as easyJet and Aegean in Europe, services that can then connect with services provided by Scoot, a subsidiary of Singapore Airlines, to connect in Athens to Singapore and points beyond. Azul and its partner, TAP Portugal, can take passengers between Brazil and the US on one side and Portugal on the other side. There are many other low-cost low-fare airlines based in many countries that are not shown on this map. For example, Southwest and jetBlue, in addition to a number of LCCs based in Mexico, serve cities in Mexico and the Caribbean. However, do any of these airlines provide a booking service that can enable a passenger to connect multiple airlines to build an itinerary through inter-line connections? How about a platform that not only enables inter-line reservations on low-cost airlines but also arranges the transfer of baggage between multiple airlines? There is white space for a platform to provide these services, including ease of shopping. Think

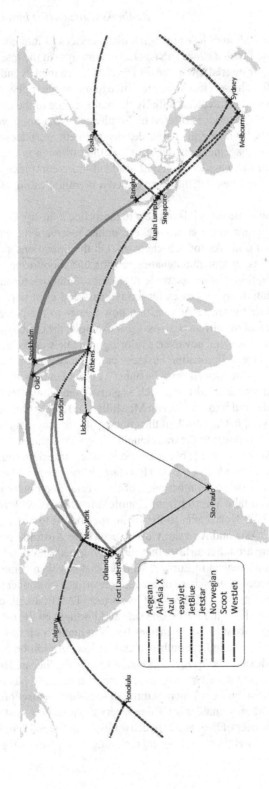

Figure 6.2 Services offered by low-cost low-fare airlines in selected markets around the world

Source: Map drawn by Aviation Strategy Ltd., UK, with the map drawn using an equidistant map projection based on London.

about Apple's iPhone. The value of the iPhone was not just in the core product itself, but in the platform created through the availability of apps and devices, not to mention the payment system and the open operating system.

The breakthrough will be the development of a platform by a third party (because it is difficult to imagine it would be developed by an airline or a traditional distributor). Asset-heavy businesses such as airlines are not likely to be the developers and operators of platforms. The challenge is going to concern data ownership, the chicken and the egg. Who has the data, who owns it and will share it, and at what price? It is also about making the data available to other parties on the platform, and that gets involved with regulations too. Gary Doernhoefer provides, in Chapter 7, a thoughtful piece to help travel-service providers (airlines, hotels, and car-rental companies) develop and adopt a practical data strategy.

Although there are already organizations – Dohop and Air Black Box, for example – that can enable a passenger to make connections with low-cost carriers for a fee, in the end, the platform is going to go further and enable the development and offer of a seamless travel journey. Dohop, founded more than ten years ago, began as a travel search engine specializing in the area of aggregation of information on connections between low-cost carriers. The company does not make the reservation itself but refers the user to the airline's booking system. Its revenue comes from the fee per click. Air Black Box (ABB) is a multi-airline travel booking system with features that go beyond the capability to make reservations. It facilitates the sale of ancillary products and services. ABB is reported to be supporting the newly formed Value Alliance in Asia. It could be the beginning of a platform for low-cost door-to-door travel services.

For higher-end travel, the full-service carriers could offer not only point-to-point service but also 24/7 concierge service. A group of carriers within an alliance could coordinate their products and services to optimize not only their customers' experience but also the efficiency and effectiveness of their operations. Within a platform, there would be not only airlines but also comprehensive OTAs (Ctrip, for example), organizations that provide 24/7 concierge services (Lola, for example), and providers of special services. Recall AccorHotels' purchase of onefinestay. In a similar sense, in late April 2017, Delta announced a partnership with BLADE, a digitally-powered aviation company that arranges on-demand helicopter services between Manhattan (from one of the three heliport lounges) and JFK Airport, to improve the customer experience. Passengers arriving by helicopter are met at the airport and escorted through the check-in process. A meet-and-greet service is also provided to incoming passengers to facilitate the connection with the helicopter services.

Consider the possibilities of a smaller like-minded group of carriers within an alliance. Figure 6.3 shows a route map of eight carriers in the oneworld alliance: American, Iberia, British, Qatar, Qantas, Cathay, JAL, and LATAM. The percentage of the key markets covered by these eight carriers (solid lines) is truly impressive. Let us assume for a minute that if these eight carriers work through a platform, a ninth carrier, Ethiopian Airlines, can enter the group through some sort of an arrangement, filling in significant gaps within Africa.

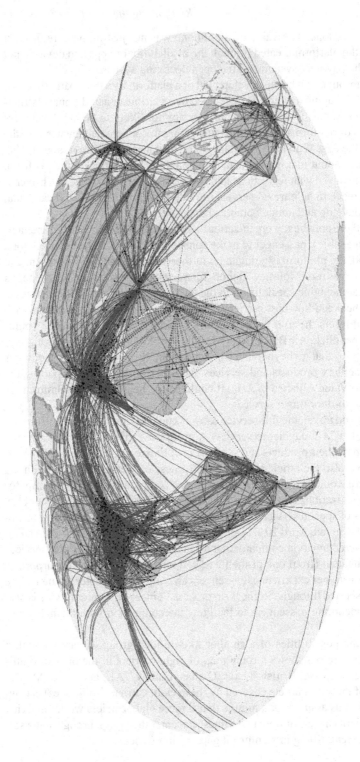

Figure 6.3 Network of eight selected carriers within the oneworld alliance and Ethiopian Airlines

Source: Map drawn by Aviation Strategy Ltd., UK, using an equidistant map projection based on London

Within digital transformation, the key driving force would be related to the aggregation of content, a process that is at a relatively rudimentary stage among the alliances. There is lot of information on schedules, but not much on the consistency of the detailed product attributes across the alliance or the reliability of different parts of the operations across the alliance. Moreover, comprehensive information is not readily available on a mobile device. To get true integration and a mobility solution framework would require airlines to collaborate with innovative technology firms, both established and start-up, that are committed to solving conventional problems. The object would be not only to provide a seamless experience, but also to provide travelers with digital tools to take care of problems that arise. For example, a passenger could improve her itinerary within the platform by going out from one airport and returning by another. The passenger could have flexibility in stopover points, similar to what airlines based in Iceland are offering.

The digitization process would enable an airline to grow and sustain its bottom line. However, the digitization process does not focus only on extending the current core business – for example, by flying to new destinations, or by bringing in a new strategic alliance partner, or by introducing a different product either at the high end or the low end, or by introducing a new channel for sale of distressed inventory. These initiatives simply extend the core product in conventional ways, a process that leads to extending competition in the conventional way and the continued pursuit of market share. Such initiatives also promote the strategy of acquiring competitive companies (consolidation) and put pressure on vendors and labor to reduce costs. Digitization can enable an airline to expand through a platform in related businesses where margins are high and where value can be enhanced for existing or new customers. Airlines clearly have explored this strategy in the sales of ancillary products and services. However, this area can now be expanded much more through the digitization process and platform development with the use of existing resources and with the least amount of risk and the greatest potential to provide added value for existing and new customers.

A digital workplace

In the digital environment, it is not just consumers who are always connected and desire instant access; employees have the same desire. If airline employees are required to provide a meaningful experience to customers, then they must also be able to communicate, interact, collaborate, and share information within the organization, across functions and up and down within a function. This criterion calls for a major transformation of the conventional workplace environment, not just to increase efficiency but also to promote innovation. Think about a workforce environment that facilitates an increase in agility and flexibility for faster time-to-market, crowdsourcing for more innovation, and a significant improvement in work-life balance that would attract and retain desired talent. The digital environment must implement strategies for employees to deal with "information overload" and the capability to interact and collaborate to improve not just customer satisfaction and experience, but also employee satisfaction and experience. As for experience, just as it needs to be consistent and seamless for customers, it needs to be the same for employees. The human resource department needs to identify employees with similar interests and shape a community of interest in order to foster innovation.

Creating a digital workforce environment is not a new concept for airlines. It started a few years ago, when airlines began to provide pilots with iPads that held the flight manuals, eliminating the need to carry heavy hard copies and allowing the pilots to get updates almost instantly. Aircraft manufacturers have also been using sensors and transmitters to bring about significant improvements in areas relating to maintenance. The predictive developments in the Internet of Things will reduce downtime significantly for aircraft, an enormous benefit for the airline industry given that it is capital-intensive and aircraft downtime is expensive.[1] More recently, some airlines began to equip their flight attendants with iPads with the capability to access a broad spectrum of relevant information to improve the customer experience, as well as internal communications. However, how is the workforce environment changing within individual corporate functions, say within the sales department? How much access does a sales professional have to individuals in marketing, product development, customer service, and, perhaps most important, revenue management? How much of a challenge is it for sales to resolve an instance that requires collaboration among sales, loyalty, and revenue management?

New forms of transportation

Could new forms of transportation disrupt the airline industry? Based on the exponential growth in the advancement of technology and the platform-based and networked businesses, the answer appears to be yes, in the short- to medium-haul travel sector. Consider the potential impact of shared and autonomous vehicles and now the real potential of Vertical Take-off and Landing aircraft (VTOL) providing on-demand services from a distributed network of "vertiports" as well as the emergence of 10-to-50-seat hybrid-electric aircraft that could fly to and from the existing under-utilized regional airports. According to a 2016 research report by Morgan Stanley, although fully autonomous vehicles may be a few years away, competition to airlines in their short-haul business sector is already here in the form of intercity ride-sharing options. Within the United States, short-haul markets (less than 300 miles) make up about 25 percent of the domestic departures of US airlines. In these markets, the new forms of transportation could produce significant pressure on yields.[2]

According to a report by Uber, the company is exploring the future of on-demand services in urban markets, using, for example, VTOL aircraft and a network of "vertiports," small pieces of land for VTOL aircraft take-offs and landings with facilities for charging the aircraft. The report provides some eye-catching travel scenarios: San Francisco's Marina area to San Jose in 15 minutes, compared to two hours in a car; São Paulo's city center to suburbs in Campinas, saving four hours of time round-trip; Gurgaon to New Delhi in six minutes (compared to 90 minutes in a car). Although the report lists a number of market-entry barriers (such as the regulatory certification process), on-demand aviation has the potential to radically transform mobility in urban areas.[3] Google is also reported to be investing in the concept of flying cars.[4]

However, much closer to reality is Uber's thought leadership in electric-powered flying cars, as well as its focus on customer service and customer experience. Uber's concept would take us to the final goal of door-to-door travel. Consider this concept with the commercialization of autonomous cars. Uber is reported to be considering the use of small electric aircraft for on-demand urban transportation. The aircraft would have the ability to take off and land vertically. They would bypass airports completely, not to mention reduce congestion on roads.

Zunum Aero, a start-up based in Kirkland, Washington, USA, is planning to design a hybrid-electric aircraft (10–50 seats) that could fly to and from existing under-utilized regional airports. According to the data contained in the company's press releases, there are about 5,000 regional airports in the US, and about 95 per-cent of the passenger traffic is to and from about 2 percent of the airports. Accord-ing to the company, the hybrid-electric aircraft, with a range of up to 700 miles, could be ready by the beginning of the next decade, depending on the certification of newly designed electric aircraft by the US Federal Aviation Administration (FAA). The aircraft is expected to lower emissions. The lower operating costs of aircraft and the regional airports, coupled with the ease of ground travel to and from these airports, could re-invent short- to medium-haul travel within the US. According to the company, airline fares could be reduced by about 50 percent in markets under 700-mile stage lengths. As with the VTOL aircraft discussed above, there are also challenges facing the introduction of these small aircraft – for example, hybrid propulsion and lower seat-mile costs for small aircraft. However, one cannot overlook the opportunity available from the use of thousands of under-utilized regional airports in the country.

The question is not *whether* these new forms of transportation will emerge, but *when* will they emerge. Their time is not that far away, considering the following:

- Daimler, the parent company of Mercedes-Benz, in collaboration with Bosch, a global developer and supplier of automotive components, is exploring the introduction of driverless (robot) taxis. The partnership could easily develop hardware and software to introduce driverless public vehicles – taxis, where the vehicle comes to a user rather than a user going to the vehicle. Self-driving taxis are not that far out. The Japanese government is envisioning and supporting their availability for the Olympics in 2020.
- Domino's Pizza is testing concepts, in partnership with other businesses, in which pizzas are not only ordered through robots (possessing conversational capabilities), but also made by robots, and finally delivered by robots. The robot revolution is progressing fast, given the advancements in artificial intelligence technology.
- The introduction of new aircraft is also not that far away, given that recent advancements in technology could reduce the time required to develop commercial aircraft from, say 6–8 years to 2–3 years.

Is the airline industry ready to adapt? A quotation often attributed to Charles Darwin is, "It is not the strongest of the species that survives, nor the most intelligent that survives. It is the one that is most adaptable to change." Although Darwin may not have said these exact words, the point about adaptation applies here.

Closing thoughts

- Focus first on managing the core elements of the business before attempting to develop digital strategies. Observations show that the gap between even the conventional airline strategies and their optimal execution continues to exist, and, in some cases, it is even growing. This gap is partly the result of tension between the current constraints within which an airline operates and the desire to transform fundamentally to address effectively the end-to-end journey challenge relating to connected customers. Stevens and Barlass provide insights, in Chapter 7, on how to maximize value from large assets.
- Advance the first element of the business – the airline's network, fleet, and schedule –by developing a digital operating system, which itself calls for a data hub and a digital hub-and-spoke system. It is with the use of a platform system that an airline can undertake the network, fleet, and schedule exercises on a truly dynamic basis. This would represent a step change.
- Simplify revenue management, the second core element of the business, through the use of much more comprehensive and real-time data; analytics, for harnessing customer and business intelligence; and enabling technologies (particularly artificial intelligence), for making smarter decisions.
- Innovate quickly to respond to customers' changing expectations, behaviors, and preferences. "Smart" technologies, including data, are empowering buyers to communicate with sellers on many fronts. Moreover, customers are not just looking for products; they are looking for (a) reduction in complexity and (b) outcomes and solutions.
- Make a decision on where is the power relating to data (the intangible asset). Does the power come from having it, owning it, or sharing it? Data sources are increasing, given the expansion of online sources and the Internet of Things. Customers are willing to share data with trusted airlines if the airlines are willing to develop personalized interactions. Airlines should be willing to share data to meet, if not exceed, customer expectations.
- Combine technology with human interactions to solve situation-based problems. This combination will increase the seamlessness and consistency of customer service and experience. Moreover, such a technology-human interaction will build true loyalty to the brand.
- Look at customers' expectations from outside in, a process that has, with few exceptions, been missed (or under-estimated in the haste to capture direct business online, reduce costs, and re-think operations). Although this has now become more or less conventional wisdom, it requires more than a catch-up program. It involves a fundamental shift for the organization – its culture, its talent, and its systems – as well as a much faster pace of change.

- Learn how to observe how airline customers assign value to products and services. Discover how to measure that value. Explore ways of getting feedback as to whether the airline is providing the right value. Three major reasons for an airline to re-design its services around its customers' experience are passenger trends, big data and analytics, and platform-based collaboration.
- Become prepared for the emergence of digital competition from outside of the airline industry. Scan the environment in the context of (a) the sharing economy, (b) social media, and (c) mobile technologies – areas that are forecast to bring about innovation in the distribution of travel products and services. Such an analysis calls for the smart use of information to create an *intelligence imperative* to offer smart and experientially-based services on a personalized basis.
- Recognize the value of platform-based businesses based on the success of new businesses and given the observation that capital is flowing toward the platform-based enterprises because of their demonstrated growth, global scalability, and huge addressable markets.
- Keep in mind the four critical aspects of the digital environment: developing a digital mind-set, leveraging digital technologies, identifying and implementing digital strategies, and creating a digital workplace. Simultaneously focusing on all four aspects will facilitate the development of a platform-based business in the context of a digital environment.
- Think about the execution aspect of the development of a digital platform. Although the theory of platforms is sound, in the end it is all about execution. Managers need to not only focus on all four aspects of the digital environment simultaneously, but also manage successfully the transition from the conventional system to the platform system. Monika Wiederhold, in Chapter 7, points to the need for senior management to foster a culture change to broaden the organizational mind-set to drop constraints.

Notes

1 There are two potential challenges for digitization. First, some members of the unionized labor force may not be in favor of certain changes. Second, there needs to be an open dialogue with OEMs who do have enormous data that could be helpful to airlines relating to operations.
2 "US Airlines and Shared Mobility: Will Auto Disruption Travel to Airlines?" *Morgan Stanley Research*, October 6, 2016.
3 "Fast-Forward to a Future of On-Demand Urban Air Transportation," *UBER Elevate*, October 27, 2016, pp. 1–4.
4 Ashlee Vance and Brad Stone, "Welcome to Larry Page's Secret Flying-Car Factories," *Bloomberg Businessweek*, June 9, 2016.

7   Thought-leadership pieces

1   Loyalty at the forefront of the transformation curve

Evert R. de Boer

General Manager Global Business Development, Travel
Aimia, Inc.

Airline executives look longingly at Uber and Airbnb – but the ultimate asset-light, platform-based, digital business sits right under their nose: the frequent flyer program (FFP). In many aspects, loyalty programs have witnessed a great rate of change compared to the core airline business – and even compared to some other traditional businesses. In fact, the origins of the first FFPs can be traced back to disruptive events in the regulatory and technological contexts in the late 1970s.

In the first section of this paper, we will look at how FFPs were the product of disruptive change. When FFPs were first launched, many in the industry considered them as a bit of a marketing gimmick and of little strategic value. But over time, and perhaps against the odds, they managed to survive by pushing the boundaries of the original FFP model – effectively reinventing themselves. Interestingly, through that reinvention, they took on some of the aspiring characteristics that we ascribe to some of the most successful (digital) disruptors today. The second section will explore the reasons why FFPs have been able to embrace digitization, and change more than the airline, by reviewing three critical areas. The first reason offered is the difference in core business drivers between the FFP and the airline, where we can observe some stark contrasts. The second reason is FFPs' growing ability to acquire and manage data in a meaningful way. And in third place, we look at how FFPs have turned themselves into network players, forging successful partnerships with an increasing network of companies, built around the consumer. In the final part of the paper, we will explore the impacts on the FFP of some of the scenarios that have been floated as potential outcomes of disruption in the airline industry. Lastly, we will look at how the FFP can best support the airline in an uncertain and disruptive environment.

The FFP: born out of disruption – and with a proven ability to reinvent itself

FFPs have witnessed a tremendous amount of change over the course of their existence. Seven years after the first FFP was launched by American Airlines in

1981, Airbus achieved the certification for its first A320 aircraft. One year later, in 1989, Air France became the first operator of the A320. By 2017, Airbus had delivered more than 7,000 Airbus A320 series aircraft, and Air France maintained a fleet of forty-two A320s, with an additional three on order.[1] Although Airbus made some changes to the aircraft, including wingtip fences, and increased fuel capacity for the A320-200 series, the aircraft is fundamentally the same as it was 25 years ago. The same can be said for other aircraft types, such as the Boeing 747-400.

During that same time, FFPs underwent significant changes, in many ways allowing them to deal with changes in the environment. Going back in time, it was a major disruption in the regulatory and technological environment in the United States that preceded, and enabled the launch of, FFPs. On the regulatory front, the Airline Deregulation Act was signed into effect in 1978 by US President Jimmy Carter. It paved the way for more intense competition between airlines by opening markets and routes. As a result, airlines scrambled to find new competitive tools to attract and retain customers. At the same time, the introduction of new central reservation systems with enhanced functionalities allowed the airlines to better track their individual customers. American Airlines, United Airlines and Delta Air Lines all launched programs in 1981, followed by their global counterparts in the 1980s and 1990s. A similar pattern could be observed in Europe around the time when the European Union's "Third Package" of liberalization measures took effect in January 1993, opening the European aviation market to more competition. Air France, Alitalia, KLM Royal Dutch Airlines, Iberia, Lufthansa and Scandinavian Airlines all launched their FFP in the period 1991–1993 in an effort to become more competitive. The programs that we witness today bear little resemblance to their original counterparts. And that is a good thing. The structural design of the original FFPs was unable to adjust to the growth in the programs, as well as the changing conditions offered in the airline environment. FFPs have been able to reinvent themselves, ensuring their survival and ongoing relevancy for all stake-holders. The first critical change that materialized over time was the realignment of rewards to the actual value of the customer. Many of the programs started with a distance-based currency, effectively rewarding members based on the miles flown. This turned out to be a relatively poor proxy of customer value, so FFPs and airlines started to look for new ways of measuring the true value of customers. In 2004, Air New Zealand became the first airline to introduce an accrual structure based on revenue instead of distance flown. Not every airline has opted to go for revenue-based accrual, and instead some have introduced more refined accrual structures, awarding less or more miles (or points) depending on the specific fare class the member traveled on. The second change that would prove to be of critical importance for the survival of the programs was the programs' ability to secure awards seats beyond the distressed inventory that was allocated to FFPs under the original model. As the programs grew, by attracting a wider audience through offering an ever-expanding range of non-airline partners, at the same time the load factors increased across the board, creating a double whammy effect, leaving many programs faced with the dilemma of too many miles chasing too few seats. By entering into new agreements with revenue management, effectively buying seats at commercial rates, the programs were able to secure a sufficient supply of award seats. At the same time, FFPs became more sophisticated in using the available supply of reward seats, effectively matching seats with the individual customer value (something that would set them on the path of using data insights to determine allocation). FFPs also embraced awards outside the traditional airline offering, improving the customer value proposition as well as driving down the cost per mile redeemed. In some cases, these non-air categories can account for a significant part of the redemptions. According to Lufthansa, almost one out of every three miles redeemed is used for awards other than flights.[2] Other changes and innovations introduced over time include sophisticated cash and miles offers, compelling elite qualification structures, and, last but not least, comprehensive partnerships with companies outside the airline domain, creating an extensive network of inter-related companies around the consumer.

The most successful programs changed not only their structure, but perhaps equally important their marketing philosophy. Against a backdrop of increased consumer choice and raised expectations, programs had to significantly "up their game" in many ways. Marketing executions are now done at nanosecond level, and the more advanced programs have fully embraced digital, social, and mobile. Facing stagnant marketing budgets, in combination with declining results from older execution mechanisms (think for example of declining open rates for emails), FFPs were forced to reinvent their approach to marketing and data. The traditional approach, using basic data sets and generic targeting, has made way for a pin-pointed strategy, based on a much better understanding of the customer life cycle and touchpoints, enabled by better models and marketing automation technology.

The FFP as a digital intermediary avant la lettre

Imagine a business that does not own any of the physical assets required to deliver the final product. This business furthermore is highly scalable, with its main operating platform sitting in a cloud environment. It facilitates an exchange between consumers and producers, carefully matching preferences with selected products using data analytics. Based on the extensive transactional data, and rich behavioral information, the business is able to form a 360-degree view of the customer. Now it does not hold any physical stock, and it sells a suite of highly targeted products mainly through digital channels, including online and mobile. It makes extensive use of big data and predictive analytics to shape, measure, and optimize the customer value proposition. It may sound like a vision of a distant future, but in reality this is what some of the most sophisticated FFPs are doing today. They match consumers who have a strong appetite for travel and rewards with an ever-increasing range of suppliers (including those outside the traditional travel space). They operate mainly online – Eurobonus, the FFP of Scandinavian Airlines, for example, sells 80% of its redemptions through the online channel.[3] By funneling the wide range of data into their data hub, and by using sophisticated analytics, FFPs are able to offer highly targeted and relevant offers to members. FFPs don't own any of the assets required – they don't own planes, or hotel buildings – they simply enter into agreements that allow them to obtain the services as required.

In putting data (information) at the center of every aspect of the FFP business model, one could argue that they follow the same path as some of the most success- ful digital disruptors, such as Uber and Airbnb. By following what Battelle[4] coined an *information first* approach, they built their business systems around flows of information, and potential information, instead of fixed assets. Every aspect of the business is built around the data that is available. Offer strategies, for example, are built on individual customer data, weighing competing offers to find out what messaging will create the best results, and incorporate learnings both from previ- ous executions as well as actual implementations.

The core business drivers of the FFP are fundamentally different from those of the airline

Opposites attract, they say – and in the case of the FFP and the airline, this could very well be the case. In examining the underlying drivers of the FFP and the air- line businesses, some stark contrasts can be observed. But how, some will say, can you compare the FFP and the airline as if they were separate units – is the FFP not but a part of the airline? Certainly the FFP was born as a function deeply embedded in the airline, but over time it underwent an increasing degree of separation, not too dissimilar to other functions, such as the catering business, ground-handling services, or reservation-system software providers. Although these functions are intrinsically linked to the airline business, they do not necessarily have to be part of the airline in order to provide the best performance. One could even argue that the FFP, with the majority of miles now being earned outside the airline for leading programs, has been one of the most successful functions in crossing traditional air- line boundaries. The analogy here would be a catering company that successfully managed to diversify its revenues from selling just to airlines to selling to other institutions requiring catering services. Let us examine the difference between the airline business and the FFP, assuming that the FFP is run as a separate entity. Firstly, on the financial side, airlines continue to offer unpredictable earnings in the long term. Although the current oil price, and, to some level, capacity disci- pline in the US, have helped to realize a strong performance in the last few years, airlines continue to struggle to deliver acceptable returns, with many failing to generate positive ROIC-WACC spreads. FFPs, on the other hand, generate strong and consistent cash flows. In addition, loyalty programs are less cyclical compared to airlines – and sometimes even operate anti-cyclical. It means that during eco- nomic downturns, loyalty programs will continue to deliver solid results. Airlines continue to be exposed to swings in the price of oil, making significant impacts on their cost side. FFPs don't share that same type of exposure to a single factor. Sec- ondly, there is the well-known fact that airlines operate in a substantially complex operating environment. As Michael Porter described in a report commissioned by IATA, airlines exercise little bargaining power over the stakeholders in the value chain, such as aircraft manufacturers, global distribution systems, airports, and other suppliers. Likewise, the homogenized products make consumers price sensi- tive, and many innovations lead to short but unsustainable competitive advantages.

An FFP, on the other hand, operates in a very different environment. The loyalty business is a relatively simple business model that offers to a great extent control over the levers of profitability. Thirdly, unlike the airline business, the loyalty business is not capital-intensive. It is easy to scale up or down, using an infrastructure (loyalty platform) that could easily be hosted in a cloud environment. Markets seem to underwrite the difference in business drivers and assign different valuation multiples to airlines and FFPs. A comparative analysis performed by EY in 2014 showed that the average EV/EBITDA multiples of loyalty-management companies reflect a 79% premium over the average EV/EBITDAR (Earnings Before Interest, Taxes, Depreciation, Amortization, and Rents) of a selected, representative airline peer group.[5]

FFPs have built richer data sets and stronger analytic capabilities

The third area is today's use of data in FFPs, which in many ways is more advanced than the other airline functions. Data collection isn't necessarily the issue – airlines possess a wealth of data on their customers. Their challenge is to connect the data "dots" in a way that helps them develop a complete view of their customers. A significant portion of airline product distribution occurs though third-party channels, which limits the airlines' ability to build insight. FFPs have been on the forefront of acquiring and managing data, delivering insights to manage their business, and enhance the customer experience. In many ways it owes this privileged position to the quality of the data that is available to the FFP. Sources of data include transactional data, booking data, behavioral data, and social, mobile, web, digital, and location data. With today's loyalty penetration rates in excess of 50%, the FFP no longer just represents a niche subsection of the airline's customers – instead, in many cases it provides access and deep insight into the majority of the customers.

Traditionally, airlines build products and services for scale, rather than to address the needs and values of individual customers. That is, they create relatively uniform products and sell them to as many customers as possible at the highest possible price. Traditional airline revenue-management models continue to see the world in black and white, reducing every sale to a reject or accept decision. Even the most sophisticated origin and destination bid-pricing systems continue to turn a blind eye to the individual customer's characteristics. It is telling that a common use of customer value in a revenue-management setting is the sledgehammer approach of offering a guaranteed seat on sold-out flights to members of the elite tier of the FFP. FFPs, on the other hand, have developed more intelligent approaches to decide on availability questions. The scarcity of reward seats forced the programs to come up with a better approach to deciding on award availability. In today's most sophisticated programs, the individual member profile is a key factor in deciding who gets access to the most attractive, classy award-seat inventory. Instead of framing it as a binary question (whether the particular RBD is available or not), the leading FFPs take into account factors such as status, recent interaction history, and lifetime value. Conversely, some programs are willing to subsidize more expensive award items, because they understand that the short-term investment will pay off in the form of long-term revenues from that member. This realization has also increas-ingly led to innovative ways of recognizing member value. Under the archaic rules of the past, customers were evaluated purely on the number of miles flown in a certain period. Today, many programs have implemented other forms of qualifying, in an effort to recognize the most valuable members. They look at the present value of the expected future revenue contributions from the member, allowing them to make a more informed decision. Although the FFP is in a privileged position when it comes to the ability to identify a particular customer (the member must be logged on to find the best results), airlines also are increasingly capable of recognizing customers through new (digital) technologies.

Another example is the advanced marketing automation that FFPs are deploy-ing. Using the rich pool of data available to them, they are starting to deliver on the "right message, right channel, and right sequence" adage. This would not be possible without the integration of data from outside the airline, namely from partners. This latter category is increasingly being made available by partners, as they realize their interests are aligned when it comes to building an attractive and relevant customer proposition. It does put the onus on the FFP to generate tangible and incremental results for partners, something that the leading programs are increasingly able to demonstrate. One interesting aspect of the automated mar-keting systems is that they integrate transactional data with behavioral data. In that context, an interesting debate is taking place over whether airlines should focus on analyzing existing transactional data versus acquiring and leveraging behavioral information. Airlines are continuously investing in using their transactional data to optimize their physical network and operations. Here we could learn a les-son from leading retailers. Retailers have long adopted revenue-management best practices from the airlines to manage their businesses, and many of the world's most successful retailers have evolved these practices even further – by infusing their revenue-management decisions with highly detailed customer insights. The real value lies in marrying transactional data with behavioral information. By focusing on one dimension only, any company would run the risk of significantly sub-optimizing its business. By marrying transactional data with behavioral infor-mation and customer-journey analytics, they can make effective and optimized decisions about almost every aspect of the business. Think for example of special offers, but also real practical matters relating to the physical store environment, such as store layout, to minute details such as the number of brands of a particular product that should be offered on a shelf.

How FFPs have evolved into successful network players

FFPs today operate as part of a complex ecosystem of interlinked company rela-tionships. In more ways than one, the survival of an FFP hinges on its ability to forge successful partnerships outside the airline. When American Airlines entered into the first FFP partnership in 1982, it set in motion an irreversible trend to expand the network through linkages with partners. In 1997, when Scandinavian Airlines, Thai Airways International, Air Canada, Lufthansa, and United Airlines launched the Star Alliance, the first global alliance, it bore particular relevance for frequent flyers, as the alliance introduced common service tiers (Star Alliance silver and gold), facilitating the provision of benefits to frequent flyers across the network. But the programs have arguably been equally successful in creating partnerships outside the traditional airline realm, delivering lasting and successful partnerships. This type of partnership is centered around the direct accrual of miles on non-air partners, but it increasingly incorporates an element of data analysis and sharing. The scale of the outside partnerships has become fundamental to the success of the airline and the FFP. Delta Air Lines, for example, is predicting that its American Express partnership will produce a contribution of $4 billion by 2021.[6] In addition to the direct accrual of miles for partners' services, FFPs have been able to tap into other pools of loyalty currencies through conversion agreements. By connecting the dots between various categories, FFPs have effectively built an ecosystem of miles-earning opportunities across a significant share of everyday spending. These partnerships are, of course, important because of their financial contribution to the FFPs and the airlines – in some cases, they even acted as a lifeline during turbulent times. But the creation of these partnerships, evolving into comprehensive networks around the member, also enables something else, which may be even more important in the future. The combined intelligence from across the partner range affords a view of the customer that is hard to match by any other single player in the ecosystem. It provides the FFP and the airline with a proprietary competitive edge, by taking advantage of two key aspects. Firstly, the FFP has a unique perspective on the customer, enabled by the rich data from across the partner ecosystem. Secondly, the width and depth of the customer touchpoints offered in the expanded partner ecosystem is virtually unmatched. Nowhere else could you find the combination of transactional, financial, and socio-demographic data that is offered in the FFP ecosystem. The changing nature of the partnerships reflect the recognition that this opportunity is getting in the FFP world. In the olden days, the FFP would sign an agreement with a partner, and the extent of the relationship would be limited to sending transaction files and invoices going back and forth. Today's most successful programs have dedicated teams of analysts working side by side with partners, delving into combined membership data in a quest to unlock customer insights that can make a real impact on the partner business.

The future of FFPs

Extrapolating some of the current thinking around disruption in the airline industry through the lens of an FFP yields some interesting scenarios. Of course, looking into the future based on what we know today misses the point of innovation, but let's, for argument's sake, look at a few scenarios:

- **The end of distressed inventory** – Assuming that data-analytical and networking capabilities will drastically improve, we may ultimately see no more spillage. In other words, every seat on the plane is sold at the right price to the right customer, leading to a load factor close to 100%. This outcome could be realized under the scenario where airlines would be able to run timetables purely built on the forecasted demand of high-value customers. Under this scenario, FFPs can no longer rely on leftover or distressed inventory, because there simply is no such inventory anymore. It does not mean that the programs cease to exist – however, it does mean that the commercial relationship between the airline and the FFP changes. The FFP will have to buy seats from the airline at the right price. But by that time, the analysis will also reveal that sacrificing short-term yield to drive a stronger member-value proposition will pay off in the future.

- **The rise of the super-informed consumer** – As airlines get access to better information, using stronger analytical tools, the same will go for consumers. Today already, consumers have access to a wide, but dispersed, variety of tools that can help them make decisions related to the travel journey. Think for example of fare watches predicting whether fares will go up or down, award-availability-monitoring tools that help members keep track of award seats being made available, and various kinds of alerts for special fares and offers, but also optimizing tools in relation to earning of miles. Expedia recently embedded a product offered by a company called 30k, which displays the number of miles a particular itinerary would yield using a selected FFP. As these tools become more integrated and user-friendly, consumers will be armed with real-time and complete information helping them to make an optimal and informed decision. What it means for the FFP is that the bar is raised across the board, fueling the need for better and more relevant messages and customer-value propositions.
- **Extreme fungibility of loyalty currencies** – The third scenario is a world in which loyalty currencies become completely fungible, meaning that as a result of connectivity and partnerships, you can convert any one currency into any other currency. To some extent, we see some of that already today. Credit-card points can be converted to hotel points, hotel points can be converted to frequent flyer miles, and so forth. Some people predict an increasingly important role for loyalty currency marketplaces, where members can freely exchange currencies, akin to the exchange of foreign currencies. Under this scenario, we may see the rise and fall of certain currencies and the start of a whole new world of currency trading. Program operators will have to consider the trade-offs of participating in such a new and open world, making careful decisions on how to engage. A number of industry observers are pointing to blockchain technology as the disruptive force that will enable this increased fungibility and many other changes.[7]

How can an airline's FFP best support the airline in the future?

So change is coming. What will change and when it will change remains up for debate – and no one can know for sure what is going to happen. What is clear, however, is that in a disruptive and uncertain future for airlines, FFPs can continue to play a key role, perhaps even a bigger role than they do today. That potentially more prominent role is founded on three characteristics of FFPs that were identified in the previous section. Firstly, FFPs offer fundamentally different business dynamics than the core airline business. Secondly, no other component in the travel value chain has either the richness of data or the data-analytical capabilities that FFPs do. Thirdly, FFPs have the greatest ability to act as a catalyst for change, and embrace new technologies and innovations from outside the airline industry. FFPs are naturally positioned to act as a conduit with the outside world to extend the boundaries of the airline business.

In assessing how an FFP can best be structured as a catalyst for change, it is useful to examine the different kinds of FFPs there are today. FFPs can be categorized into one of three typologies: legacy, advanced, and autonomous programs.[8] The advanced and autonomous types of programs offer the greatest potential for airlines. Legacy programs represent the original category of FFPs, and their common characteristics are a focus on high-yield, high-frequency travelers and the use of distressed inventory for award seats. In this type of program, the bulk of the miles are earned by flying, and the partner lineup is limited to travel-oriented companies, such as hotels and car-rental partners. Legacy programs typically sit within the sales and marketing department of the airline, and the vast majority of the employees in the department have an airline background. The results generated by the legacy program are not reported separately but roll up into the overall airline results. Given the inherent limitations of the legacy model, airlines still deploying this type of FFP may find themselves less able to exploit the opportunities that disruption will offer in the future. The second type of FFP is the advanced program. In many ways, these FFPs build on the foundation laid by the legacy programs and widen their scope both in terms of member focus and in terms of partner lineup. By offering more partners outside the airline, including financial services and retail, the advanced program becomes more attractive and relevant for those consumers who cannot match the frequency and spending of the original frequent flyers. The additional earning options give them enough earning velocity to reach an award level in a reasonable time. With the additional demand for award seats, the advanced programs can no longer rely solely on distressed inventory to satiate the demand. As a result, and enabled by the increased revenues from selling more miles to outside partners, advanced programs start to enter into agreements with the airline to buy additional inventory at agreed commercial rates. It allows them to offer more award seats to members and also to introduce more dynamically priced awards instead of the fixed, classic award charts. Advanced programs may choose to report their reports separately, as a segment within the airline. The third type of FFP is the autonomous program. By entering into arm's-length commercial agreements with the airline, the FFP can operate as a stand-alone business that is suitable for outside investment. In a number of cases, the shareholders of the airline decide to sell off part of the business to strategic investors or to float part of the business on the stock market. The majority of miles are earned on non-air partners, whereas the majority of redemptions still take place on the airline, creating a positive balance of trade with the airline. The new company can make more autonomous decisions around technology and marketing investments, and it attracts resources from a wider talent pool beyond the airline, including retail, fast-moving consumer goods, and financial services.

Conclusion

In a world where every airline innovation is easily copied (think for example of new lie-flat seats, better IFE systems, on-demand dining, Wi-Fi connectivity, premium economy seats, and LCC subsidiaries), airlines need to look for sustainable competitive advantages. And as Jack Welch famously said, an organization's ability to learn, and translate that learning into action rapidly, is the ultimate competitive advantage. Here is where the FFP can play a key role – both in learning insights, as well as acting on them in a meaningful way. Although the future may hold many uncertainties, some things we know already. Firstly, people will continue to love to travel. It means that travel in the form of rewards will continue to captivate consumers' imagination – no technology will alter that. Secondly, there remain tremendous growth opportunities, especially in Asia and Africa. Loyalty programs are only starting to scratch the surface there. But to fully reap the benefits that the FFP can offer, we need to overcome some of the ingrained perceptions about the programs. FFPs have been enormously successful – not only in terms of growth and reach, but also in financial terms. There have been instances in which the implied value through market capitalization of an FFP has exceeded that of the associated airline. Some observers in the industry have scoffed at this notion, calling it the proverbial tail that is wagging the dog, implying that this is neither desirable nor realistic. But if airlines are going to succeed in a wildly disruptive environment, we need to embrace these kinds of new and unfamiliar strategies, as the airlines need to break free from inertia and the status quo.

It is also time for airline boards around the world to give the FFP the attention it deserves. Based on its unique characteristics (its structurally different business dynamics; its ability to acquire, manage, and use relevant data; and its ability to embrace and exploit change), FFPs deserve a more prominent place at the table. Although it is encouraging to see that leading airline groups such as IAG and Lufthansa Group have created special entities for their FFPs, an arguably far bigger share remains reluctant to make the necessary changes and investments to let the FFP flourish, either inside the airline or with outside support. The FFP is uniquely positioned to create the deepest digital relationships and use those relationships to create value for all stakeholders. It has potentially access to more and better data, but, more importantly, it continues to hold the keys to the most desirable award category: high-value travel redemptions. In an uncertain future, with competing priorities, airlines must carefully consider where they will place their bets. The FFP is uniquely positioned to help the airline ride the waves of disruption and create real value for all stakeholders.

About the author

Evert de Boer has researched and worked in airline-loyalty strategy since 2000. He has collaborated with more than 15 airlines globally on frequent flyer programs in management and advisory roles and has published numerous articles and white papers. He is the author of *Strategy in Airline Loyalty: Frequent Flyer Programs*, which will be published in early 2018 by Palgrave Macmillan.

Notes

1 CAPA Fleet database.
2 Lufthansa, "Miles & More Company Portrait." Accessed March 6, 2017, from www.miles-and-more.com/mediapool/pdf/00/media_1038159100.pdf
3 Scandinavian Airlines, "20 Years of Loyalty With Scandinavian Airlines," April 2012. Accessed April 11, 2017, from www.sasgroup.net/en/20-years-of-loyalty-with-scandinavian-airlines/
4 John Battelle, "Living Systems and the Information First Company," October 2014. Accessed April 5, 2017, from http://battellemedia.com/archives/2014/10/information-first-company.php
5 EY, "Frequent Flyer Program: Ready for Take-Off." 2014. Accessed April 13, 2017, from www.ey.com/Publication/vwLUAssets/etude-ey-sur-les-programmes-de-fidelite-des-compagnies-aeriennes/$FILE/etude-ey-sur-les-programmes-de-fidelite-des-compagnies-aeriennes.pdf
6 Delta Air Lines, "Delta – A Durable Business Model," Speech presented at J.P. Morgan Aviation, Transportation and Industrials Conference, New York, March 2017. Accessed March 21, 2017, from http://s1.q4cdn.com/231238688/files/Conferences/2017/Delta-Air-Lines-J.P.-Morgan-Aviation-Transportation-and-Industrials-Conference.pdf
7 See for example Dan Kowalewski, Jessica McLaughlin, and Alex Hill, "Blockchain Will Transform Customer Loyalty Programs," *Harvard Business Review*, March 2017.
8 Evert R. de Boer and Sveinn Vidar Gudmundsson, "30 Years of Frequent Flyer Programs," *Journal of Air Transport Management* 24 (2012): 18–24.

2   A high-level checklist for developing a data strategy

Gary Doernhoefer

Vice President & General Counsel
Journera

> *"Most people use statistics the way a drunkard uses a lamp post, more for support than illumination."*
>
> *– Andrew Lang, 19th century poet and anthropologist*

One of the biggest challenges in travel today for service providers, including airlines, hotels and ground transportation, is to develop and adopt a thoughtful, thorough and practical data strategy. A data strategy should plan to benefit every aspect of the travel business, making operations more reliable and efficient, improving budgeting and planning, increasing employee productivity, and improving the company's ability to provide personalized, timely and convenient value-added services in addition to the basic service. This paper will use the customer-service benefits of a data strategy in many examples, but the broader focus should not be lost. A successful data strategy should not reinforce silos; it should help break them down.

The customer-service opportunities in travel springing from new data capabilities are just getting started. Highly differentiated products provide a fertile environment for personalization using the growing availability of data and data-management tools. Hotels have offered differentiated products and services – suites, television and movies, free breakfast, parking, airport transfers, internet, 24-hour room service, onsite bars and restaurants, fitness centers, pools, spa services, meeting facilities and so on – for a long time. Airlines are relatively new to product differentiation, starting from basic, safe, air transportation with some differentiation in fare types and now "unbundling" services such as baggage checking, and adding in-flight entertainment and Wi-Fi, varying seating alternatives and selection, frequent flyer perks, boarding priorities, airport lounge access and other amenities trying to suit the preferences of travelers from the parsimonious to the prestigious. As the range of options in all types of service increases, it creates a challenge and an opportunity. Retailers need to avoid inundating the consumer with too many choices and complicating the shopping process. Instead, the service provider must work to identify the unique blend of custom additional services each consumer is most likely to want, and to offer them at the right time. This retailing opportunity should be win-win – the more accurately the retailer can align its product/service offer to the preferences of its consumer, the better the shopping and travel experience will be for the consumer, the service provider can provide better service while capturing the incremental revenue from the custom elements of the trip and receive feedback on which services are valued by its consumers.

Success will be driven by data – its collection, analysis, reporting, communication and use. The key to today's data strategy is to move an organization along the data spectrum, from descriptive analytics – arguably Twain's lamp post, to predictive and on toward prescriptive.[1] This paper establishes a very high-level roadmap to developing such a data strategy. Every company will be different and will fill in the details based on its own circumstances. There are likely to be elements your organization needs to add to this framework. Nevertheless, the topics and questions presented here may be a useful starting point or checklist for travel companies contemplating the difficult move from legacy systems to a data-driven enterprise.

Offering a drink to a drowning man

A manager tasked with developing a data strategy might be tempted to start by asking what it is the organization wants to accomplish with the application of data. One of the lessons of big data is to suspend that temptation because it may establish unnecessary limitations on the strategy. There is a somewhat controversial phrase that became popular with big data, "Let the data speak for itself." Although this aphorism has been subject to interpretation and criticism, the valid message is that big-data techniques allow the identification of correlations, insights and potential predictive results that may be unexpected and, had a specific query been made, would have been overlooked. Accordingly, the best first step on the road to the successful implementation of a data strategy may not be to list the desired results, but to consider the sources of data. In the simplest terms, data sources will be internal or external to your company.

Most travel-service companies are already awash in their own data, so asking a manager to look for more data sources may be akin to offering a drink to a drowning man. In a 2014 article in *Fortune*, United Airlines' vice president of e-commerce and merchandising, Scott Wilson, estimated United had roughly a terabyte of customer data in the system at any given time. This might lead a manager to think the last thing she needs is to seek out more of it. There may be a tendency to start on the next step of trying to make sense of what is already at hand. A good strategy will resist this temptation as well and approach this question more strategically.

It may be fine to start with an inventory of existing internal data sources and types, but it's important not to let that current inventory become a constraint, despite however much data is already identified. At the outset, be slow to discard a potential data source as irrelevant to a broad data strategy. In addition to a current data collection inventory, consider a strategic look at operations and customer experience – maybe informed by practices in other industries – which may identify additional valuable data that isn't currently collected, or that is collected but not utilized. A recent data success story from Hyatt Hotels offers a great example.

In short, the Hyatt story tells of an observant housekeeper who deduces that a particular guest is doing yoga in the hotel room and ensures that a yoga mat is provided for the remainder of that guest's stay. The data success story is that this information gets reported and captured in the guest's profile; that profile is made available across the Hyatt system and is used to provide a yoga mat for this guest every time the guest stays in any Hyatt hotel.[2] The lesson is that the search for critical data that can impact customer service requires a thoughtful, detailed examination of the customer experience, not limited to available data sources. The volume of data currently available, even though already overwhelming, still may not contain the right pieces of information.

Some data sources will be external to the company. Most retailers are already aware of companies that compile data about customers from other sources, such as Facebook and LinkedIn. Those sources may not offer the detailed preferences that support personalization. Travel-industry participants might want to also consider data from other points in their distribution channels and complementary travel sources.

For example, an airline might make excellent use of channel data from an online travel agency or other aggregator. An airline might want to know when it was in a search results set, which competitors were also present, the frequency with which it received a booking and, when it did not receive a booking, what factors were present in the successful offer that were not in its offer – price, available seat preference, etc. In short, data from the search process, particularly when presented against competitors (unlike a search on the airline's own site) might be particularly useful.

A second category of external sources should include complementary service providers. Travel often involves multiple service providers that together offer the services required by a single consumer on a single journey. Sharing data across airlines, hotels and ground transportation providers could create a unified, personalized picture of a consumer's journey that would allow all service providers opportunities to offer useful services at the right times. For example: a hotel that knows the guest's departing flight isn't until 5:00 p.m. affords it an opportunity to offer late checkout; an airline that knows the rental car has been returned hours before the departing flight could offer an earlier flight or lounge access. There are likely to be a wide variety of correlations in consumer preferences among the travel verticals as well. Travelers in business class might be more likely to desire an upgraded car service, rental car or hotel room, for instance.

Once the organization has identified sources of data to be collected and developed the culture and tools for collecting it, it needs a system in which to store and process the data. The logical starting point is to look at data storage and processing systems already in place and, if multiple systems exist, whether they can be integrated. The trick here is determining whether some or all of an existing system can meet the strategic need with minimum duplication and without constraining essential functions or growth. Some managers might be tempted to start here, pursuing the promise of modern computer processing first, and backing into a data strategy to fit the system. It's easy to do. System vendors aggressively sell their systems, and managers are forced to routinely fend off calls. Starting with a strategy, reducing that to requirements, and then assessing system alternatives will offer better results.

System architecture or application recommendations need to fit the company requirements and are well beyond the scope of this paper (and this author's knowledge!). But we can identify some key things for a manager to consider that will influence an expert's recommended solution.

1   Who will use the output of the system will determine reporting or visualization requirements. Customer-service output intended for implementation by service-desk staff is very different than output consumed by a small group of technical

or strategic planners. Similarly, whether data output will be needed in widely distributed locations or only within centralized headquarters may impact system choice. Equally important to "who" is "how many." Some serious efficiencies can be achieved by careful consideration of all the departments, divisions and areas in a company that need to receive the same data output.

2   In the past, data systems were mostly about storage and retrieval. Today, managers should assume most data captured will be used in some kind of advanced analytics, pushing toward the predictive and prescriptive end of the spectrum. The functional differences between storage and rapid retrieval versus relational database applications have been a historical factor in airline systems based on a system called transactional processing facility, or TPF. TPF offered enormous scalability and rapid data retrieval in an era with much more limited computer power, but it offered little or no relational data processing capability. Managers selecting systems today need to think hard about the potential for future processing capabilities, even if only certain data is stored today.

3   Does the system need to act in real time, in any or all aspects: receiving data, processing it, and distributing results? The airline industry already functions with combinations of real-time data, such as seat availability, and high-latency information like flight schedules, which need to be relatively predictable and constant over long periods. A clear view of these needs for different functions will help an airline select the best, cost-effective system.

4   Are the data contents structured, like cells in a spreadsheet, or unstructured like social media? There are strategies for managing each, and for integration, if that is necessary.

5   And finally, the choice of any system today needs to anticipate, as well as possible, the growth and needs of the future. Clearly there will be more data coming, likely in different forms and formats. Scalability and flexibility will be vital. Kevin Iverson, chief technology officer at Journera, a travel-industry data platform, describes the need for system flexibility: "It needs to be able to cost-effectively scale so there is not an organizational incentive to limit what you store. It needs to be flexible enough that you can process the data effectively to answer the questions you know about now, but also enable the organization to ask questions it doesn't know are valuable yet. The other aspect of flexibility is around the change to allow new technologies and techniques to be applied without having to start over."

"If you torture the data long enough, it will confess."

– Ronald Coase

Among the most treacherous steps in developing a data strategy are the decisions about what to collect and process and how long to keep it. This decision can be treacherous because of the highly dynamic environment of data and data analysis. It will be easy to choose not to capture data today that the company might find very useful next year, just because conditions and data-management capability have changed. On the other hand, today's low data-storage and data-processing costs are not a good excuse to avoid serious deliberation about what data you should capture and process – "because we can" is not a strategy. There can be indirect costs beyond merely the price of storage in the cloud or elsewhere. For instance, no matter how seemingly benign the data is, there is likely to be some requirement of data security and some risk if data is hacked or leaked. The harm may only be reputational, but it's still a risk to be managed, and costs will be incurred. Collecting and processing data the output of which you will never use needlessly exposes the organization. Regulatory issues, such as the European Commission's concept of data protection "proportionality," may also limit the types of personal customer information you can collect and store.

One good test when faced with a decision of what data to capture, store and process may be to consider at least a use case the output would support. Use cases impose the practical requirement that data processed achieve actionable information – some insight, observation or conclusion upon which a company can do something to improve service, increase efficiency, develop a new product or service or meet some other tangible business objective. In some cases, data processing may lead you in unanticipated directions. In other situations, a business need will compel targeted inquiries. Both need support, and a use case test, coupled with a good imagination, may help draw the line.

There may be two lessons from Mr. Coase's quip, depending on how you wish to interpret it. The first may be that good data science requires determination and diligence to achieve results. While there is a caution here against collecting and storing useless data or wasting time processing data that do not produce actionable results, a mantra of the big-data movement is "fail fast." Another is that even failure produces useful knowledge. If the data do not immediately offer useful insights, you may need to keep trying. On the other hand, bias in statistical analysis is a well-known enemy of good data science. Mr. Coase's admonition could also be interpreted as a warning against generating inaccurate results as a result of the "torture" of data with the bias of supporting the sought-after confession.

Applying a general standard for the collection and processing of data based on a use case, rather than requiring a full business case standard, may be best, particularly at the early stage of the data strategy. A use case is likely to identify at least a plausible tie of relevance between data and the business's objectives. A use case simply posits a potential actionable outcome, without regard to its current cost, return or practicality. In contrast, all of that would be required to make the business case and may exclude many more types and sources of data, some of which are likely to be relevant later. A use case is less likely to be committed to a particular answer from the data, one that may be needed to support a business case. A use case is more likely to merely seek a correlation without implied causation, something that can be studied further if the data is kept. This is a better way to support a data strategy than risking forcing an outcome to fit a business case.

"If you can't explain it simply, you don't understand it well enough."
– Albert Einstein

An effective data strategy must include planning for the communication of the "actionable output" of data processing to the part of the organization – down to the individual or system – that can make use of it. Actionable output means information that can be used to make a decision or take an action. An example might be a report that shows a trend in baggage fees. Interesting, but not yet actionable. The same data breaking down whether the booking, a pre-trip communications or airport kiosk generated the most baggage fees is actionable as a consumer-communication strategy. Data on the consumption of in-flight catering items would be useful for budgeting. But actionable data on which items sell out on flights by time of day could lead to changes in catering practices that improve customer service and increase revenue.

Like the data-collection step, there is both a technical and a cultural aspect to making output actionable. Part of the system selection should have anticipated the location and type of user expected to consume the processed data output. The "where" is addressed by internal networks with appropriate consideration for data security, efficiency and ease of access. There's no point in generating brilliant data products and then impeding their use by making them difficult or inconvenient to either access or understand. With current wireless and mobile communication capabilities, the data should be easily available wherever it is needed, right down to the aircraft mechanic using a diagnostic maintenance app to access records on a mobile device or a flight attendant in first class having access to customer loyalty status and preferences. Further, data-visualization tools have improved dramatically in recent years, along with the art of human interface design. Making the data output easily accessible and easily comprehensible by its end user must be a part of the data strategy.

> *"Culture eats strategy for lunch."*
>
> *– unknown*[3]

Another lesson may be that until services are delivered by robots, a successful data strategy relies on a fundamentally data-focused culture. Having employees who are sensitive to providing a service – in our Hyatt case, a yoga mat – is important, but the data strategy also requires that employee to identify and capture that data so that the positive experience gets replicated. Good managers will have to think about how to make this practice routine. Randy Bean, CEO of NewVantage Partners, describes this perfectly:

> The greatest business challenge for most mainstream corporations is not about technology; it is the process of cultural change. Cultural change represents a business problem, requiring a business solution and business approach. Business adoption of big data requires addressing issues of organizational alignment, change management, business process design, coordination, and communication. These are issues that involve people and communication and understanding.[4]

The pithy saying "Culture eats strategy for lunch" succinctly captures the challenge. Books on managing corporate culture could fill a library. For this purpose, it is sufficient just to add to our checklist that a data strategy must be developed in parallel with a data-driven cultural focus – a combination of human sensitivity, instilled by company culture, and technology working together. Otherwise, the best data strategy, selection of technology and flawless implementation risks failure at the data-input and data-use ends of the process flow. Preparing your organization for the shift to a data-driven organization may be uniquely difficult. It requires thinking in new ways and using new tools. Kevin Iverson of Journera emphasizes the recruiting challenge: "[The people you want] are in high demand and only interested in joining a team where the importance of data is understood, so you need to make sure you have a firm plan that addresses the cultural aspects before moving into full press recruiting mode."

> *"True intuitive expertise is learned from prolonged experience with good feedback on mistakes."*
>
> *– Daniel Kahneman*

Nearing the end of our process-flow checklist, an essential component of a successful data strategy is to ensure a feedback loop. There was a time when organizations could undertake a study, develop an IT strategy and budget, execute and then make incremental changes for a few years before repeating the process to catch up again. At the current pace of change, those days are gone. Today's data strategy needs to incorporate excellent communications on utilization of data, development of new needs, data sources and opportunities, and constant assessment of new processing techniques, communications, data-presentation solutions, recruiting and education to ensure continuous improvement.

> *"Data is the new oil."*
>
> *– Clive Humby, at the Association of National Advertisers Senior Marketers Summit, Kellogg School, 2006*

Only better. Unlike a barrel of oil, which gets refined into gasoline and burned, data has value *and can be replicated at essentially no cost.* That barrel of oil can't be in two places at once. Data can, giving it the potential to be even more useful and more able to generate value than oil. The point, however, is that strategic thinking about data-processing needs has gone from cost center to revenue generation. So, the final step in a company data strategy is to look for external opportunities to monetize the data in addition to its internal consumption that drives efficiency, innovation and revenue opportunity. Looking externally, travel-service providers might first investigate the value of their data to adjacent markets, such as the value of airline data value to a hotel or a car-rental business. For instance, a hotel that knows an arriving guest lands in the city at 8:00 a.m. may want to offer early check-in, or a half-day rate – and such an offer might be greatly appreciated by the guest. That hotel may find sufficient value in the airline's data that it will pay to receive it. That's the motivating principle behind Journera, a B2B travel industry startup led by CEO Jeff Katz, the initial CEO at online travel agency Orbitz. Journera is constructing a platform that will allow travel-service providers from the various travel verticals to identify common customers and exchange travel information about them, even in real time.

The data age arrived several years ago, and companies in all industries are scrambling to catch up. The pace of data-capability development is not waiting. The sooner a company undertakes strategic planning for the digital world, the sooner it will begin to reap the benefits.

Notes

1 See Jeff Bertolucci, "Big Data Analytics: Descriptive Vs. Predictive Vs. Prescriptive." Accessed from www.informationweek.com/big-data/big-data-analytics/big-data-analytics-descriptive-vs-predictive-vs-prescriptive/d/d-id/1113279
2 https://blogs.informatica.com/2016/09/07/using-data-to-delight-guests-how-hyatt-wins-customers/#fbid=-RSUIN8qVrR
3 The source of this catchy phrase seems in dispute, but there's general agreement it developed from the less graphic "Culture *beats* strategy."
4 www.forbes.com/sites/ciocentral/2016/11/08/another-side-of-big-data-big-data-for-social-good-2/#3d6db9e06628

3 Radical digitization in the airline industry

Stefan A. Jenzowsky

Senior Vice President, Head of New Products
Siemens Convergence Creators, Vienna/Berlin

Embarking on a voyage to the future is like embarking on a voyage to the past: it feels like traveling to a strange, albeit somehow familiar country. Let us assume we could travel back in time 50 years. Certainly, we would be shocked by many things we would see. But what might shock us most would be the relative inefficiency of the world around us. We would be shocked to see lift operators in elevators asking us which floor we would like to go to. And we would be similarly shocked to see young men at gas stations ready and waiting to fill up our car with gas. We would see buses with conductors on board. But, interestingly enough, our airports and airlines would look quite familiar.[1] Now let us assume that we can go into the future. What will we see? How will the airline industry have changed? Please embark with me on this brief voyage into the airline industry of the future. Let us look at (1) what digitization and radical digitization mean, (2) how Moore's Law is enabling digitization, (3) some examples of the effect of digitization in other industries, (4) some ramifications for the airline industry, and (5) some perspectives on possible future scenarios relating to the airline industry.

Digitization vs. radical digitization

We have been digitizing businesses and their processes for many years. In fact, since computers became common. Hence, we have digitized the world around us since the 1980s.

But we are now in the process of radically digitizing businesses. But what makes "radical digitization" different?

Whenever we digitize a business or a process, we basically put its core elements into software, thus on a computer. In my view, it is that simple. But the reason for doing so is different between digitization and radical digitization. Historically, we introduced computers in order to assist and help us in our duties. In the airline industry, we use computerized passenger lists, as they can be easily edited and changed until closing of the flight. And then we print out the list. In a travel agency, we use computers to look at hotel and flight options, and then we use them for booking the passenger to the flight. And computers are incredibly handy for locating and retrieving lost baggage, because they can communicate worldwide and find where the piece of baggage was last seen (or rather scanned). But this is not radical digitization. Because we do it to help ourselves and our colleagues – in order to make us faster, more efficient, to make us do our jobs easier and better.

When we radically digitize a business, we do it to disrupt it *by* making it digital. Disruption is a somewhat hip concept these days. It really means we actually strive to destroy the business as we know it. And replace it by a business that has similar capabilities – but is fully digital in nature. For the case of the travel agency, this meant we replaced the travel agent by a booking system that is used by the passengers themselves, thereby eliminating the need for a travel agent altogether. In most Western societies, we have done this already. But what about the location of lost baggage? Or the passenger list? Soon, we will replace them, too. And we will we radically digitize the taxi driver who drove me to the airport in 2017 and the bus driver, too. And what about the pilots and the entire flight crew? Probably them too. Which leaves us with one simple question: Is there a way to radically digitize an entire airline? Or even the entire airline business? Well, I believe so. And I believe that there is a good chance that we will be able to witness (or shape) this dramatic change during our lifetime.

What really happens when we put a business entirely into software? And why would we want to do this in the first place? The answer to these questions is that Moore's Law will start to work for us. As you know, Gordon Moore's brilliant observation known as Moore's Law was nothing more than a linear prediction (and is no law of nature at all). It simply states that the number of transistors in a computer chip doubles approximately every two years, thereby doubling the computer performance (or shaving off half of the cost for the computer operation). So, the driving forces for radical digitization are simply processing power (aka speed) – and cost. But the consequence of radically digitizing a business is that it can now operate at twice the speed and half the cost every two years. This means that you can, after radically digitizing a business, reliably expect to grow the capacity of your business exponentially. In other words, you can deliver twice the amount of books (or pizza!), four times, eight times, sixteen times, etc. And you can reliably predict at what point in time the book (or pizza) delivery capabilities will be large enough to serve the entire human population with books (or eradicate world hunger entirely by pizza delivery).[2]

In our world, we have witnessed the stunning explosion of computing power in countless examples, ranging from the smartphones of today, which possess more calculation power than the entire Apollo program, to modern game consoles, which surpass the processing power of yesterday's mainframe computers. The most stunning consequence of this culminating development may be the concept of Singularity by Ray Kurzweil. Kurzweil forecasts an exponential increase in global artificial intelligence, reaching the level of processing power of a single human within the next ten years. Due to the exponential nature of this development, shortly after this, the processing power of all humans will be surpassed by artificial intelligence. Once this Singularity has been reached, Kurzweil predicts that machines will be more intelligent than all human intelligence combined, thereby transforming human life altogether.

What consequence does all this hold for digital businesses? Well, the first observation is trivial: expect exponential growth. By radically digitizing a business, we put the business *itself* on Moore's Law, allowing it to grow exponentially. In a non-exponential world, with limited resources and customers, this poses some interesting challenges. How many books can people read? (or: How many pizzas can be baked?) As you can easily see, customers and resources may be limiting factors. Of course, today's book (or pizza!) delivery corporations like Amazon (or Delivery Hero) can already organize book (pizza!) delivery for the everyone in the world (they could probably shoulder 10 billion pizzas per day). Because they are radically digital businesses. But there are simply not enough book readers, authors, pizza ovens, pizza eaters, and tomatoes available. This is what limits their growth, not the capability of their business. This is the reason why electronic businesses that rely on network effects, like portals (e.g. for dating, photo sharing, and any user-generated content) and marketplaces (e.g. for used cars, houses, accommodation, books, music, video) reach enormous valuations by investors. For most of them (Facebook, Instagram, YouTube, Cars.com, TripAdvisor, etc.), their resource is (or has been initially) generated by the user, allowing them to really grow exponentially.

The second observation is less obvious: there may be a limiting factor within your business process chain. If we still need a paid author (or a pizza baker, delivery driver, or tomato supply), we have not created a radically digitized business. In phases of strong growth, we would encounter instead situations in which these human elements of our business processes simply would become overworked. They are limiting our growth – especially in periods of exponential growth. This is exactly where digital businesses and radically digital businesses differ. Thus, whenever we are leaving an element in our business which, even for good reasons, we cannot digitize, we are decoupling our business from Moore's Law. And this is totally fine – as long as no one else figures out how to radically digitize our business.

This is why Amazon and other companies invest in automated packaging, automated delivery systems, automated shipping systems, and drone delivery. The underlying expectation is visible: drone delivery is radically digital in nature. Thus, we can expect it to become twice as cheap, or twice as fast, every two years. This strategy eliminates any non-digital (human) element as much as possible. In a second strategy, Amazon was successful in transforming its product offerings. It has shifted a substantial part of its delivery of books, music, and video from physical products (books, CDs, DVDs, Blu-ray discs, etc.) to radically digital (Amazon Prime video-streaming service, e-books, etc.) by altering the product itself. Essentially, by transforming their core products from physical to virtual.[3]

The third observation is that, once we radically digitize a business, we can now *reliably* predict its exponential growth. This means that, if we find enough customers/users who are willing to share their views/photos/comments or spend their money, and enough supply, we *will* grow exponentially. This is exactly what Silicon Valley investment strategies look for: a start-up company that can disrupt an established business by radical digitization of all elements and a product test (based on a minimum viable product) that indicates customer interest, which should fuel exponential growth. These ingredients form an exponential aspiration – and an exponential business plan, which reliably predicts exponential growth. In the world of radical digitization, business plans have to look like hockey sticks.

Of course, Moore's Law may be nothing more than a self-fulfilling prophecy. But as this self-fulfilling prophecy impacts business planning and financing of the computer industry, as well as business planning and financing of any digitized industries, it may work for many years to come. In other words, as long as Silicon Valley believes in it and plans for it, Moore's Law will work for us.

Digital disruption in other industries

In many industries, we have seen countless examples of the effect of radical digitization. The telecommunications industry is an excellent example, because the digital disruption in this industry impacted even large suppliers such as Siemens. The telephony world around the globe was coming out of a governmentally owned past and used to be extremely profitable, with a few strong players in each market. But aside from the changes induced by deregulation and the resulting increasing competition, it was disrupted digitally. New entrants were using purely internet-based technology and Voice-over-Internet-Protocol (VoIP). Initially almost unnoticed by the larger players, a small company called Skype was starting to offer free telephony. This happened at a time when private-consumer telephony was the core product and a major revenue generator for telecommunication providers worldwide. Someone had altered the core product of this multi-billion-dollar industry and was giving it away for free! How could this happen? The secret was very simple: not only was Skype offering VoIP telephony, they actually used the internet as the underlying infrastructure. In other words, a telephony carrier without any network had emerged. Whereas traditional telecom companies had thousands of employees managing their telecom network, Skype had none. And while traditional telecom companies were spending millions of dollars on marketing, Skype was spending nothing. The company's founders had managed to radically digitize the core product of an industry – and now could give it away for free. Instead of charging consumers for the core service, they actually invented innovative business models in which consumers were paying for calls in and out of the Skype system or even for the answering-machine function. Today, with more than 300 million users, Skype is the largest telecommunications provider of the world by minutes and users. And it is still growing.

But the most profitable product of the telecommunications industry was not telephony. It was the short message service (SMS). With relatively low costs associated with the service, and based on SMS centers, which could handle an enormous amount of SMS, the SMS was a golden cow to the telecommunications industry. From 2008 onward, Australian mobile telephony provider Telstra would transmit more than 800 SMS messages per consumer per year, all of them either paid per usage or as part of a rate-plan package. In the UK, subscribers send almost 200 SMS messages per month. In 2010, South African provider Vodacom sold and transmitted more than 5 billion SMS messages. And since 2006, the number of SMS messages had almost doubled in all markets. It actually increased every year. Until 2011. In October 2011, Apple announced its new upgrade to the iOS operating system. And this upgrade contained a new offering called the iMessage, which was an SMS – for free. Moreover, consumers who wanted to send an SMS message from their iPhone were automatically shifted to the iMessage if the recipient also used an iPhone. Within two months, worldwide use of SMS started to decline rapidly. Apple, considered a close and highly valued partner to the mobile operators, had digitally disrupted the SMS business, the most profitable business their partners had. Within some months, Android followed suit, disrupting and almost eliminating SMS messages between Android phones. And, of course, WhatsApp – which today is about 50% more used than SMS. Overall, market analysts such as Ovum conclude that, due to the disruption of their SMS business, mobile operators lost out on $32.6 billion in revenue in 2013, projected to increase to $86 billion in 2020 (compared to the original SMS business).

Another product that is radically digitized right now is broadcast television. The digital replacement product is called OTT, short for Over-The-Top television. In the year 2015, we were witnessing a historic shift: it was the year in which, during some single days, US consumers were watching more streamed video than broadcasting. Indeed, the lead medium of our age, television, is being disrupted by radical digitization. Over-The-Top offerings, such as Netflix, YouTube, Amazon Prime Video, and Apple TV, may seem very much like television to the individual user – but in fact they are radically digitized replacements to television as we once knew it.

Of course, the production, curation, and programming of a television channel is a complex and intellectually demanding task, because it has to take consumer target groups, advertisers, viewer flow, and many other aspects into account. In addition, traditional television channels need to be transported to the consumers, too. In many territories, such as most of Europe, this is largely paid for by the broadcaster. In others, including the US, cable or satellite fees play a large role in financing TV distribution. In any case, specialized companies, such as cable or satellite TV providers, bring broadcasting to the consumer. In contrast, Over-The-Top television providers leave the entire distribution to the internet, utilizing internet-based content-delivery networks. In other words, your internet provider brings television to you, too. Thereby, these new television providers are acting over the top of traditional distribution systems, hence the name. In addition, they are also acting on top of the regular television offerings, establishing their own billing relationship with the consumer. One consequence, known as cord-cutting, is already affecting the balance sheet of traditional cable operators: the amount of homes that are paying for television cable bundles is decreasing in all Western societies.

In light of radical digitization, the idea of replacing curation and programming in Over-The-Top providers is more interesting, because now you can leave all these tasks to computers. Computers can now curate television programming. In Over-The-Top-Television, you can put together a television offering that is precisely geared towards your personal preferences and that is uniquely made for you as a consumer. With OTT offerings such as Amazon Prime Video and Netflix, you have the choice of hundreds of thousands of videos you could watch tonight. And with recommendation technologies, OTT providers will give you the few choices that fit your interests, mood, or preferences. These recommendation technologies offer you what you want to watch, in relative privacy. In short, today recommendation computers are beginning to replace the editorial composition of television. And, with digitization at work, the number of television offerings will be ever-increasing, down to automated offerings tailored for very small target groups – or even tailored to the individual user. We are entering the era of truly "private" television.

How should traditional businesses react to radical digitization? How did broadcasters react to the seismic change in their industry? After careful analysis of the capabilities and future scenarios, most traditional broadcasters have concluded that they will not be able to counter or stop the move to OTT and individualized television. Instead, they have decided to embrace the new possibilities and drive the change themselves. Today, most broadcasters and most cable operators, exactly the companies disrupted, have started their own Over-The-Top offerings. These offerings operate under the company's own brand or even specific brands created just for this purpose. It seems like sometimes you have to disrupt yourself. My company, Siemens Convergence Creators, used to be active in television distribution. And as the changes ahead became visible, we decided to provide Over-The-Top technologies to broadcasters. We approached one of the largest broadcasters in the world, India's Zee TV, and started to build their Over-The-Top offering. Within a few years, it grew to be one of the largest Over-The-Top offerings globally.

As you read this, the disruption based on radical digitization is making quick advances into another sector –finance and banking. For instance, radically digitized companies such as Lending Club are starting to offer services that look and feel very much like consumer banking. But they are no bank. They are digital services, which are offering credits/loans or saving opportunities to consumers, which is identical to what a bank does. But traditional consumer banks operate in a non-digital environment, operate branch offices, and have often thousands of employees who basically need to live off the difference in interest rates between taking and giving money. These fintech start-up companies, of course, operate no branch offices, have much fewer employees – and are now beginning to radically digitize consumer banking itself.

Ramifications for the airline industry

In recent years, the airline industry has changed massively. With the advent of low-cost airlines, heavy investments in process redesign and digitization, and better and more efficient equipment, air travel has been truly democratized: It has become affordable for the masses in most developed societies, fostering intercultural exchange, understanding, and international business relations and trade. Thereby, aviation has made a profound positive impact on the development of our societies and economies, creating the first "world-wide web" long before computers. And the airline industry has made massive improvements in safety, reliability, and efficiency, combined with heavy investments and efforts in digitization. It has digitized most of its consumer interfaces, as well as its logistics and processes. But, so far, this digitization in the airline industry has not been radical in nature.

For example, let us look at the check-in process: The paper boarding pass has been (partially) replaced by a smartphone app. But often, my smartphone gets manually scanned. And when I want to check a bag, I usually meet people. Or let us look at the luggage-recovery process: When I try to recover misplaced luggage, I usually deal with people who re-enter my known personal data into a computer – as if my address and phone number would not be existing in my frequent flyer profile. Although the interaction with agents of the airline could be an emotionally positive and reassuring experience when I have lost my luggage, it usually is overshadowed by external factors (such as the 24 people in front of me who have all lost their luggage).

Can we radically digitize these aspects of passenger aviation? Only if we put the whole process on Moore's Law – if we digitize the whole process. This means there should be no human interaction in the process. All aspects should be fully digital, from self-service by the consumer (e.g. passport details/freight data/bag tag printing) to error handling (e.g. rerouting). I am convinced the airline industry can put this into practice in already today. But this is just the beginning. We also would need to change all underlying business processes.

For instance, in luggage handling: of course, consumers could print their own luggage tags. Then, such luggage tags should be scanned and physically routed by automated systems (as they already are today). And, of course, this is governed and monitored by a safety and security system. But now handling the luggage, putting it into or out of the aircraft, is usually a manual process. For the sake of argument, let us assume we can eliminate this manual step by some new and clever technology. What would result? If we really could radically digitize luggage transport, and the systems would be designed for exponential growth, we could expect to deliver much more luggage every year. Or do it much more cheaply. If we could find enough customers willing to send luggage, thousands of micro-parcels could be running through that system, changing the economics of luggage delivery entirely. Maybe I could send a single book from Berlin which my friend in Albuquerque could pick up at the airport. And, as the cost of a radically digitized business is constantly reduced, in a few years, it should cost only a few cents to send a single book. As long as there is excess capacity, the airline industry could become a viable competitor to consumer-facing logistics providers – simply by radically digitizing the way it handles luggage.

What really makes the lost-luggage experience difficult is the fact that I as a consumer know that all data should already be available and I could be offered a self-service luggage-recovery function in my app. Such a function could offer me the option to state the status of lost luggage, could allow me to enter my data (if necessary) and preferred delivery address, and could tell me where my luggage is and when to expect it. We could eliminate the entire lost-luggage counter at an airport by a simple app function, thereby bringing us one step closer to radical digitization. In the case of rerouting due to missed connections, we also could develop a self-service system. I am convinced that, in case of missed flight connections, future consumers will be much happier finding their own alternatives (such as taking a later flight, rerouting, or renting a car) than having to wait in line in order to find someone re-entering known data and suggesting limited alternatives. I believe that the handling of misplaced luggage and rerouting are areas ripe for radical digitization.

Finally, let us look at the role of the pilots and flight attendants. Couldn't we consider a database of trained and certified passengers (e.g. frequent flyers) who could ensure the safety of a flight? If necessary, such passengers could be undergoing the same safety and security training and certification as regular flight attendants. Thus, they could ensure on-board safety equivalently. But they would still be passengers, going on that very flight for a different reason – they are trying to reach a destination. A digital system would always make sure that enough safety-trained passengers were on each flight.

I believe that the role of pilots in the future could be looked at, too, as we are nearing an interesting point in the history of aviation: currently, the number of drones is increasing almost exponentially. And except for the low-end toy category, most of them have a self-flying artificial intelligence built in. This means that we are nearing the historic point (perhaps already reached as you read this) when most man-made aircraft are not guided by humans anymore. But commercial aviation seems not to take notice. I understand that the primary role of flight attendants and pilots is to ensure on-board safety. But that was the primary reason for having a lift operator on board an elevator, too.

Recently, it was announced that human-transport drones will be introduced for commercial passenger use in Dubai. This interest in human-transport drones is not only driven by the mere fact that they now can be built. It is driven by the fact that it removes the need for human interaction. Imagine an Uber-like business based on booking, paying for, and summoning a drone on your smartphone – and fulfillment by an automated drone system. Like Amazon, they are changing the product itself. This *is* a radically digitized passenger-aviation business in its infancy. It only consumes energy; it has zero human interaction. It has all the ingredients to grow exponentially. And in my view, it may even digitally disrupt passenger aviation.

A voyage to the year 2032: how could radical digitization change the airline industry?

Travelling to the future is like travelling to the past: it feels like being in a strange foreign country. As progress around us is accelerating, we do not need to go 50 years forward; 15 years will suffice to bring us to an unknown strange country that will feel almost like an exotic planet from a science-fiction tale. So, what can we see when we travel to the strange country called the year 2032? We may see an airline with a human head count of zero. From today's perspective, it does look reasonable to assume that we will enter the age of unmanned commercial passenger aviation based on unmanned airplanes with a few safety-and-security-trained passengers on board, or based on human-transport drones for short-haul flights that may be able to dock to larger objects based on lighter-than air-technology (e.g. airships) for longer distances. Of course, we may also see alternative transport systems like the Hyperloop, essentially a high-speed pneumatic post-conveying system designed for humans. As sci-fi as the Hyperloop concept may feel for us today, fundamental physics favors it: Due to magnetic levitation and the minimal air resistance in the near-vacuum tube, a Hyperloop capsule travelling at supersonic speeds would still have an excellent energy efficiency. And, in our view of the year 2032, do we see "flight" attendants in a Hyperloop capsule? Maybe in 2032, the idea of a flight attendant on board an airplane will feel as strange as the idea of a conductor on board a bus (or a lift operator on board an elevator) feels today. And maybe, in the future, the roles of pilots and flight attendants could be fused, just as we have fused the role of bus drivers and conductors.

Many future scenarios mix fleets of self-driving cars (e.g. by Uber), shared cars, and other mobility providers to construct a seamless multimodal transportation experience, because self-driving cars will have a profound disruptive impact on all human transportation industries. Although there is considerable hype around self-driving-car technology today, we may still underestimate the impact that self-driving cars will have on public transportation, parking (e.g. airport parking), and the automotive industry itself. Self-driving cars, once they reach full autonomy for defined use cases (referred to as autonomy levels 4 and 5), will be able to bring you to the airport, drop you off, and return home, thereby eliminating the need (and existence) of airport parking facilities, thereby disrupting the businesses of airports directly. In fact, we may see the end of paid parking garages in our lifetime. Or your self-driving car may go to work as a taxi while you are at your job. This concept, driven by companies like Uber and Voyage, will fundamentally increase the amount of car sharing while fundamentally decreasing the amount of cars sold, disrupting the automotive industry itself.

Automotive-industry consultants, such as Mario Herger, predict that by 2032, due to self-driving-car technology, the last driver-license holder has already been born[4] and that human driving will be confined to special hobby areas, much like horse riding today. In any case, the self-driving car, as it eliminates human intervention, will have a strong impact on the concept of hub-and-spoke airlines, as the traditional mixed calculation of short-haul and long-distance flights may not work in the future. Self-driving cars will replace short-haul flights. But they will hardly impact long-distance or transcontinental aviation. Consequently, airlines will face disruption and fierce competition on one side of their hub-and-spoke business, while the other side may stay relatively stable. This will certainly lead to new constellations, such as intermodal mobility and mixed business models between shared-ride companies such as Uber and airlines, allowing the shared-ride companies to infringe on the airline-passenger business somewhat. Think of mixing the business models of Uber, Surf Air, and a low-cost (but long-distance) airline, and you may get an idea of the future of passenger aviation. In my view, airlines will be impacted by autonomous vehicles – but less severely than buses, trains, taxi drivers, or the automotive industry.

This scenario shows also that the airline industry may be on its way to developing fully adaptable consumer products. From the passenger-interaction perspective, every journey will start on a smartphone or similar personal device. Although we may look at an interactive map and stay connected to the internet, we may change transport systems seamlessly, adapting to new traffic situations and delays by automatic rerouting. In fact, when we enter the self-driving car that picks us up at home, we may not know whether our travel that day will include a flight component, as the car may decide during our journey to continue driving if there is a delay on a flight connection – or it may reroute us to another airport. Consequently, the airline may become an adaptive-transport provider. And, as a result of these changes, two classes of airlines may emerge: efficiency and experience platform airlines. Whereas the efficiency airline will be organized around its core competencies of efficient (i.e. cost-efficient and time-efficient) travel, experience-platform airlines may promise a better experience on the same route (more passenger comfort, less intermodal changes, high-end entertainment, scenic routes with better views). However, it is by no means certain whether in the year 2032 the experience airlines will be airlines at all.

Blockchain-based businesses

In the year 2032, we will see businesses that have no incorporation, no employees, and no address. Hence, they will not pay taxes, because some businesses that undergo radical digitization could end up as blockchain-based algorithms. As blockchain technology by nature tends to eliminate traditional institutions and middlemen but still provides the fundamental bases of a business (currency, accountability, trust relation, exchange of goods, and record keeping) engraved in an algorithm, blockchain-based businesses are perfectly radically digitized. As an example, the Distributed Autonomous Organization (the DAO), an organization (or: algorithm) for venture-capital funding, was launched in June 2016 and received $150 million in crowdfunding in the same year. The owners of DAO shares acted like venture capitalists, with a joint company and a joint bank account. But still, in conventional terms, there was no company – and no account at any bank. In fact, as the DAO had no employees, no CEO, and no address, it also had no country of residence. Consequently, the DAO had no legality to be considered, no laws to follow, and no taxes to pay. This is no organization in the conventional sense. Still, as blockchain-based algorithms get more complex, more businesses, such as banks and insurance companies, can be put onto (rather: substituted by) the blockchain.

How will blockchain technology impact the airline industry? We can easily envision a booking engine that exists only as a blockchain algorithm. It would be booking flights, collecting money, and keeping records of your booking, your payment, and your itinerary. All these are tasks that a blockchain algorithm can perform perfectly well. But could we even put an entire travel agency onto the blockchain? For example, let's think of a travel agency that composes travel, ground transportation, and hotel accommodation and offers this as packages. These tasks are perfectly suited to be executed by an admittedly complex blockchain algorithm. Thus, there may be blockchain-based travel agencies in 2032.

But what about an entire airline? Can we replace an airline by a blockchain algorithm? Yes, absolutely. If we view an airline as an entity that is sourcing airplanes and personnel as well as fuel (or even wet-leasing all this) and offers seats and cargo capacity on certain routes, then the entire airline could be replaced by an (admittedly very complex) algorithm. In the year 2032, we will see blockchain-based airlines bid for slots at airports, offer and share seat contingents, and offer routes based on demand predictions. And algorithms can be astonishingly good at demand predictions. Actually, in 2032, most airlines may be blockchain-based algorithms.

Consequences

These predictions may feel as strange as the country they are coming from. But let us briefly look at the impact on society and economy if some of these ideas become reality in the next 15 years. One of the most obvious consequences of radical digitization is the elimination of human labor. Jobs will be replaced by machines. Not because machines make no mistakes. Not because machines are cheaper, do not need holidays, and do not get tired. Jobs will be replaced because humans simply cannot keep up with exponential growth. Although all efficiency gains will be most welcomed, radical digitization will be the true driver. Therefore, in my humble view, many concepts of wealth redistribution (such as social basic income or helicopter-money concepts) may become more prevalent in the next 15 years. Although the elimination of jobs may be extremely consequential from a social perspective, we may also have to look at it from a psychological perspective, because employment and people's sense of meaning and self-esteem are so tightly coupled. Clearly, money alone will not fix the societal shift that we are facing.

Of course, taxation is an important issue, too. When we replace a human job with a robot, we are also shifting the tax base. Whereas today about half of the payment a human employee receives is recollected in taxes (such as income tax, sales taxes, and luxury taxes) and social-security contributions, the tax-recollection rate of a robot replacing this job is much lower, as it mainly depends on profit. In addition, profits can be shifted easily between countries and jurisdictions, allowing for a level of tax optimization that exceeds that of an employee. Today, the aviation industry enjoys a tax advantage for kerosene, especially when compared to other transportation providers. Of course, this is due to the fact that the airline industry is in a great position for tax optimization (by its having the option of filling the fuel tank elsewhere). Obviously, in a future world of multimodal transportation, where an airline becomes less and less distinguishable from a transportation provider such as Uber, this tax advantage may come to an end. Tax concepts that are discussed already today, which locate the tax duty with the usage, may burden the aviation industry in the future.

Looking at the future consequences of radical digitization, standing still is not an option. We certainly will not be able to fight progress by laws and security concerns. And most certainly, nimble and smart start-up corporations will always find a way around regulations and local laws – if necessary, by moving to another jurisdiction (like Skype, when it was outlawed in the US). And then they will grow at an astonishing, exponential speed (like Skype, when it became the largest telephone company on Earth). Usually, this is the moment when the established industries are caught by surprise (like the established telecom providers) and try to imitate the disruption that radical digitization has caused. But then it is too late.

Of course, established companies, regulators, and legislators can try to fight progress. But historically they have not been successful. In 1865, after heavy lobbying of the horse-carriage owners, the British parliament issued the Red Flag Act a law that restricted the upcoming automobiles to a speed of 4 miles per hour and requested a "Red Flag Man" to walk in front of the vehicle. When the Red Flag

Act was finally abolished in 1896, the automobile had won. Let's not try to create the next Red Flag Act. None of us will be able to fight radical digitization. It will happen anyway. Radical digitization eats businesses. Indeed, we have no choice: Let us go forward boldly to radically digitize the airline industry, now. And let us confidently embark on that voyage to the strange country called "the future".

Notes

1 Of course, 50 years ago a long-range airplane's cockpit had four to five (usually male) staff; now an A380 might be flown safely by two people (their gender playing no role at all). And today, some airlines offer the First Officer seat to pilots who need flight hours to keep their license. But these changes do not represent radical shifts; they reflect the changing of societal and economic norms over the last 50 years.
2 Sadly enough, we have radically digitized only the book-delivery business (by making the book itself electronic), as well as the movie-delivery business (by making the movie itself electronic), but we have not yet found a way to radically digitize pizza delivery, resulting in the absurd consequence that we now can easily deliver action movies to everyone in sub-Saharan Africa but are still fighting hunger there.
3 This is not about digital versus analog products. Please note that CDs, DVDs, and Blu-ray discs were always digital but still physical products, and that ordering, packaging, and delivery were always digital.
4 See the aptly named blog *The Last Driver License Holder...* (https://thelastdriverlicenseholder. com/) or Mario Herger's book of the same title.

4   The flexible flyer: turning the airlines' operating model downside up (from fixed schedules and variable fares to variable schedules and fixed fares)

Dietmar Kirchner

Senior Aviation Advisor
Frankfurt, Germany

"Scheduled airlines" are the top level of the airline industry, having evolved over time from charter and other non-scheduled roots. The whole business model is built around airlines designing a network (network planning), crafting a schedule by maximizing the aircraft utilization (schedule planning), uploading a schedule almost one year ahead into the reservation systems (schedule publishing), developing complex and ever-changing fare structures (pricing), taking reservations on published flight numbers (distribution), optimizing the combination of fares to maximize revenue per flight (yield management), and finally flying according to the published schedule (very rarely switching airplane sizes for demand reasons).

Obviously a lot of research, prognostic effort, day-to-day number crunching has to go into network planning (to find the right markets), scheduling (to develop a minimum cost – maximum utilization schedule), pricing and yield management (to maximize "skimming" the market). In this model, a schedule once published has to be considered as fixed cost; demand only triggers the marginal cost of passenger-related fees plus a small proportion of payload-dependent fuel cost. Therefore an additional passenger is considered to be "marginally profitable" even at a very low fare.

"Downsides" in this business model are very sophisticated, and thus expensive predictive IT systems (which still fail, as every prognosis does); ever-growing complexity of fares and fare rules, leading to individual and situational fares per customer contact (completely undermining brand credibility); load factors of around 80% (one out of five flights practically being empty); and, most importantly, a high percentage of passengers travelling on "fill-up fares".

Insufficient yields produced by a large number of passengers are the main reason for the insufficient results of especially the "classic" airlines over the last decade.

These "classic" airlines were not able to turn the complexity of their dense hub-and-spoke systems into a real advantage over the simply-knit LCCs, who seem to have the more successful operating model all over the world. The setup of alliances with really global reach, multiple hubs, and high-frequency presence in most markets so far is not really exploited as a competitive advantage. Even on the North Atlantic, where alliances are very powerful with their JV concepts, new entrants like Norwegian or WOW together with old niche players like Icelandair have grown tremendously. And all the "classic" airlines are doing is copying, with their own LCC spinoffs named "Level" or "Eurowings".

The "flexible flyer" business model

The express-parcel operators (FedEx, DHL, UPS) have developed a system that knows no reservations, PNRs, published schedules, or multiple day-to-day fares.

Yet they have higher commitment levels towards arrival quality than the passenger airlines.

Their main ingredients are:

1   Flexible capacity and schedules
2   Pricing rewards for demand flexibility
3   Real-time allocation of shipments to ground transportation and flights

Taking the lessons of the express-parcel operators to the passenger-airline world requires adaptations in four areas:

Scheduling for flexibility

Scheduling is done using four capacity layers:

1   New-technology aircraft with minimum operating cost are scheduled for maximum utilization, providing a capacity that will be filled even on the foreseeably weakest days.
2   Older-technology aircraft are scheduled to provide extra capacity on those seasons, days, and hours that foreseeably have a higher demand.
3   Backup-level capacity is called from specialized suppliers to allocate peak demand which is foreseeable at maybe two days' notice.
4   Backup-level capacity (last-minute) is called in with 12 hours' notice.

Layers 1 and 2 may be produced by the airline itself, layers 3 and 4 by third-party airlines specializing in flexible short-term operations.

Pricing rewarding flexibility

Today airlines give no credit for flexibility once a passenger is booked on a flight (there are only restrictions for changing bookings associated with lower fares). In the new system, fares vary only by three easy-to-understand parameters:

1   Space (describing the living space in the cabin as defined today by pretty equal cabin classes), measured in the multiple of a standard economy seat (examples: Economy (1), Premium Eco (2), Business (4), First (6))
2   Speed, measured as the variation from the minimum travel time between two points
3   Flexibility, measured as the maximum number of hours a passenger can wait (at home, in the hotel) until he wants to be called to the airport

Other than that, fares are constant over the year (maybe with the exemption of peak travel days – like Christmas, Chinese New Year, etc.).

The new reservation system

Passengers "order" a flight, indicating origin and final destination and defining their variables.

> Example 1: I want a seat (Size 4) on Warsaw to Orlando on May 15 any time, six hours' extra time acceptable.
>
> Example 2: I need two seats (standard) anytime between tomorrow and two days later from Madrid to Singapore. I do not mind eight extra hours against the minimum travel time.
>
> Example 3: I want to go from Boston to Portland tomorrow morning, arriving as soon as possible. I do not want to leave before 6:00 a.m., and I want double space.

The new reservation system has two layers:

1 Long-term travel requests (Example 1) are stored in the **long-term system (demand "cloud")** which is organized on a point-to-point citypair basis (not flight numbers) with the space, flexibility, and speed requests attached. Passengers paying the top priority fare are immediately booked on the most suitable flight. All other passengers are allocated into the departure control system, using an algorithm that maximizes airplane load factors and minimizes passenger inconvenience.

2 The **departure control system** is filled sequentially: First the high-speed non-flexible passengers on the nonstop and minimum travel time flights, then the more flexible ones with long- and short-term requests (Examples 1 and 2). In most cases, 12 hours is enough time to notify a passenger at home or at the hotel to leave and make a flight. If there are still passengers left, backup airplanes will be requested from backup operators. Extra sections will be flown to accommodate a maximum of "overhang".

Fare setting

Although fares are set by the market and the competition, there should be some rules to relate the fares to the airlines' cost base. Otherwise unsustainable fares can lead to losses, even at extremely high load factors.

Each fare group should stand "on its own" and not rely on cross-subsidization.

Fares that grant priority over all other groups have to cover the fully allocated cost of the airline (Baseline Capacity) plus a 15% margin at a load factor of 75%. Normally fares in the market for such a product are considerably higher. It is up to every airline to either become more attractive in that segment or stay with the market and collect most of the profit in that segment.

Fares that launch an extra flight have to cover the fully allocated cost of that flight (Seasonal Capacity) at a 75% load factor. This allows planning and deploying seasonal capacity on a profitable basis.

Fares that have minimum priority must cover the operational cost of an extra flight (Peak Supplemental Capacity) at an 85% load factor, as short-term "over-flow" capacity has to be justified.

If market fares are substantially below those fares, the route will not be flown.

Cons and pros

Arguments against such a system

As with everything new, there will be a number of arguments put against such a system:

1   "This system will generate fewer passengers than before, as today's extremely low fares will largely disappear". Answer: As today's "fill-up fares" do not provide a sustainable basis for industry growth anyway, this should be considered as an advantage.
2   "Especially congested airports do not have the flexibility to accommodate flights at short notice." Answer: As the "flexible flyer" system does not offer fares at marginal seat cost (only at marginal flight cost), there will be slightly less passengers than today. So airlines will file for the foreseeable maximum operation, yet have many flights on a "demand pending" mode.
3   "Classic airlines are not capable of producing on-demand flights." Answer: The most flexible part of the production will be "outsourced" to operators specializing in providing flexible capacity (like today's regionals providing lift to the major airlines' networks).
4   "Passengers like to know their flight data well in advance". Answer: Already today more and more airlines are using the Optiontown-Tool "*Flexibility Reward Option*" to incentivize passengers to become more flexible. However, this tool is not part of a larger change of business model.

Challenges

In order to change to this business model, airlines have to touch many areas at the same time:

•   Fleet planning (Create a mix of new and old airplanes; most classic airlines already have such a mix.)
•   Supply chain (Make contracts with the flexibility-providing sub-operators.)
•   Scheduling (Develop robust yet adaptable schedules for non-peak and peak times, which are easily scalable.)
•   Crew planning (Develop simple patterns of duty, stand-by, and off periods.)
•   Reservations (Create inventory around "virtual" citypairs to collect travel intentions, which requires the establishment of a reservation system using virtual flight numbers, from where to re-assign the passengers to real flight numbers when the departure control system is filled.)

- Pricing (Develop a simple, cost-based, customer-centric fare structure.)
- Ops system (Develop a real-time customer-centric itinerary management system.)
- Partnering (Use your alliance partners to offer a real global network, managed jointly, that provides multiple travel options on most citypairs.)

Some of these changes require additional IT. Using trip-management systems such as Uber and Lyft might be a way to store, manage, and control passenger itineraries. As for launching ad-hoc flights, airlines can use the procedures they have built to launch backup capacity in cases of irregularities. (Launching an extra flight technically is the same as replacing a "stranded" airplane.)

The migration into the new system should not be done at once. An airline might start using that model on a citypair with eight to ten daily flights; an alliance might start by migrating their JV in one area.

Advantages

Especially large alliances can finally offer many options for almost any citypair by combining all itineraries possible (Example: On April 1, Star Alliance offers 23 different routings on Los Angeles–Oslo, leaving LAX between 6:00 a.m. and 7:20 p.m.). Many travelers are willing to fly on any of those routings as long as there is an attractive price and they are notified 12 hours in advance on which one to take. If demand out of California to Europe turns out to be larger than the scheduled baseline capacity, Star could operate one extra B747-400 SFO-FRA, using those hubs to collect overflow West Coast demand and then distribute them throughout Europe.

Below is an example of a high-volume route in a **domestic regional environment** which is served about every hour with a typical load factor of 80%. In the new system, a carrier may schedule some flights "on demand". Thus flexible passengers may be pushed to an earlier or a later flight (without paying "Denied Boarding Compensation"). On peak days with even more demand, additional capacity may be called in from the "Flex Operator". Thus load factors will be close to 100%, although around 20% fewer flights will be operated.

Capacity can be fine-tuned every day, based not on predictive algorithms but on real passenger demand. Instead of offering "fill-up" fares on all flights that have a poor load prediction, only the last flight has some potentially "distressed inventory".

Also, passengers willing to pay for full flexibility and minimum travel time will always find a suitable seat (even at 12 hours' notice), as all other passengers will be allocated after them.

In case of operational disruption (e.g. not making a connection), passengers will be re-assigned according to their requested final destination, prioritized again by the fare class chosen.

In this model, only the baseline schedule, together with the foreseeable peak capacity, can be considered as fixed cost; all ad-hoc capacity will be triggered by ad-hoc demand at sustainable fares.

Passengers willing to pay only "fill-up fares" will be diverted to carriers operating under the traditional model, which will further dilute their yield.

Large network carriers, together with their alliance partners, are finally able to use the strength of their global networks as a competitive advantage, as only they can offer the flexibility options to price-sensitive customers and "maximum speed" options to time-sensitive travelers.

Example

An airline operates a string of six flights (capacity = 100) about every hour. Total load factor is 80%. Nine percent of the passengers are not flexible and pay the top fare, 18% are somewhat flexible and pay the "standard" fare, 40% are flexible and pay "discount", and 15% pay a "fill-up" fare which is below a sustainable level. The first flights have a high demand on high-fare passengers, later discount passengers prevail:

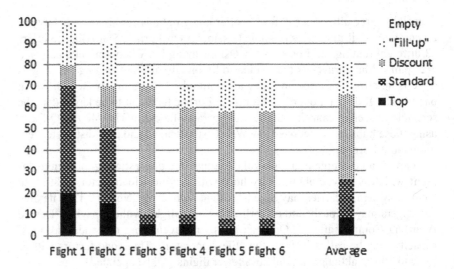

Figure 7.1 Today

In the new model, the above passengers will be stored in a demand "cloud" indicating their flexibility over time ("want to travel within three hours starting at 7:00 p.m."). "Fill-up" fares will not be offered anymore, because capacity will be adjusted to demand willing to pay "sustainable" fares.

Now scheduling comes in and plans for the minimum number of flights to accommodate the contracted demand, observing the flexibility rules given by the passengers.

In our case, two out of six flights need not to be operated, thus achieving a total load factor of 98%. Revenue is less because the "fill-up" passengers are

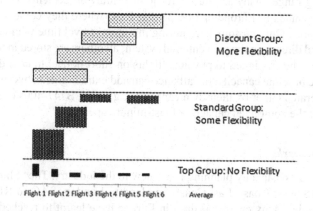

Figure 7.2 Demand "cloud"

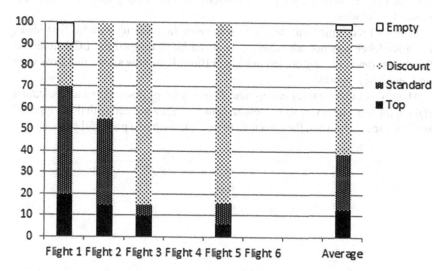

Figure 7.3 Tomorrow

missing, but since their respective costs are also disappearing, the "loss" will be minor. Yet the operating cost of two flights (fuel, landing and handling charges, maintenance, and most of the crew cost) will be avoided, a cost saving between 15% and 20%.

Possible first steps

The above example shows how the new system works on a high-frequency citypair. Most airlines have more than one of those heavy-traffic routes in their network and could select one to test-run the system.

On long-range, many alliances have joint-venture agreements for a larger area (like US/Canada to Europe or Europe–Far East) where they could start offering citypair fares. Only customers requiring minimum travel time with no flexibility are booked directly in the conventional system; all others are stored in the "demand cloud" and then assigned to physical flights on short notice. In case demand surpasses the baseline capacity, the alliance can add extra flights between their major hubs, operated either by their own capacity (e.g. using B747-400s or A340-300s) or call for the contracted capacity of last-minute operators.

Closing remarks

Demand-based capacity planning is not new to the industry. The "Shuttles" of the 1970s (US West Coast, East Coast, Scotland to London, SAO to RIO, etc.) are one example. Many charter airlines in Europe have learnt to reschedule at short notice according to the booking data of their customers, the tour operators. And then, of course, there are the parcel carriers, who have been using that business model for decades.

FedEx's Fred Smith was laughed about when he came up with his first ideas, Herb Kelleher was not taken seriously when he developed the LCC model at Southwest (and O'Leary copied him), and Bjorn Kjos now shows that Low Cost on Long Range works.

Mentioning these names means that it takes a lot of leadership and dedication right at the top. However, all successful companies are aligned with those types of leaders, especially when they manage to find and inspire a powerful team.

5 Meeting the expectations of today's connected and empowered passengers: on-demand, real-time, end-to-end

Raymond Kollau

Founder
AirlineTrends

> *Major consumer trends airlines should take into account when designing a future passenger experience that meets the needs of empowered consumers*

Airline passengers' expectations are not only shaped by how well an airline performs compared to its direct competitors. They are also fuelled by standards set by experiences that consumers have in other industries –retail, hospitality, electronics – because innovative products and services in one industry eventually raise the bar for all industries.

This sentiment is echoed by Ron Verweij, Manager of Research and Technology at Zodiac Aerospace:

> The benchmark for customers is not only the experiences they have with airlines and at airports. The benchmark is set by the likes of Apple, Amazon and Zappos, who are centred around staging the best customer experience over and over again and who have lined up every detail in their organisation to deliver simple, consistent and burden-free experiences over every channel and touch point. This means airlines and airports need to tune into the customer from a holistic perspective when designing passenger services, so they operate more from the outside-in.

An example of an airline that has embraced this holistic service-design approach is Cathay Pacific, which states:

> Customers do not view experiences via a single lens. Their expectations are constantly evolving and are viewed relatively, as they expand beyond the category and are shaped by cumulative experiences. Consumers have access to information via the internet anytime, anyplace and, as product life cycles are becoming ever shorter, 'new and improved' quickly becomes 'expected'.

And when Air New Zealand looks for inspiration on how to please customers, it doesn't copy rival airlines like Qantas Airways or even partners like Virgin Australia. The Kiwi company, known for its entertaining safety videos and quirky image, turns to the latest technology from Silicon Valley and innovative hospitality-industry players like Disney, Celebrity Cruises, and Four Seasons Hotels. "If you want to drive innovation you have to go outside and then go inside," says Air NZ chief executive Christopher Luxon.[1]

This article provides an overview of the consumer trends – especially those that tap into basic consumer needs such as choice, control, convenience, and transparency – airlines have to take into account when designing their future passenger experience. Unlocking these basic needs in innovative ways is a large driver behind the success of digital disrupters such as Amazon, Uber, and Airbnb.

The on-demand economy

Smartphones make it quick and hassle-free to order goods online, make a restaurant reservation, or flag a taxi via Uber. The fact that many products and services are now only a click away has generated a sense of entitlement to fast, simple, and efficient experiences, because it taps into consumers' appetite for greater convenience, speed, and simplicity. For example, analysis from Uber shows the longer Uber has been in a city, the less willing to wait for a car everyone becomes.[2]

This so-called on-demand economy provides a good analogy as to why airlines should make the transformation from a focus on operational excellence (processes) to a focus on serving their passengers' needs (customer-centricity).

As *Business Insider* puts it:

> The On-Demand Economy is defined as the economic activity created by technology companies that fulfill consumer demand via the immediate provisioning of goods and services. Supply is driven via an efficient, intuitive digital mesh layered on top of existing infrastructure networks. [. . .] The businesses in this new economy represent the manifestation of years of technological innovation and an evolution in consumer behavior.[3]

Food and beverage

In the food and beverage industry, Starbucks' new pre-order app quickly has become a very popular time-saver. Looking to solve a customer 'pain point', Starbucks last year extended its digital wallet service – which the company introduced in 2009 – by letting customers pre-order and pay via their phone and pick up their order at a nearby store at a dedicated counter. With Starbucks' "Mobile Order & Pay," customers can avoid long lines at peak hours and ensure quick service. Some customers may otherwise even have skipped their visit to the Starbucks store, so Starbucks is generating more sales by improving convenience for its clientele.

In North America, airport restaurant operator OTG Management has installed thousands of tablets at major airports such as New York JFK, Minneapolis–St Paul, and Toronto Pearson. Rather than make travelers leave the departure areas to go to a restaurant, passengers can order food and drinks via a custom application on Apple iPads installed at dining areas near the gates. A server then delivers the food to the customer's seat within ten minutes. Furthermore, prior to completing their order, customers using the new dining stations will be informed of their meal delivery time to ensure their order is received before their flight departure time.

In-flight services

A growing number of airlines – including Virgin America, Air New Zealand, Japan Airlines, Norwegian, and Azul – allow passengers to order meals, snacks, and drinks via the in-seat IFE system in between regular meal services. Qantas and EVA Air are among the carriers that offer passengers the option to purchase duty-free via the Panasonic eX3 IFE systems.

The next step is to include on-demand ordering of food, beverages, and duty-free via an airline app so passengers can use their own devices and can also be targeted with more personalized offerings.

These on-demand services allow for retailing to occur throughout the entire duration of a flight and let passengers order whenever they feel like it, rather than the limited time when the flight attendant walks the aisle, announcing "Duty free goods in a tone that shows she fully expects zero sales," as trendwatcher James Woudhuyzen likes to put it.

To summarize, customer expectations shaped by the 'on-demand economy' are forcing airlines to flip the current dominant service model and provide service at the moment the customer wants it. They can also work with other brands to match these expectations, as for example the partnerships of airlines with Uber and Airbnb illustrate.

The end-to-end customer journey

This brings us to the second theme: Airlines should look further than just offering a flight. As the main author of this book, Nawal Taneja, has argued for a long time, airlines should not just sell a mass product (tickets). They should offer personal travel experiences. "To gain competitive advantage, it is essential to know more about the customer's wishes and preferences in order to offer tailored experiences."[4]

Passengers, spoilt by the availability of user-centric apps on their smartphones, are raising the bar for airline apps to become more relevant as well. A growing number of airlines are working to evolve their apps into a 'digital travel companion' in order to extend their service beyond just flying passengers from A to B.

Uber as a platform

This approach is most visible today in the digital partnerships that airlines such as United and American have forged with Uber. In 2014, Uber announced it would open up its application program interface (API) so any app developer could integrate the on-demand car service into an app. Basically, all it takes is a few lines of code and an Uber button is part of the app. So if you're an airline or a restaurant-booking application, you can create a situation whereby your flight delay is automatically communicated to your Uber driver so that your pickup is correctly rescheduled.

Further expanding its open digital ecosystem approach, and positioning itself as having a wider purpose for its customers – beyond providing basic transportation from point A to point B – Uber recently launched Uber Feed, which allows users to integrate mobile notifications and content from third parties into their Uber app.

The idea is that while passengers are in an Uber car on the way to their destination, other apps and services can push them content during their ride, content that can be customized since data about the destination and duration can be used. When a user gets into an Uber, the Uber app will turn "into a rich feed of cards," designed to grow engagement in the Uber app itself. Needless to say, this approach provides a nice parallel how airline apps can evolve in the future.

Lufthansa as a digital travel ecosystem

Lufthansa is one of the airlines that has embraced this open-platform mentality, and the airline's Innovation Hub in Berlin is taking a leading role in turning Lufthansa into an 'end-to-end digital travel ecosystem'.

As Sebastian Herzog, managing director and chief strategist of Lufthansa's Innovation Hub, summarizes it nicely: "While Lufthansa traditionally sees itself 'only' as an airline, digital transformation drives the connectivity and interdependence of all mobility services. In such a scenario, it is important to understand and build ecosystems while proving the ability to share data and partner."

This platform approach can also be applied to other parts of the customer journey. Scandinavian Airlines (SAS), for example, has partnered with a local co-working office to open City Lounges for its frequent flyers in downtown Stockholm, Sweden. Tapping into the big shift in how a growing number of people work today, City Lounge includes both open-plan work areas and private meeting rooms where passengers can work and network. The City Lounges cater to business travellers who often fly in and out on the same day and who want to stay productive on their day of travel, as well as freelancers who can use the venue as temporary offices to hold their meetings in the city.

Airlines as journey integrators

By partnering with third parties that offer specific services at different phases of the customer journey and integrating these services into a seamless, on-demand service, airlines can become what IBM's Institute for Business Value[5] has dubbed 'journey integrators' and provide consumers with a more integrated travel experience. New technologies and business models now offer the potential for online differentiation and the provision of value-added services and features for which travelers will pay a premium.

Real-time information and services

The ability to be connected on the ground and increasingly while in the air – combined with airlines' growing commitment to digitally led service innovation – allows passengers to be in the know about the progress of their journey in real time. Common examples are real-time departure and gate information, proactive notification in case of delay, and quick responses to information and service requests by passengers via social media.

Furthermore, a host of startup companies have come up with data-aggregation solutions that let passengers calculate travel time from their home or office to their departure gate, including the time they need to wait at airport security and navigate the airport.

One area that sees a lot of 'real-time' innovation is the handling of checked baggage. Baggage service has come a long way from the only option of staffed check-in desks, and options now include self-service baggage check-in and drop-off, letting passengers print their own baggage labels at home, and, at a few air-lines, digital bag tags that allow passengers to track the location of their baggage in real time.

Real-time tracking

Taking a cue from the pizza-delivery business – back in 1973, Domino's Pizza introduced a guarantee that customers would receive their pizzas within 30 min-utes of placing an order or they would receive the pizzas free – Delta in 2011 became the first airline to make the baggage process more transparent for pas-sengers by launching its 'Track Checked Bags' service.

Available for domestic flights, Delta passengers can use the 'Track My Bag' functionality on the Delta mobile app to scan their baggage tag with their smart-phone camera. And, because Delta has equipped its entire domestic fleet with GoGo's inflight Internet, passengers can even check while in the air whether their bag has made it on their flight using the free access to delta.com and the mobile app.

Furthermore, turning its operational excellence into a passenger benefit – the airline has integrated RFID chips into its luggage labels to further reduce errors – Delta guarantees fliers' checked luggage on domestic routes will arrive at the bag-gage carousel within 20 minutes when travelling on domestic flights. The airline will give 2,500 miles to customers whose bags take longer than that to reach the carousel.

Early adapter Delta has now been followed by Lufthansa, which – besides allowing passengers to track their bags via the Lufthansa app – also offers a digital baggage tag in partnership with luggage brand Rimowa. Qatar Airways recently became the first airline to be certified by IATA for its capabilities to track baggage in real time at every stage of the journey.

Passenger-experience transparency

Besides instant gratification via on-demand services and real-time information, another major trend is 'radical transparency'. As consumer-trends agency Trend-Watching puts it: "Billions of people worldwide expect to find out pretty much anything they want to know, often instantly."

Airlines have long relied on awards and recognitions from industry watchers and major publications to reassure customers of the quality of their products and services, in very much the same way that professional critics and ratings firms have put their seal of approval on restaurants and hotels for decades.

But the rise of the Internet has disrupted that 'expert-review' dynamic. The active participation of consumers on ratings sites which evaluate everything from films to books to consumer goods to services, and of course travel, means that today's consumers trust popular opinion over ratings. With more access to information, more sensitivity to price, and less sensitivity to advertising, customers are getting harder to win and keep. Or in the words of *The Experience Economy* authors B. Joseph Pine and James H. Gilmore: "The experience is the marketing."

A growing number of online travel agents and airlines have partnered with third-party data providers TripAdvisor (FlyScore) and Routehappy (Happiness Score) to help customers learn more about the quality of their flight. By sharing candid details of the passenger experience, airlines could move beyond commodity pricing and beyond competition solely on fares, instead giving customers fact-based metrics about their products which would justify a higher fare.

There is an important precedent for this change in consumer mind-set in the hospitality sector. Today's informed and savvy travellers are making their hotel choices based on 'reputation pricing' – the correlation between a brand's online reputation and the premium it can charge. This shift from 'sticker price' bookings to bookings based on the quality of the experience has been one of the big positive effects of TripAdvisor on the hotel industry.

Instant feedback

A few forward-looking airlines are also embracing this transparency trend. As part of the third phase of the program – which focuses on digital innovation – Ryanair recently added a 'Rate My Flight' feature to its app. Passengers who want to rate their flight have to download the regular Ryanair app and allow for push notifications, and then they are sent the survey through the app upon landing.

The 'Rate My Flight' survey asks passengers to evaluate each element of their flight, from boarding through food and drink provision to crew helpfulness and overall service standards. Ryanair says it uses the feedback to tweak and improve its offerings as much in real time as possible.

Digital frontrunner KLM shares the feedback it gathers directly from passengers with customers who are looking to book a flight with the airline. KLM shows star ratings and reviews in the search flow of the KLM website. Customers searching for a flight can see actual reviews from previous passengers who have flown that flight in the past, based on reviews collected from KLM passengers using the airline's 'Rate My Flight' feature.

The ratings and reviews are not filtered – except for when crew or passengers are mentioned by name or unsuitable language is used. KLM says that by adding reviews from real people, it aims to be transparent to future customers but also to its crew on their performance.

From cabins to virtual classes

Another consumer expectation fuelled by the online revolution is customization. These days any item can be customized to suit one's specific needs, ranging from fashion accessories such as shoes, bags, and bikes to more mundane items like personalized tissue boxes.

In an effort to generate high-margin ancillaries by providing passengers with more options for customizing their travel experience – and looking to escape the current commodity trap – the airline industry is rapidly evolving to become retail-focused.

Airlines are in the process of learning from online retailers – especially when it comes to offering the right product to the right customer at the right time. Airlines know they have critical data on passengers, but the key is figuring out how to monetize that information.

Because the lack of sales sophistication of many of the global distribution channels (GDS) is preventing airlines from distributing more customized fares via third-party channels, IATA is working on revised standards – called the New Distribution Capability (NDC) – to reform how airfares are combined with personalization tools independent of the direct or indirect distribution channel.

Virtual classes

The future of the aircraft cabin is set to go through significant changes as customers are able to share their preferences with airlines, and airlines will be expected to meet their individual needs.

According to an Amadeus/Oxford Economics report:

> The increasing number of airline optional services and new technology for determining what passengers want on their flights could even end up blurring the distinction between cabin classes, creating what amounts to personalized 'virtual classes' instead.
>
> For example, some passengers in today's economy [class] would have access to a wide variety of [paid] electronic services, such as Wi-Fi, gaming and entertainment. Others might prefer quiet or distraction-free zones. The integration of these different subclasses with other specialized paying services (such as improved meal services or preferred seating arrangements) could result in further effective fragmentation.[6]

Quiet zones and sleeper seats

A few airlines are already experimenting with this concept of 'virtual classes'. Passengers flying Virgin Atlantic's Upper Class on its A340s have the option to book a seat in the 'snooze-zone', which will locate them at the front of the Business cabin. After takeoff, the cabin lights are immediately dimmed, and no meal is offered by cabin staff, to allow for maximum sleep time. Instead, passengers can choose to take their meal on the ground in the Virgin lounge prior to take-off.

Long-haul low-cost carriers AirAsia X and Scoot have created 'Quiet Zones', which are located in the Economy cabin at the front end of the aircraft and bar kids younger than 10 years old. Passengers opting for the zone – which is located directly behind the Premium cabin – will be asked to keep noise to a minimum. The fare for a seat in the 'Quiet Zone' is around $15 more than the regular Economy fare.

And because not all seats in the same travelling class are created equally – airlines are already monetizing extra legroom seats in Economy – Swiss International Air Lines has introduced a fee of between 99 and 199 Swiss francs to pre-reserve one of the popular solo Business Class seats on its A330 and B777-300ER aircraft. These so called 'throne seats' are a quirk of the staggered Business Class configuration adopted by Swiss and are prized by solo travellers, because they are flanked by a pair of useful side tables.

South Korean low-cost carrier Jeju Air has an offer called 'Side Seat', which allows travellers to purchase one or two seats next to their own seat in an effort to sell last-minute seat inventory. Passengers can only book the additional seats at their departure airport on the day of the travel (up to 1 hour before boarding).

On longer routes onboard Jeju Air's B737-800s, the airline also offers passengers the option to purchase a 'Sleeping Seat Package'. If a passenger purchases two 'Side Seats' (for a fee of $100) in addition to his or her main seat, a pillow and blanket are added, as the passenger will have a row of seats to himself. By raising the armrests of the middle seat, the passenger can then stretch out horizontally on three seats.

From in-flight entertainment to in-flight engagement

Rapid developments in consumer electronics have been fuelling consumer expectations towards the entertainment offered aboard airliners. As Tony Tyler, former CEO of Cathay Pacific, already observed years ago: "The bar is being set very high by Apple and others and our customers don't understand why we can't match it."

Thus wireless IFE and onboard connectivity is quickly gaining traction. Because traditional closed in-seat IFE systems now are based on the open Android standard, the number of in-flight entertainment options has grown rapidly.

IFE as an open platform

What these different systems have in common is that they give airlines a great deal of control, allowing them to move beyond just offering passengers entertainment. Jeff Standerski from Rockwell Collins nicely summarizes the evolution of traditional IFE systems:

> Passengers' expectations have evolved from a passive 'Please entertain me' to a proactive 'I want to entertain myself.'
>
> Today, we've moved to IFEC, where the C stands for Connectivity. This is an improvement because many aircraft enable passengers to plug in a personal electronic device, and others enable passengers to purchase broadband connectivity for an even better experience. But even IFEC is woefully inadequate to describe what passengers now expect during their flight.

Our industry needs a new term to describe a holistic experience that is equal in every way to how people leverage their devices on terra firma. The future of the passenger/cabin interaction is beyond one of mere entertainment and can be more accurately described as one of deep and ongoing engagement: In-Flight Passenger Engagement (IFPE).[7]

Ultimately this development means that this in-flight engagement platform – be it in-seat systems, in-flight wireless portals, or mobile apps – will become another touchpoint in the airline-travel ecosystem. This concept is echoed by Panasonic, which asks, "What if the inflight (wireless) IFE portal or airline app becomes an integrated touchpoint as part of an end-to-end airline service, entertainment and merchandizing ecosystem?"[8]

For example, with the proliferation of e-commerce – retail is now all about self-service – it is understandable that passengers have come to expect self-service and an on-demand environment while in the air. So, when it comes to in-flight connectivity, airlines need to think more like Starbucks: Rather than making money from selling Wi-Fi connectivity, airlines should be turning to third-party merchants with last-minute inventory – such as hotels, restaurants, duty-free retailers, transportation companies, and sellers of event tickets – to develop a retail environment as part of their in-flight Internet portals.

Finnair's 'Nordic Sky'

Finnair, for example, has put its new 'Nordic Sky' in-flight portal to work as a channel to offer new services to flyers, as well as boost ancillary sales. The portal can be accessed on passengers' own devices and gives all passengers free access to Finnair's web site, plus Finnair services such as destination information, customer care, and pre-order duty-free shopping – with purchases being delivered to passengers' seats on their return flight.

This onboard retail strategy is a departure from the tired trolley product push which has been part of the in-flight experience for decades. Technology allows Finnair to promote shopping opportunities while letting passengers enjoy the journey and letting cabin crew focus on critical functions of passenger service and cabin safety.

And the airline is also working to turn the in-flight portal into a helpful platform that helps passengers plan their experience on the ground in advance. Passengers can already use the in-flight portal to order taxis via Cabforce on inbound Helsinki flights or book destination services such as trips, dinner cruises, and concert tickets with Viator Destination Services. The airline is also considering letting passengers pre-order their groceries in flight.

Design thinking and continuous innovation

Nowadays, success depends on how fast and responsive an airline organization is, in order to prepare for a digitally disrupted marketplace. Airline executives continuously face the challenge of keeping up with and interpreting the latest digital trends and innovations and then translating these into a product and service innovation to improve their customers' experience.

"The process is the product," as TrendWatching writes in its latest report. "If everything happens in real-time, nothing is ever final and always in permanent beta."

Design thinking

In a response to this turbulent environment of demanding customers and rapid technological change, forward-looking companies are working to incorporate 'design thinking' approaches into their organization.

Due to the remarkable success rate of design-led companies, design has evolved beyond making objects. Organizations now want to learn how to think like designers and how to apply design principles to the workplace itself.

Tim Brown, CEO of design agency IDEO, describes design thinking as "a method of meeting people's needs and desires in a technologically feasible and strategically viable way. [. . .] Design thinkers rely on customer insights gained from real-world experiments, not just historical data or market research."

Another central element of design thinking is to minimize the uncertainty and risk of innovation by engaging customers or users through a series of prototypes to learn, test, and refine concepts.

KLM X

In the airline industry, KLM and Delft University of Technology recently signed a 'Design Doing' cooperation agreement, with the aim of developing new products and rethinking existing KLM processes. The partnership is applying the 'KLM X' strategy of testing and optimizing new products or processes in a real-life situation, with genuine passengers at a real airport and in real aircraft, rather than in a laboratory setting.

An early example of design thinking at KLM is the airline's 'smart boarding' concept, which sees passengers being issued with a boarding number at the gate, based on their seat position on the aircraft. When boarding starts, the numbers are displayed one by one at five-second intervals on monitors at the gate, allowing only one person at a time to board the plane.

According to Jan van Helden, product strategy manager at KLM:

> Our breakthrough idea was to translate the seat number into a sequence number. The trick is using an algorithm to change the seat numbers into sequence numbers. The algorithm decides which passenger goes where in the sequence. Calling the numbers on screens is a system that is familiar in different cultures because it is done at the post office and the butcher shop, in some restaurants and pizza counters and in highway (access) flow control, on the ramp, where they let one car through each minute. All of these things were an inspiration.[9]

Lufthansa's FlyingLab

On a similar note, Lufthansa has come up with the concept of a 'FlyingLab': regular scheduled flights on which passengers can test new products and services ideas, ranging from wellbeing concepts, to virtual reality devices, to videoconferencing.

"The aim of the FlyingLab is to try out new things quickly and easily," said Dr Torsten Wingenter, Head of Digital Innovations at Lufthansa. "If we find an exciting product, we can discover quickly if it appeals to the target group. Lengthy tests can be counterproductive. We are making use of the same disruptive thinking that start-ups use: to quickly test a prototype and then to decide promptly whether to introduce the idea or to discard it."

Summary

Airline passengers' expectations are not only shaped by how well an airline designs its passenger experience versus its direct competitors. They are also fuelled by standards set by experiences that consumers have in other industries, because innovative products and services in one industry raise the bar for all industries.

Of course, most passengers will continue to choose their flights based on criteria such as price, the availability of direct routes, frequencies, corporate contracts, and frequent-flyer membership. However, a growing number of experienced and informed travellers are becoming more value-sensitive, and they will pay for a better experience.

Liberalization of the aviation industry means that passengers now have a choice between many airlines and business models, and airlines increasingly must compete on the overall experience in order to win and retain customers.

Innovation in the airline-passenger experience today is largely driven by the rapid developments in personal devices, connectivity, and 'big data'. Always-connected travelers and rapidly evolving technology creates a huge opportunity for airlines to come up with customer-centric products and services.

Customer expectations shaped by the 'on-demand economy' are forcing airlines to flip the current dominant service model and provide service at the moment the customer wants it. The benchmark is set by the likes of Apple, Amazon, and Uber, which are centred around staging the best customer experience over and over again and which deliver simple, consistent, and burden-free experiences.

By partnering with third parties that offer specific services at different phases of the customer journey and integrating these services into a seamless, on-demand service, airlines can become 'journey integrators' and provide consumers with a more integrated travel experience.

Notes

1 Jamie Freed, "Air New Zealand's Innovation Inspired by Silicon Valley, Disney and Four Seasons," *Sydney Morning Herald*, November 27, 2015. Accessed from www.smh.com.au/business/aviation/air-new-zealands-innovation-inspired-by-silicon-valley-disney-and-four-seasons-20151126-gl9cae.html

2 "Uber Expectations as We Grow," *Uber blog*, January 2015. Accessed from https://newsroom.uber.com/uber-expectations-as-we-grow
3 Mike Jaconi, "The 'On-Demand Economy' Is Revolutionizing Consumer Behavior – Here's How," *Business Insider*, July 13, 2014. Accessed from www.businessinsider.com/the-on-demand-economy-2014-7
4 Nawal K. Taneja, *Airline Industry: Poised for Disruptive Innovation?* (Abingdon, UK: Routledge, 2016), p. xxvii.
5 "Travel 2020: The Distribution Dilemma," *IBM Institute for Business Value*, 2010. Accessed from www-935.ibm.com/services/us/gbs/thoughtleadership/ibv-travel2020.html
6 "Travel Gold Rush 2020," *Amadeus/Oxford Economics*, October 2010. Accessed from www.amadeus.com/amadeus/documents/corporate/Travel-Gold-Rush-2020-EN.pdf
7 Jeffrey A. Standerski, "The Changing Face of Connectivity." *AviationWeek*, April 6, 2016. Accessed from http://aviationweek.com/information-management-solutions/changing-face-connectivity
8 IFE, "Onboard Innovation: Viva La Evolucion!" *Future Travel Experience*, March 2014. Accessed from www.futuretravelexperience.com/2014/03/onboard-innovation-viva-la-evolucion/
9 Raymond Kollau, "Airports and Airlines Look at Other Industries for Ideas to Speed Up Security and Boarding," *AirlineTrends*, January 2014. Accessed from www.airlinetrends.com/2014/01/26/airports-airlines-looking-sideways-security-boarding/

6   Competition and digitization

Dianchun Li

Chief Commercial Officer
Hong Kong Airlines Ltd

"This is the best of times, but also the worst of times." This is just the right sentence to describe Hong Kong's aviation industry. In the past decade, Hong Kong's aviation industry created a great glory, but what about the rest of this decade and the next? Obviously, it is much more difficult now.

Aviation in the Pearl River Delta emerges

In recent years, with the rapid development of the Pearl River Delta (PRD) region's economy, airlines' networks have been developing a lot compared to a few years ago. But these changes also bring a lot of competition and a pressure to Hong Kong's aviation infrastructure.

In the past decade, Hong Kong was in a very competitive environment. It was not so easy to achieve today's results. In fact, due to the high frequency and low fare (on average 10%–20% lower comparing to CAN), "fly via HK" was once the first choice for people from the Pearl River Delta to travel abroad. Fifty percent of the tour group would choose "fly via HK". But today, the number of international routes of Guangzhou Baiyun Airport have increased from 40 to 80, which means another international hub in has been built in the Pearl River Delta. Only less than 10% of the

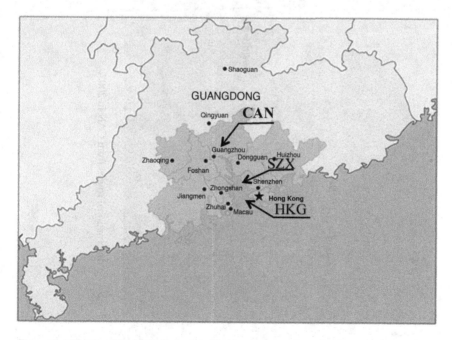

Figure 7.4 The Pearl River Delta region (dark) and three competing international airports

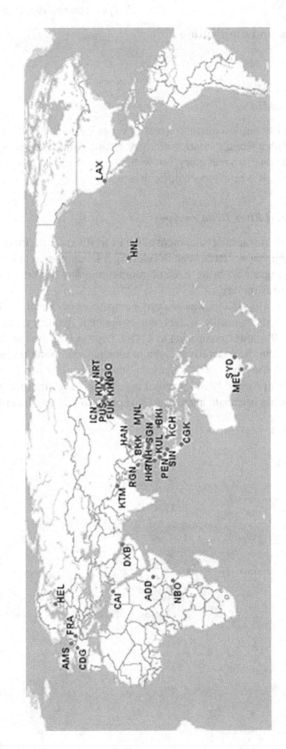

Figure 7.5 International routes from CAN in 2007

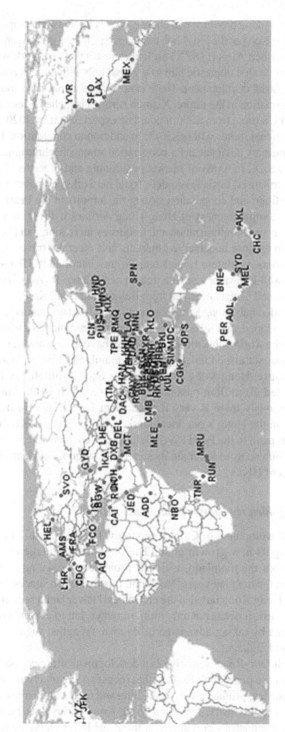

Figure 7.6 International routes from CAN in 2017

tour group in Guangdong province will choose "fly via HK", a 40% drop. Guangzhou has replaced Hong Kong as the No. 1 hub transferring Chinese passengers to Oceania.

Similarly, Shenzhen Airport (SZX) no longer restricts its network within China but is transferring from a domestic hub to a global hub with the government's support and the industrial development. There is no doubt that SZX has more room for its global transformation in the future. Xiamen Airlines launched Shenzhen–Seattle, which is the first US route from SZX. It could be expected that by 2020, the number of SZX's international routes will reach 48. In addition to competition, I think there are also complementary advantages for cooperation among the three airports, namely HKG, CAN and SZX, in terms of market positioning and in terms of developing strategies, infrastructures, business models, route networks, airspace resources, etc.

Facing competition and cooperation among the airports in the Pearl River Delta region, the core competitiveness of Hong Kong Airlines will rely not only on its capacity growth, network optimization and frequency increasing, but also on its blue ocean strategy to explore underserved markets and meet the travel needs of passengers in these markets. Before Hong Kong Airlines launched its HKG-OOL, Gold Coast was not a well-known or a popular tourist destination. Tel Aviv is another dark horse that Hainan and Cathay operated from Beijing and Hong Kong recently. As an international aviation hub, Hong Kong has its unique advantages: its aviation industry has been long developed, the city is highly internationalized and has a wide accessibility to the rest of the world – this means passengers have quite a few transfer options.

In addition, the established linkage between mainland China and Hong Kong is of great significance. Hong Kong's population is only 7 million, but Hong Kong airport transported 70 million passengers in 2016, which is 10 times the local population. Obviously there is very limited room for HKIA's further growth if it focuses only on the Hong Kong local market. In the future, HKIA's hinterland market should expand to the Pearl River Delta and even the whole mainland population of 1.4 billion so as to maintain its super-hub stature. Connectivity is a core competitiveness of HKIA.

Grasping the 'golden ten years' of mainland China

With the rapid development of China's economy, Hong Kong as an international portal is seeking its new growth point. The ultimate advantage of HKIA is its strong feeder from the mainland, which is projected to have an overwhelming travel demand in the next ten years. No doubt, it is the key to success. Hong Kong serves not only Hong Kong but also the entire Pearl River Delta region. To expand its aviation business, it needs not only more runways, but to expand Hong Kong's business to China by taking advantage of its own strengths, such as culture, the legal system and languages.

The 'One-Belt One-Road' initiative is a development strategy and framework, proposed by Chinese premier Xi Jinping, that focuses on connectivity and cooperation among countries, primarily between China and the rest of Eurasia. The entire Hong Kong aviation industry, including Hong Kong Airlines, is benefiting from this policy. Some industries previously in the Pearl River Delta are now moving to other developing countries, such as Vietnam, Myanmar and Cambodia. So new routes to these countries are opening, and increasing frequencies will definitely be beneficial. HKIA and its carriers performed very well in the past ten years. With the emergence of new opportunities and new competitors, we need to take precedence and further refine the business to suit the new competitive norm, involve and practice in China's next golden ten years. Digitization is one trend that I want to explain in the next few pages.

International routes, especially long haul, are of vital importance to Hong Kong–based airlines in the competition, which is also one of the keys to HKIA's success in the past ten years. Hong Kong Airlines, for example, in 2016 and 2017, launched services to the Gold Coast, Auckland, Saipan and Vancouver, which attracted a lot of leisure travelers in the Pearl River Delta to fly via Hong Kong again. This proved that Hong Kong maintains its leading position in Asia as a global hub. Looking forward to Hong Kong Airlines' future, to become a world leading airline, optimized network, new technology implementation and excellent customer experience are three key components.

Hong Kong as a global logistic hub

Some say that Hong Kong's role as a global logistic hub is declining. Its container business has already been surpassed by Shenzhen. But this does not necessarily mean Hong Kong's role as logistic hub has been replaced. In terms of air-cargo volume, HKIA still ranks in the global top three (the other two are Memphis and Shanghai Pudong). However, it is hard to say in the long run whether Hong Kong will retain its position, because it is facing greater challenges than ever before. One of the biggest threats is Shanghai, which has a well-developed international network. Shanghai is China's economic center and is highly urbanized. It is very likely that Shanghai will eventually replace Hong Kong as the new logistic hub in China. On the other hand, competition is for better cooperation. Competitions widely existed among airports as well as airlines in the Pearl River Delta region, but their ultimate goal is to serve the people and the local economy.

Airlines face the threat of substitution

Airlines are now changing their strategies and adjusting to adapt in the new environment and to meet some new standards – for example, in early 2000, load factors of 60%–70% were common. But nowadays the average load factor has risen to 75% or even 85%.

Regional airlines tend to operate in a relatively noncompetitive market, with limited complexity and controlled risks. However, network airlines cannot adjust easily, nor can they adapt to the fast-changing market. Our passengers' expectations regarding the quality and scope of services provided are higher than ever before. There are also more alternative travel methods available. That is to say, airlines will 'push' their potential customers to their competitors or even push them to choose other transportation means, if the travelers' needs cannot be fulfilled.

This kind of substitution is not a new phenomenon. Airlines ignore this threat because they focus too much on their traditional business and have used the point-to-point speed superiority enabled by advanced aircraft. Customers are sensitive to travel time for very-long-haul trips, and travel by air has a clear advantage. But delay or interruption can occur in each step, such as while booking, at check-in, at the long security queues, or due to bad weather delay. Low reliability greatly reduces the perceived efficiency of air travel, making more and more travelers reconsider their travel options, with the emergence of high-speed railways. Shenzhen-Fuzhou and Guangzhou-Changsha/Wuhan are typical routes that are most impacted by the high-speed railways. The city pairs are usually within two flying hours. Overnight high-speed trains leave in the evening and arrive in the morning, which ideally saves one night's accommodation for the traveler. They are, thus, diluting some medium-haul travelers (e.g. Shanghai-Shenzhen/Guangzhou).

The implementation of telephone-conference and remote-meeting systems also reduces business-trip demand – one consequence is that airlines are reducing their first/business-class seats in response to the declining demand. There is an urgent need for airlines to face the substitution.

Challenges to profitability and the digital innovation of the tourism ecosystem

Airlines have the highest profit pressure compared to other players in the tourism ecosystem. Travel agencies, including online travel agents, earn the greatest net profit. The reason is simple: customers value personalized travel advice and solutions more than the transportation service itself. As a result, they tend to spend more on travel services than on airline tickets or hotel rooms, which leads to significant net-profit differences between upstream and downstream travel companies. If airlines are looking for more revenue opportunities to increase their profit, it is high time they expand their services across the whole industry to increase their share in the full range of travel expenses, rather than air transportation.

The traditional tourism ecosystem's value chain is relatively stable and provides customers with limited choice. Due to information asymmetry and technical barriers in the past, travel-service providers – airlines, hotels, agencies – control the vast majority of the value chain and have significant bargaining power. So they are unlikely to provide differentiated services based on various custom needs.

Thanks to the Internet (including mobile access), travel-service providers found a new way of communicating with their customers, without the involvement of intermediary agents. On the other hand, customers take initiative and they have more ways to be involved. Their behavior is undergoing an unprecedented change. Towards this end, the Internet is no longer purely a sales channel; it is a communication platform. Information barriers have been gradually broken. Service providers have been able to easily access customers via mobile and social media. The rapid development of the Internet spawned a comprehensive and dynamic tourism ecosystem and served various functions in travel aspiration, travel plans, product search, booking, destination service, on-the-journey assistance and post-travel feedback, etc. Google flight search is one example that integrates multiple functions mentioned above. The app 'Umetrip', developed by TravelSky, provides flight status, online check-in, pre-seat selection, flight feedback and delay-lottery modules, which makes this app quite popular among Chinese frequent travelers.

Digitization in modern society has been fast and will continue to develop in an unstoppable way. There are companies realizing it (e.g. Google and TravelSky) and taking advantage of it, but unfortunately they are not airlines. Airlines should be better prepared and attach enough importance to the digital transformation caused by mobile networks and social media to integrate this 'digital spirit' into their business and strategy.

The digital era of airlines

Baidu, Ali, Tencent and Ctrip are inevitable topics when talking about the Chinese tourism industry. In 2013 and 2014, these four companies set up their own travel platforms, integrating their respective merits – Baidu's search function, Ali's purchasing function and Tencent's social-media function. Data can be viewed as the source or power of the Internet. The new travel ecosystem is also driven by data. As the No. 1 search engine in China, Baidu owns mega-data that characterize each person. Naturally, Baidu can make use of that information to better target its customers and treat them as individuals.

Ali has the biggest e-commerce platform in China. Its travel products displayed on its flight platform enable the booking process like online shopping: it is more natural and convenient and can be easily customized. Its 'score system' makes 'purchase-travel-feedback' a closed loop seldom seen before – in fact, much can be done after the airline has delivered its customer to the destination. Tencent, on the other hand, is the leader in social media. Its WeChat official accounts can promote a new destination. Some Chinese airlines also use their WeChat official account to supplement their call centers. In China, people won't install every airline's app, but they will have WeChat installed in their mobile phones because WeChat is seen as an essential component of a smart phone in China (like WhatsApp in some other areas).

Different companies use their own advantage to develop their own travel ecosystem which could not only benefit their consumers but also benefit their business partners. This type of cross-industry collaboration strategy is often able to get more market success factors.

Today's travelers have more choices than ever before. Many professional service providers offer tailor-made products to meet the needs of different passengers. The so-called strategy "meeting changes with constancy" will no longer be effective. It has been replaced by diversified products. This means that convincing customers to accept the standard services provided by the airline is not as easy as before, and the cost is higher. Can I save money by rejecting a free meal in the economy cabin? Or can I have the luxurious meal without paying for a full business-cabin service? Obviously, airlines can only rely on digital and Internet technology to provide such travel resources along the travel process. As a consequence, airlines, partners and a variety of travel-service providers can provide customers with a set of services, or a menu-based service model, which can increase the profit of an airline and increase the satisfaction level and loyalty of its customers simultaneously.

Adopting the new digital technology, Delta is committed to improving the value of its service by improving the customer experience at all of Delta's touch points. Throughout the whole process of service, Delta provides customers with customized products and value-added services. Such innovative improvements created more revenue for Delta and also enhanced the customer's travel experience. Recently, Ryanair's chief marketing officer said that Ryanair plans to make its B2C website, ryanair.com, the "world's largest travel product website". On the website, the company will sell not only Ryanair tickets, but also third-party tickets, other tourism products and even cruise products. Ryanair even plans to put other airline's inventories on its own website and app in order to attract the attention of more customers.

Hong Kong Airlines revamped its fare structure based on hotels' fare strategy. They differentiate the fare by various inbound and outbound data, seat allocation and service embedded. For instance, one sub-class corresponds to a specified time and allocation that once sold out, a higher sub-class will be available. The sub-class will be adjusted based on the sales data and dynamic prediction. This change will bring millions of incremental sales. Hong Kong Airlines also uses data-mining technology from social media to inspire new routes and provide services that differentiate it from its competitors.

Airlines are taking different strategies to meet the digital trends and respond to the challenges of new tourism ecosystems. Despite the disadvantages of operation pressure and heavy assets, airlines still occupy a unique advantage, as they can maintain frequent and face-to-face contact with customers. And also the interactions they have with their customers during every long journey give them sufficient time to come up with new ideas about the requirements and demands of their customers. Thus, as "traditional carriers", airlines are taking advantage of their core strengths to try to generate more efficient service as well as ancillary revenue.

For airlines, the digitization process has generally been slow

We all recognize that airlines' digitization will bring opportunities to improve operational efficiency and customer satisfaction as well as create new growth in revenue. The digitization process so far, however, has been slow and usually small in scope: for example, an airline may gain the capability to send customized messages to customers' mobile phones or email. In my opinion, there are some factors restricting the process.

First, there is no independent department or section to lead or execute the digital strategy. Existing functional departments focus on their core KPIs, so the digital revolution is within their own department. The business sector focuses on digitization in the areas of distribution, ancillary revenue and booking; the ground- and cabin-service sector is more concerned with providing customers with 'one-stop service'; the flight-operation and engineering sector will take digital integration into daily operations and the metal itself. But there is a lack of information sharing among these sectors, partly because integration between different functions seems too costly and complex, as well as very low urgency.

Another factor is the fund allocation. With the expanding fleet and network, increasing capacity and competition, airlines' profit margins have been further compressed. So airlines have to further reduce their costs that consume most of the technical funds to be used in maintaining the existing system to ensure a more reliable and safe flight. Digitization does not affect daily operations, so the investment may be very limited. So the underlying reason is not insufficient money but the lack of financial institutions' understanding of the potential return of airlines' digitization. Increasing profits by lowing operating costs cannot create new revenue opportunities or adapt the business model to the new environment. Airlines must introduce new revenue sources to enhance their profit. And digitization is one possible way.

Summary

Airlines are in a fast-changing world, facing a variety of unstable business environments, sophisticated competitors and increasingly highly demanding customers. Nevertheless, there is reason to believe that airlines can still rely on their inherent advantages to expand their services horizontally – to be innovators in the tourism ecosystem, bring more value to their customers and obtain higher business profit – rather than merely move passengers from A to B.

7   How much a threat from long-haul low-cost carriers?

Keith McMullan and James Halstead

Managing Partners
Aviation Strategy Ltd

Back in the 1990s, the European Majors, as they were then, knew about US low-cost carriers, Southwest mainly, but were unconcerned, because they thought that such models would not work in the intra-European market, and this perception was reinforced by the failure of the first wave of new entrants, such as Air Europe. Then in the early 2000s European LCCs, led by EasyJet and Ryanair, started to take off, expanding rapidly, placing mega-orders for new A319s and 737-800s, and introducing ruthless fare competition. The LCCs were able to use their unit-cost advantage to attack the Majors' short-haul point-to-point traffic (even if they didn't compete directly on airport-to-airport routes) and threatened to undermine the Majors' network economics. The Majors' response – cost cutting, route rationalisation and establishing lower-cost subsidiaries – has been slow and painful.

Now we see the emergence of long-haul low-cost carriers (LHLCC) in the initial form of Norwegian Air Shuttle operating across the Atlantic and into Asia, potentially posing a serious challenge to established European, US and Asian Network carriers. Yet it is not at all clear that the incumbents see Norwegian and other new entrants as viable. Could they be making that same mistake as in the 1990s? Could the new low-cost business models in the long-haul airline sector have the potential in the next 15 years to be as disruptive to established network business models as the low-cost model has been to their short-haul operations in the past 15 years?

There is a wide range of long-haul airline operations that could be classified as low cost. These include the well-established long-haul divisions of Charter operators – TUI, Thomas Cook, Air Transat – and the lower-cost subsidiaries of Legacy carriers – Scoot, Jetstar, Eurowings, Boost, Level. However, the most significant market disruption will almost certainly come from an LHLCC that has evolved from an existing short-haul LCC: AirAsia X and Norwegian are the leading contenders at present, and they dominate the LHLCC orderbooks for new 787s and A330/A350s, but none of the LHLCCs has yet proved its financial viability.

The traditional view of the Network or Legacy carriers has been that the LHLCC cannot work, or at least that they can see off the challenge of new entrants; what worked for LCCs in short-haul markets will not work for LHLCCs. There are several, apparently convincing, reasons for their confidence. First, the Legacy long-haul carriers have the option to offer deep discounts in the densely configured Economy cabins of their widebodies, relying on Premium-Class passengers to "cross-subsidise". Second, long-haul aircraft already operate at maximum daily hours, and there is little opportunity to improve asset utilisation through quick turnarounds; curfews and time-zone differences also limit scheduling optimisation. Thirdly, there are few attractive long-haul true O&D markets, and short-haul feed of some sort, or group travel consolidation (the traditional charter-package holiday), is essential on all but a handful of routes.

However, while barriers to entry to the long-haul market remain high compared to starting up in the short-haul sector, the rewards from disrupting the established market are potentially greater. The incentive for start-up increases in markets where there is a high degree of consolidation, notably the North Atlantic, where in recent years leading carriers have been able to achieve "virtual mergers", with antitrust immunity enabling combinations such as BA and American, Air France/ KLM and Delta and Lufthansa/United to coordinate fully on pricing and capacity. The status quo for the Legacy carriers may be more fragile than it currently seems, which may partly explain the sharp legal reaction to Norwegian's plans.

How might the LHLCC model succeed?

When Bjørn Kjos, Norwegian's CEO, is asked to explain his confidence in the Norwegian long-haul operation, he usually replies that they have done the math. Although we have absolutely no access to Norwegian's budgets, we too have carried out a modelling exercise for a new LHLCC, partly based on experience gained from start-up business planning for two successful short-haul LCCs (as a result of which we are also acutely aware of the differences between a theoretical spreadsheet and airline reality).

Our model is fairly simple conceptually but is built up over five years on a route-by-route basis with detailed cost allocation. The main scenario uses new 787s on the thicker North Atlantic routes from a London base. It does not set out to directly copy Norwegian's model, though it does incorporate some key aspects. Also, it does not attempt to replicate Norwegian's global network with routes to Asia as well as North America. Nor have we factored in Norwegian's innovations with 737 MAX 8s on thinner transatlantic routes.

The bottom line, however, is that the LHLCC looks more than viable, delivering a system unit cost (cents per ASK) located well below the trend line in the far right of Figure 7.7.

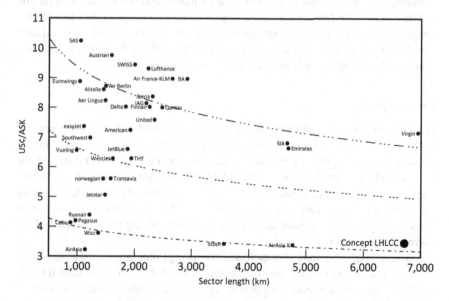

Figure 7.7 Airline unit costs vs. stage length

Gratifyingly, the exercise produced the type of returns that would make sense to a short-haul LCC. The profit margin (after all costs but before taxes) touched 20%, which is the gold standard for the most successful LCCs, such as Ryanair.

It is perhaps not surprising that the LHLCC long-haul operation is forecast to make 20% margins on the North Atlantic, as some of the US Legacy carriers are reporting similar numbers at the operating level – the result of extensive consolidation, "capacity discipline" and unit revenue maximisation. It would seem that the North Atlantic, currently at least, represents a more promising market than Asia/Pacific, where the other highly ambitious LHLCC, AirAsia X, has had to face multi-airline competition on price-sensitive, leisure-dominated routes. It has struggled to establish a viable core network, though, after years of losses, it has reported a net profit for 2016.

Some key issues

In working through the LHLCC operational and financial model and thinking about the competitive environment, some key issues emerge.

Seating density

It is well nigh impossible to squeeze more utilisation out of a long-haul schedule, in contrast to short-haul LCCs which produce around 30% more hours a day than short-haul Legacy aircraft feeding global hubs, but the counter-balancing efficiency gain for the LHLCC comes from seating density – roughly 30% higher compared to traditional carriers. (At the extreme, Cebu Pacific gets 460 seats onto its A330-300 compared to, say, Cathay Pacific's 250).

The Legacies have started to take note: from 2018 BA's Gatwick-based 777s will be reconfigured from 280 to 332 seats, which will equalise, BA claims, the operating cost per Economy seat between its planes and Norwegian's 787s. The problem is that the Legacy carrier ends up with an Economy product that to passengers is indistinguishable from that of a new entrant LHLCC, and it is unlikely that BA or any of the other European carriers would be willing to replicate this seat density on higher-yield routes out of their main hubs.

Onboard products

BA is reported to be considering duplicating the new short-haul Economy product on long-haul flights – basically, this means paying for food and drinks. Making onboard service a profit centre rather than cost has been an integral part of the LCC model, but when a Legacy carrier adopts this policy, the consumer perception hardens, they understand that they are buying a commodity, and price becomes all-important for Economy travel. And our modelling suggests that it is feasible for a start-up LHLCC to have sustainable Economy pricing at around half of the current Legacy offer.

However, our modelling also indicates that filling Premium as well as Economy cabins is vital for an LHLCC on the Atlantic. Without this income stream, it is difficult for the operation to achieve decent returns. This is undoubtedly a challenge, but business travel is price-sensitive, and there are important passenger segments that LHLCCs will appeal to by offering fares at, say, 25% of the published tariff of the Legacy carriers. Business travellers from small and medium-sized enterprises without access to the corporate rates (maybe half the published prices) negotiated by conglomerates and banks will be a target for LHLCCs. Corporate travel departments will soon also cotton on to the potential cost savings.

Fleet selection

In the scenario of our model referenced here, we have assumed a fleet of new 787-9s, but these could be A330s or even second-hand 777s. The 787 pricing is estimated at $129 million per unit, a 33% discount from Boeing's list price, but nothing exceptional.

What would be really disrupting would be an LHLCC obtaining 50%–60% discounts from a manufacturer, just as Ryanair and EasyJet managed when they placed mega-orders for 737s and A319s in the depth of the recession that followed the terrorist attacks of September 11, 2001. Such a severe downturn is unpredictable, but if or when it does happen, then the Legacy carriers would again be left very exposed to low-cost new entrants. Ryanair has specifically stated that it is likely to enter long-haul only when it can purchase aircraft at deeply discounted prices, as it did in 2002.

Airport charges

Perhaps surprisingly, airport policy does not yet play as prominent a role in LHLCC strategy as it does in the short-haul sector, although Norwegian has started to fly 737s to some secondary airports in the US – Providence (for Boston) and Stewart (for New York). But what is missing as yet is a substantial symbiotic relationship with a base airport. This is, for example, a key element in Ryanair's strategy – negotiating discounted rates in return for guaranteed volume growth, most notably at its main base, London Stansted. We have hypothesised such an airport agreement in our modelling, which implies per-passenger charges of less than 20% those in force at Heathrow and less than 50% those applicable at Gatwick.

LHLCCs cannot be purely point-to-point operators; they also need feed. Norwegian has been actively pursuing transfer traffic to feed its long-haul operations and not just from its own services, but also interline agreements with other LCCs. The idea of a large-scale *intraline* operation at Stansted connecting short- and long-haul traffic should give the Legacy carriers palpitations.

Labour costs and overhead

This is the segment of the cost pie where LHLCCs should have an unbridgeable advantage over the Legacy carriers.

The LCC model, short or long, does not necessarily mean low cockpit pay, but it does require efficiency (for example, about one-third of Ryanair salaries are productivity-related). Actual remuneration per pilot might well be equal to or above those at a Legacy carrier.

Cockpit-crewing levels are necessarily higher on a long-haul operation – say, 7.5 crew per aircraft, compared to 4.5 for a short-haul LCC operation. The problem for the Legacies is that they have a multiple of these normal ratios. Cabin crew are somewhat different. Without the traditional seniority scale, salaries tend to be lower than the Legacies' but more than enough to attract young staff, in contrast to the Legacy system which ends up with expensive and mature crew.

Lean management means *really* lean at genuine LCCs. For example, Ryanair, with a fleet of about 340 aircraft, employs 110 managers and 334 administrators. It provides the exacting benchmark of about 30 employees per aircraft. For the Legacies, the ratio of employees to aircraft is well over 100:1 for total operations, short- and long-haul. With start-up operations, heavier crewing requirements and a much smaller fleet, an LHLCC ratio might be around 80:1, but it could be much lower if there was cross-utilisation of management between short- and long-haul operations. Then there is the looming question of unfunded pension liabilities, a big problem at Legacies but not an issue at a start-up LHLCC. Further costs savings come from a clean IT set-up (as opposed to adding onto Legacy systems) and from inexpensive buildings.

In passing, it is interesting to note that Ryanair is a late adopter, not an innovator. Its managers (some of whom have been in place since the 1980s) originally studied Southwest's operations and markets before relaunching the airline as an LCC; internet distribution and yield management, the airline admits, it learnt from EasyJet; improving its product and customer services, it admits, it was a reaction to the success enjoyed by EasyJet and Vueling. Ryanair is now learning from the successes and failures of Norwegian and other LHLCCs.

Long-haul market perspective

Long haul, despite the high profile, is a relatively small part of the airline industry. From our analysis of the global schedules, it is remarkable that long haul (defined for this purpose as flights of over 5,000 kilometres) account for only 8% of the total number of seats and 4% of the number of aircraft movements. Indeed, 90% of all seats are flown on sectors of less than 4,000 kilometres. Long-haul routes are also relatively concentrated: the top 20% of the 1,700 or so long-haul city-pair routes account for over 60% of the total number of long-haul seats, and the top 10% account for 40%.

The majority of long-haul routes are operated using widebody jets; but 1% of long-haul seats are operated using the A320 or 737 and a similar proportion by the 757.

The largest long-haul route area is the North Atlantic, with more than twice as many seats as the next largest, Europe-Asia, itself 10% larger than the Transpacific. It is notable that London plays an important part, being present in 8 of the top 30 long-haul city-pairs. The London–New York route is the densest by far (with some 5.5 million seats scheduled in 2016), closely followed by London-Dubai – but as Emirates had a 65% share of the seats on the route, this may be viewed as a surrogate for routes from London to other parts of the world through Emirates' hub in the Gulf.

To gain an idea of the potential for LHLCC incursion, we analysed the top 140 long-haul city-pair routes in detail – which account for 40% of the total seats – and allocated a market share that the new LHLCCs might reasonably be able to target on each route. We tended to allocate a higher share on leisure-oriented routes to/from markets where short-haul LCCs were well established. We have tended to ignore routes involving the major international hubs or those with a significant superconnector presence, on the basis that a significant portion of the capacity represents connecting traffic; and we have favoured routes of less than 10,000 kilometres.

We arrived at a potential global LHLCC market penetration (in terms of seats) of 17% to 23%. On select routes, the market share could run between 30% and 40%.

We then worked out how many aircraft would be needed to operate these routes – using for the sake of argument 787-9s with 344 seats in a two-class configuration – and extrapolated the result to the whole market.

The result of the exercise was to suggest a long-haul low-cost widebody fleet size under current demand conditions (i.e. not allowing for growth or demand stimulation) of 250 to 450 aircraft worldwide (this compares with a current global widebody fleet of around 2,800 aircraft, not all of which are used on long haul).

The implication is that a relatively small number of widebody LHLCC aircraft could cause a major industry disruption, especially if effectively deployed in a long-haul sector with a high concentration. For comparison, the top ten independent LCCs which radically changed the short-haul market currently operate over 2,200 aircraft in total.

Competitive impact

In summary, Legacy network carriers are likely to be vulnerable to attack from the new LHLCC business model.

- In the first phase, the new entrants will aim to grab point-to-point traffic on primary routes. This will partly be at prices already publicly available as deep-discount Economy fares on Network carriers.
- Their incursion may also tend to soften network carrier yields by providing an alternative to the more price-sensitive Business/Premium leisure passenger.
- As the long-haul low-cost networks expand, they will probably move to develop minor point-to-point routes – perhaps on relatively low frequencies – undermining traffic that would otherwise have flowed through the network hubs. This, in effect, parallels the development of the Superconnectors in developing hub-bypass operations.
- As with the short-haul LCC sector, it may not be these innovator airlines which succeed, but they might well prepare the ground for successful "second movers".
- As in the short-haul market, long-haul LCCs can co-exist with Network carriers. But LHLCCs, even if they are limited to, say, a 20% share of long-haul, could seriously undermine the most profitable segments of the established Legacy networks.

8   Connecting the dots at the airport: the potential of transformation with artificial intelligence

James R. Peters

Chief Technology Officer
SITA

Airports are where people get on and off planes. Although that sounds simple, the complexity of managing the multiple participants that need to be orchestrated to deliver the passenger this basic experience is a huge challenge. These participants include airlines, air traffic control, ground handlers, security, police, immigration, maintenance and engineering, retailers, food and beverage, catering, cleaners, fueling, and of course, airport staff, to name just a few.

Much of the technology used to deliver this airport experience has not changed a lot in the last few decades. Yes, there is some computer automation behind the scenes, and you can do self-service check-in/bag drop, but for the most part, the process is completed by people facing people and people moving machines around. I think this is set to change. Looking forward 10 years, biometrics and autonomous vehicles, all enabled by artificial intelligence and the Internet of Things, will facilitate a major change to how airports operate and how passengers will get on and off planes. Let's connect the dots!

Artificial intelligence: smarter code, smarter systems

AI technology has gone through several phases since the 1950s when several university professors set out to teach a computer to think on its own. Their initial hubris had them predicting that they should be able to complete the job within two years, if not within their generation. (*https://en.wikipedia.org/wiki/Dartmouth_workshop*). Since then, opinion of AI has gone through several cycles, from deep skepticism to optimistic excitement. With recent developments driven by efforts such as "deep learning", self-driving cars, computer vision, Natural Language Processing and cognitive computing, we see predictions that within the next five years, self-driving cars will be on the road, and computers will be capable of recognizing not only faces but whole scenes and the objects in a picture or video.

The term "artificial intelligence" is applied broadly to many types of computing problems and solutions. Some common elements to its different incarnations include the use of advanced mathematical algorithms and the requirement for lots and lots of data to train the system. Fortunately, the explosion of data on the Internet offers a bonanza for researchers, and with the addition of data from physical sensor networks – that is, the Internet of Things – a tipping point has been reached that enables new types of AI applications, such as autonomous vehicles and secure biometric verification systems.

The key-trends ecosystem shows how this data flows in an airport environment. There are three key endpoints – Passengers, Staff, and Things – that can be sensed and connected to cloud-based services. Information in the cloud can

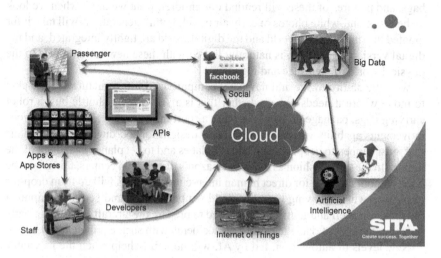

Figure 7.8 Key-trends ecosystem

be accessed via APIs (application programming interfaces) by developers who create applications that are accessed by staff and passengers from app stores. Their interaction with these apps creates data about what they are doing and what they want to do. All this interaction data is pushed back into the cloud, along with all the sensor data of networked Things, where it can be analyzed and AI applied that will feed data back to Passengers, Staff and Things to help them do what they want to do better.

Admittedly, this is a busy picture, and the explanation a little technical, but, hopefully, you get the idea of how this flow of interactions, sensor data, and user data creates a "virtuous cycle" that allows things to be done better and smarter, ultimately improving the passenger experience, while increasing staff effectiveness and optimizing operations.

A good example of this is SITA's "Day of Travel" app for airports, which, using beacons, can determine where a passenger is in the airport and serve him or her information on nearby retailers and points of interest. Based on what options the user selects, the app can get smarter about what to display in the future. This is being successfully used in Miami International Airport and Nice Côte d'Azur Airport.

Computer vision

A key aspect of AI enables a computer to "see" well enough to know you are you when it "looks" at you and to know what is around it to enable it to navigate equipment safely from one spot to another. Computer vision and camera optics are now reaching the stage where a computer can look "deep" into a scene and pick out very fine detail, such as the unique scuffs and marks on your luggage, such that it is conceivable that in the future there won't be a need to put tags on bags, and pictures of these will remind our children what we think when we look at the black-and-white photos of early air travel. Future generations will take it for granted that the physical world and the digital world are tightly integrated, and the digital version of your trip is naturally linked with these new technologies to the physical world of your face and luggage.

With the ability to see and navigate, computerized infrastructure will be able to move where it needs to be, whether this is a self-driving shuttle bus, a robot carrying bags, baggage drop-offs or other airport infrastructure. This autonomous movement capability will allow radical new designs for coordinating all the things that must happen to get people on and off planes and to get planes in and out of the airport. In the same fashion as today's Amazon's distribution centers, things will be done without the need for direct human intervention, so bags will go from drop-off to pick-up without having been handled by a person. Ground-service equipment will position itself automatically as needed to prepare the aircraft for flight, greatly reducing the cost of damage caused by accidents with such equipment today.

New levels of automation, fed by AI, will hopefully help when the inevitable happens and flights get delayed or canceled, causing disruptions. Recovering from these disruptions is a major industry challenge. Using AI to better predict when these disruptions will occur and then to construct an optimized recovery plan is a significant opportunity for the industry, and something I am sure all passengers will greatly appreciate.

The challenges

Using your face as the physical representation of your digital journey, and automating the movement of all the equipment both land-side and airside at an airport, will create the ability to vastly improve both the passenger experience and the operations of all the stakeholders that operate at an airport, but this utopian vision is not without major hurdles that must be addressed by the industry before we will see it realized.

An industry Internet of Things data hub

A defining aspect to the Internet of Things concept is that physical things get a digital "cohort" or shadow, which is used to augment their purpose and function. This digital shadow is a collection of information that is maintained and linked to the physical object, such as identity, location, status, alerts, current task, and operational environment. Managing this information and utilizing it to optimize processes and operations is a new challenge companies will face as they adopt IoT solutions, but the complexity and difficulty of that challenge is magnified by the multi-stakeholder environment of an airport. Quite often this information needs to be shared effectively between the stakeholders for it to be most useful. Setting up bilateral commercial and technology agreements to share data on a use-case by use-case basis will not scale to deliver the needed collaboration. A better option would be the creation of an air-transport-community data hub that allows everyone to share securely the data from their IoT systems with the appropriate partners to better deliver their value to the airport ecosystem.

A relatively new and promising technology that can enable the creation of such a data hub is called "blockchain". It is most famous for its use in the digital currency Bitcoin. It implements what is called a "distributed ledger", which allows multiple parties to have a copy of information that is automatically synced with all other copies, so that whenever a stakeholder posts information, that information can then be used by other stakeholders. There is a feverish amount of interest and investment in blockchain development currently, especially in the financial arena. It is still a relatively immature technology for enterprise use-cases, and things like security and access control are still getting worked out, but now is the time to start exploring and testing the concepts around an IoT data hub approach for the air-transport industry.

One example is the problem of passengers getting conflicting flight information from different sources. The airline app on their phone says one thing, the signage at the gate says something different, and if you Google the flight number, you get yet another version of the facts. This is because there are multiple copies of the flight information kept by the different stakeholders in separate databases that must be kept synchronized. Latency in this synchronization process leads to the different systems having different data. Using blockchain technology would allow everyone to post their status updates to a common "ledger" that is distributed and synchronized automatically by the blockchain protocol. Any conflicting updates could be resolved via what are called "Smart Contracts", small pieces of code that implement the "rules" by which the most correct information is what is used when a query is made on the ledger for the current status (FLIFO).

Although solving what I call "the FLIFO Problem" for the industry sounds pretty awesome and magical, the reality is that blockchain technology is currently what is known as "bleeding edge" technology. At SITA, we look to do some initial PoCs and trials with airlines and airports to learn more about it and to understand when and how it may provide some of the promised benefits.

Common-use control and management systems

On top of the shared industry data hub, standards will be required regarding how multiple stakeholders can share the control and management systems running over that data. A good example is managing autonomous vehicles at the airport. They will require some kind of management system that allows you to see where a vehicle is, what it is doing, where it is going, and what it should do after it gets there. Many vendors are likely to be involved in providing such vehicles. If each vendor implements its own management system, and the airport gets autonomous vehicles from a diversity of vendors, it will be a nightmare to try to use so many different management systems, not only internally – for, say, airport staff – but also externally, with the other stakeholders, such as airlines and security, that will need some form of visibility and control over those vehicles.

Creating and agreeing upon standards regarding how to control and manage autonomous vehicles will be a key enabler for their use in the airport environment. These standards will need to address some of the physical aspects of the solution, such as power, while others will govern how a vehicle can have its digital shadow managed in a consistent fashion by multiple stakeholders.

Governments and the future of your digital identity

Getting governments and international regulatory bodies to engage and to agree upon standards for digital identity will be the biggest challenge in implementing the biometric vision of using your face as your boarding pass or as a "single travel token", where the token is the digital shadow of all your trip details and documents. There are privacy concerns that need to be addressed as to how this personal information, including your biometric data, gets stored, shared and managed. Many governments are more focused on how to do this within their own countries as a priority. The problem is, without an international view, the goal of an interoperable approach, one that will work at any airport in any country, cannot be achieved. And even if "the body is willing", it takes a lot of time to get stuff done and implemented.

There are already a number of governments and regulatory bodies working on this problem, such as ICAO's New Technology Working Group, IATA's StB-sponsored project on "One Identity", and SITA's Secure Journeys working group. Getting critical mass in the participation at the appropriate level from governments with these initiatives will be key to their timely success.

The future is "inter-modal": the rise of high-speed ground transportation

There are already high-speed ground-transportation systems in use, particularly in Europe and Asia. New developments in this area, such as the Hyperloop, as conceived by Elon Musk, will have a major impact on how airlines manage their networks and fleets. Not only the addition of new high-speed ground options, but also the self-driving car and the sharing economy, as spawned by Uber, will provide people additional travel options on short-haul trips. (A side note on self-driving cars and airports: don't expect to be getting a lot of parking revenue anymore!)

The speed at which new high-speed ground options will get deployed is not entirely knowable, and integrating the impact of how people will travel on shorter trips in this new world will require airports and airlines to take some calculated guesses as they design their facilities, locations, and fleets for the next 10 to 20 years.

Conclusion: have we connected the dots at the airport?

The basic proposition put forward here is that technologies such as biometrics and autonomous vehicles, all fueled by artificial intelligence and the Internet of Things, have the potential to have the biggest impact on how people get on and off planes and how airlines get planes in and out of airports within the next couple of decades. The airport environment is a complex one, with many stakeholders collaborating to make it work. To accomplish this transformation will require new kinds of data sharing, common-use systems, government engagement and integration of future modes of high-speed ground transportation. There is already activity in many of these areas, including the research we do in SITA Lab, initiatives by IATA and ICAO, and engagements with governments to start defining the road ahead.

The improvements possible to the passenger experience and operational efficiency drive us to keep working on these exciting new technologies as we continue to connect the dots!

9   The future of secondary airports

Parm Sidhu

Airport General Manager
Abbotsford International Airport

> *The views and opinions expressed in this article are those of the author and do not necessarily state or reflect the official policy, opinion, or position of the City of Abbotsford, its representatives, or employees.*

Secondary airports can't depend on low-cost carriers (LCCs) alone for growth. They will need to create a value proposition that all air carriers, not just LCCs, or technology companies, such as Google, Facebook, Amazon, and Uber cannot resist. An airport operator does not need to operate a terminal building; an airport's brand is nothing without an airline's seat capacity. Secondary airports will need to focus on their most basic core business and allow the air carriers and technology companies to grow their airports. The airport's role will be to provide a competitive platform for airlines and technology companies to exploit.

Secondary airports

Secondary airports can be classified as airports located in large metropolitan areas that are in close driving proximity to a primary airport. Often, they are under-utilized, but they can attract a commercial air carrier for one or more of the following reasons:

- High costs at the primary airport
- Capacity restraints or curfews at the primary airport
- Lower air-carrier fees at the secondary airport
- Underserved catchment area

LCCs such as Ryanair, EasyJet, and Southwest Airlines have exploited the use of secondary airports, due to cost savings and to gain market share exponentially at the secondary airport. Historically, most legacy air carriers have operated from the primary airport and avoided secondary airports altogether; for them, historically, operating costs increase, but overall revenue would not increase, so, at least in theory, the air carrier would cannibalize its own operations and revenue stream by having two operations in such proximity. This may not be the case in the coming years, as carriers could diversify their revenue streams and their operations and gain market share by operating from both airports.

Abbotsford International Airport (CYXX)

Abbotsford International Airport (YXX) is an example of a secondary airport. It is located about 70 kilometers from downtown Vancouver, with a total catchment area of 2.8 million people, and is about the same distance from Vancouver International Airport (YVR), which had about 22 million passengers in 2016. YXX is also only about 40 kilometers (but across an international border) from Belling-ham Airport located in Washington State in the US. About 60% of Bellingham Airport's 836,000 (in/out) passengers in 2016 were from Canada. YXX greeted about 530,000 passengers in 2016.

YXX was transferred from the Government of Canada to the City of Abbotsford for a nominal fee in 1997. Although the municipality owns the airport, all aero-nautical regulations are national and international. In the year prior to transfer in 1997, the airport processed 3,000 passengers, mostly on short commuter flights to the provincial capital in Victoria, located on Vancouver Island. However, shortly after transfer, WestJet Airlines, formed in 1996 based on the Southwest Airlines business model, offered commercial air service to YXX. YXX converted a main-tenance building into a temporary terminal building, offered free parking (which was really popular), and imposed very low aeronautical fees.

The response from the marketplace was overwhelming, with the airport greeting 76,676 guests in 1997, a record year. A new low-cost permanent terminal was con-structed; it was a simple shell that was expandable at a very low cost. The exterior of the building was like a Costco warehouse, where the value is on the inside of the building. The airport grew at a record rate and was a disruption in the industry at the time. The reasons: a low-cost airport business model with an underserviced catchment area (about 500,000 people living within 40 minutes' drive of YXX) from an air-carrier air-route perspective.

In the early 2000s, YXX gradually moved to more of a traditional airport oper-ation: vehicle parking fees were introduced, the Airport Improvement Fee was raised to $10 per departing passenger; General Terminal Fees were introduced; and various fees within the terminal complex, such as loading-bridge fees, baggage-handling concession fees, and landing fees, were introduced or increased, with consequent effect on the airlines and passenger-ticket prices.

Risks for secondary airports

Secondary airports and regional airports in North America face some risks moving forward, simply due to the likely reduction of the number of larger air carriers based in North America. Some of these reductions arose from past consolidation, and some will be due to ongoing mergers and future acquisitions (e.g., Alaska Airlines' purchase of Virgin America). Some airlines have gone out of business (in Canada, these include Jetsgo, Canada 3000, Zoom, and Har-mony), and there will undoubtedly be additional casualties in the coming years. Another factor is the shortage of pilots, especially in North America, which will particularly impact regional carriers and result in some airports losing air service. In March 2017, SkyWest Inc. president and CEO Chip Childs testified at a congressional hearing, "All of us [in the US regional airline industry] see a very significant pilot shortage." He added: "We're deeply concerned about the statistics as we move forward over the next three years. There are a lot of retirements at the majors, and we simply don't have the backfill."[1] Childs said US major airlines, which primarily hire flight-deck crew from US regional airlines, were expected to hire 18,000 pilots in the next three years, nearly the size of the current regional airline pilot workforce. He warned that the shortfall in pilots could ultimately lead to the parking of as much as two-thirds of the US regional airline fleet in operation today.[2] Air carriers (and airports) dependent on 50-seat or smaller aircraft need to ask themselves, who will fly these aircraft in the future?

Air carriers using 50-seat or smaller aircraft will be faced with significant financial costs to replace or overhaul these aircraft in the coming years. Airports also need to consider, what OEM is manufacturing a replacement aircraft for 50-seats-and-under fleets? Boeing and Airbus say the average seat density moving forward on their aircraft types will be in the range of 180 seats. Few regional airports can supply the number of passengers needed for an aircraft of this size. As a result, airports could lose frequency.

Airlines are also forming stronger partnerships with each other, whereas airports desire competition between airlines (for example, the competition in Seattle between Delta and Alaska Airlines). Without competition, it's harder to grow airport passenger volumes. Another problem for secondary airports is that the LCCs are now increasingly looking at servicing both the primary airport and secondary airport in one single metropolitan area (for example, Ryanair). This is due to connectivity or self-connections (where a passenger separately buys airline tickets), and it permits the LCC to attract a higher-yield passenger (the business traveler). In response, and composing an additional threat to secondary-airport traffic, major carriers operating at primary airports (for example, United and American) have begun to offer unbundled fares. If the number of airlines continues to shrink in North America, how will a regional or secondary airport sustain itself, let alone see growth?

The new disruptive secondary-airport model

Can you disrupt an airport model? The growth YXX saw in 1997 was a disruption with its low-cost airport model. Can it be done again in light of the new reality with an *ultra*-low-cost airport?

In 2014 YXX changed its business model to become an ultra-low-cost airport. YXX now has some of the lowest aeronautical fees, including the Airport Improvement Fee, in all of North America. YXX operates an international airport with 16 FTEs (full-time-equivalent employees) and a total operating budget of under CAN$4 million (about US$3 million) annually, and total revenue of CAN$6.5 million (about US$5 million) based on current passenger volumes. The Airport Improvement Fee at Abbotsford in 2017 will be reduced to zero. An air carrier will be able to turn a 737-700 for under CAN$550 (under US$400) all in (landing fee, terminal fee, and Airport Improvement Fee). As the Airport Improvement Fee is passed onto the traveler in the ticket price, this makes the ticket price (which also includes high air-traveler security charges, as well as ANS charges) for short-haul flights significantly higher than for longer flights as a percentage of the overall ticket price. Eliminating the Airport Improvement Fee can have a very significant effect on a low ticket price.

Under this ultra-low-cost airport model, YXX builds its brand through the success of the air carriers that operate from YXX. The more money the air carrier makes, the more capacity the air carrier will place. This will also attract additional routes and carriers to the airport. For a municipally owned airport, this will provide greater economic development opportunities for not just the airport, but also the city and the region. Under the YXX model, the airport operator manages the core business, such as ensuring regulatory compliance, managing airside and groundside, provision of utilities, and provision and maintenance of the terminal building and facilities, including baggage systems. The airlines are empowered to manage their guests, and, in the case of YXX, the guest primarily belongs to the airline.

Objectively viewed, what does an airport really control at an Origin & Destination airport? The guest did not book the flight with the airport. The airport does not control the check-in process. Pre-board screening is not the airport operator's responsibility. The boarding process and baggage are the airline's responsibilities. For the most part, the airport has very little or nothing to do with any of these processes, other than as a facilitator.

Additionally, if the airport operator can continue to keep the business model low-cost, by avoiding loading bridges, power-out stands for aircraft, and generally sticking to its core responsibilities, it can allow the airlines to manage their guests. In many cases, secondary airports don't need to exist, as most primary airports could handle additional capacity. A secondary airport's key responsibility is to empower the air carrier to add more capacity and to use the airport as an economic enabler for the benefit of all.

Creating a value proposition

Soon, we all know, many brands in aviation and other sectors will disappear. Data-rich companies already have, and will continue to have, the same power and influence as only energy/oil companies once had. Artificial intelligence (AI) will play a significant role in aviation. Data could become the new oil. AI could have a disruptive effect equivalent to that of the introduction of electricity.

The key for a secondary airport will be to offer a value proposition that a primary airport can't. One key objective for the airport operator will be to keep the assets on the books that are critical only to the core business. These are the assets you need to replace, so the goal is sustainability, recover of capital costs, and meeting or exceeding regulations to operate a safe, secure, and efficient airfield year-round. This will help determine what human capital is required for the core business. It will also determine your annual operating costs and long-term assets replacement costs. Everything else you want to consider empowering the free-enterprise market to fund. Why fund something that is not your core business? An airport's role is to be an economic enabler. Why compete with the private sector? Why not leverage the private sector to grow your assets so that you as the airport operator can stay focused on the core business? Operating an ultra-low-cost airport requires discipline and not being distracted by fun but not fundamental activities, if you want your airport to grow and to be sustainable.

Creating the business model

Companies such as Google, Amazon, Facebook, and Airbnb, as well as air carriers and others, will continue to leverage AI and their online and mobile platforms to sell seat capacity and ancillary products. One could foresee a time when the airline seat for the leisure passenger is the loss leader. About 75% of people who fly make their decision based on price. Once they purchase the seat, they can be sold various other products (baggage fee, seat selection, food, accommodations, ground transportation, and so on). Large technology-rich companies have seen a lot of success selling goods or services. The air-travel market is worth well over $700 billion. Technology companies will take their share, which will continue to grow as they overtake some brands. Try booking a flight on Google Flights to see how fast a price can change when you change the date. See how easy it is to book the flight, especially if Google already has all your credit-card and personal info. The transaction is much faster than an airline's website. Often, these non-airline portals selling airline tickets have more information on the person looking for a flight than the airline. As we move to a consumer-based economy, consumers will want real-time info, value, and fast-tracked transactions, all from a mobile platform. One can imagine one day there will be a virtual airline, a virtual hotel, and so on. In India they have virtual banks now, with no storefront:

> Mumbai, April 26 [2017]:
>
> DBS Bank on Tuesday launched a 'mobile-only bank' in India. The 'digibank' uses technologies, such as biometrics and artificial intelligence, to enable paperless, signature-less and branchless bank.
>   The bank will leverage biometrics-enabled ID and Aadhaar card to ensure that that there is no paperwork. It will provide customer service via a 24×7 artificial intelligence-driven virtual assistant, which understands natural language and has learning ability, so that it is able to respond in real-time.[3]

Technology is changing industries globally. Most consumers have not heard of blockchain, which has the potential of disrupting industries such as financial services. Who would have ever thought banking could be disrupted?
    Another recent announcement from an intermediate:

> Airbnb is moving way beyond its home-sharing roots. At the company's annual Airbnb Open conference, held this past November in Los Angeles, the company announced a slew of new features designed to turn the service into an all-in-one trip-planning platform. The biggest new announcement: Users can now book "Experiences" that range from multiday surfing expeditions to afternoon hops around a farmer's market.[4]

What does this mean? Does it mean you will now pick your accommodation or experience first, and then allow Airbnb to offer you a flight to this destination? Time will tell, but one can imagine a world where the average person has 10 apps on his or her smart phone, apps such as transportation portals, finance/insurance, legal, retail, healthcare, entertainment, accommodations, social media, news, and food and beverage portals. Every person will have many options for the portal they like best in each category. Some may choose Uber, an airline portal, Lyft, or a brand that does not yet exist. These portals will continue to flip inventory they buy on volume or simply flip without paying for the inventory and take a commission. In some cases, these companies will sell a product and sit on the revenue for 30 days or more, before they pay the owner for the product. Airlines will need to start selling other modes of transportation in order to provide value to the 75% of customers who make their airline purchase based on price. These apps will also try to sell other products that are not tied to their core expertise – for example, a transportation portal may try to sell you a hotel room.

Disruptions that will impact airports

It's unlikely an airport app will be able to provide the critical mass required to sell products, like the portals mentioned above. Airports will need to be part of a portal that is owned by someone else. Google could provide all the information one requires at an airport. This information is already available for every city, so why is the airport any different? Many people visit an airport website or app for flight information. In the future, the portal you buy your airline seat from will provide real-time information, so the need to visit an airport website or use an airport app will become unnecessary.

Potential disruption #1 – booking a flight and more

Consumers will have many different options for booking their travel experience, including flights, in the future. The chances of the average person basing his or her decision on price booking directly with an intermediate like Google Flights is likely. As Google Flights continues to improve its flight-booking product, expect to see a drastic spike in users. Moreover, the future will be full of disruptions in all areas: travel, banking, shared economy, on-demand economy, autonomous vehicles, traffic and safety, and so on. Portals will showcase a price and the total travel time round-trip from your home or your office. For example, the portal will calculate the time it should take you to get from your home to the airport, calculate airport-processing time, add the flight time, and provide the same information on the way back to your office or home.

AI will play a substantial role in the travel industry, no different than in many other industries, as it will completely change the end-to-end platform game. AI will be used to stimulate demand for travel, hotels, and all other products and services that humans interact with; the data-rich technology companies will have a significant amount of data on hand to mine for the purposes of stimulating demand for a flight, multi-modal options, hotels, and an assortment of travel packages, to name a few. Through the use of AI, companies will be able to stimulate this demand through building experience-based loyalty and highly customizing each experience, where applicable. Furthermore, AI will provide consistently more accurate analysis in determining the best means of simplifying each step of any process. There will be data on various touchpoints associated with the travel industry and the intelligence to determine the best way to streamline and/or maximize revenues at each of these touchpoints. Imagine a super-powered Siri that is able to map out a traveler's trip instantly in real time after you tell it you would like to travel to the Arctic to see the northern lights. AI will put together your trip itinerary, taking into consideration the best time to see the northern lights and what products, services, and experiences can be catered to you en-route. AI would know your starting location and your specific habits, including, but not limited to, pricing and time. While you are in the air, if your connecting flight is delayed, AI will immediately notify you that your connection is delayed; however, AI will then provide viable options of being reconnected for a fee on another carrier or another mode of transportation to ensure you make it to your destination on time. During your entire trip, AI will also be collecting additional data based on your decisions and will keep you on schedule should you make a decision that will affect your travel plans.

There is great opportunity in this for secondary airports. Airport operators need to keep their departing passengers' airport experience simple and efficient by trying to have them processed and on the aircraft within 75 minutes from the time they arrive at the airport. Efficiency is the key, as is empowering and leveraging technology companies. Many people spend more time getting to and waiting in the airport than they spend flying. Airports need to start removing barriers to provide a value proposition to a consumer-based economy. Travelers will soon start putting a value on this unnecessary congestion/nonproductive time.

Potential disruption #2 – getting to and from the airport and more

The majority of domestic passengers at secondary airports are picked up and dropped off curbside at the airport. As end-to-end platforms enter the marketplace, more and more passengers will use ride-sharing, autonomous car, public transit, or multi-modal platforms that tie the air and ground component into one seamless reservation. For example, Uber's platform could sell a package incorporating ground and air travel in one transaction. With the development of shared and autonomous vehicles, the price to move from point A to B can only come down. A family would not need a second vehicle, and ride-sharing should be able to replace this fixed depreciating cost, which would also free up disposable income for the average household to spend on more travel.

This disruption actually may not all be good news for airports:

> As advances in the auto industry make traveling by car more attractive, airlines will have to adjust to the steeper competition. Short haul flights, flights less than 300 miles, will be most significantly affected. Short haul flights cost an average of $120 above the cost of driving, and reduces door-to-door travel time by roughly an hour. These types of city to nearby city flights make up 25% of all US domestic departures.

According to a new Morgan Stanley study, if demand for short haul flights completely disappeared, it would lead to about a 15% loss in earnings. The study also acknowledged that such a change would take at least five to ten years, giving the airline industry time to adjust.[5]

The majority of the revenue of North American airports is driven by pay parking and car-rental concessions. If travelers don't have a second car, or are buying a multi-modal package, or travelling by an autonomous vehicle, they will not park at the airport. And what will happen to rental-car operators and their brands? Companies such as General Motors are already launching their own car-sharing portals. Will they sell their own vehicles to rental-car operators, or will they go after market share and put their own vehicles on the marketplace to disrupt the traditional rental-car operator's business model?

The autonomous vehicle, in complement with multi-modal operations, will start to compete with short-haul flights in the near future. This prediction further complicates the current situation of airports having many barriers that work against them on short-haul flights. In addition, given the exponential growth of technology and based on recent automobile trends, autonomous vehicles will continue to become more productive and efficient in the coming years. In the short run, the same cannot be said for the airline industry. For example, the distance between Toronto and Ottawa is approximately 450 kilometers, and as of today this route is serviced daily by multiple domestic carriers. The total flight time for this route is one hour; however, when you factor in the time from the traveler's office/home to the airport, check-in time, baggage drop-off, and airport congestion time (walking to the gate, renting a car, pre-board-screening), on average this adds two-plus hours to the one-hour flight; this does not factor in the infrequency in flight schedules and any weather-related delays, which are fairly common in the winter months in Canada. This example is a common thread for air travel on short-haul flights in that it leads to non-productive, value-lost time for the customer.

In the coming years, the futuristic technology-first vehicle will naturally become a substitute competitor for the airliners on these short-haul routes. The technology-first vehicle will save customers time and money and, in general, will be a more productive modal means for the consumer. A traveler wanting to travel from Toronto to Ottawa by vehicle could be incentivized to travel at off-peak times or choose a ride-sharing option to bring down the cost at peak times. Moreover, the traveler could use the Internet the entire time, as the vehicle would be equipped with Wi-Fi. The vehicle could also up-sell other services for a fee. For example, a sleepy traveler could purchase a sleep mode option, in which all the windows are blackened to replicate nighttime and in which outside noises are reduced to ensure a quiet environment. Likewise, when the same traveler wakes up, he/she could opt for the entertainment option, if he/she is an avid movie or music lover.

The next decade will be full of disruptions; however, by 2030 everything should start to balance out. Roads will become less occupied, cities with no traffic lights will become more prevalent, and technology-driven vehicles will transport people more efficiently and economically along the sort of routes that today are serviced by short-haul flights.

Another major impact will be multi-modal operations in which air, ground, and sea travel are sold as one package. This concept would see a traveler bike from his/her apartment to a train station, then take the train, which would take the traveler to the airport where he/she would hop on an international flight, and as the aircraft lands at the destination an autonomous vehicle would be waiting to drive the traveler to his/her final port destination, allowing the traveler to sail away on his/her dream cruise. The best part of this would be that all these modes were purchased on a seamless portal with a single click. There are many examples of an airliner servicing a nearby hub with a flight time within 45 minutes. Now, imagine this short-haul flight being replaced by a bus or another type of vehicle. Why would an airliner deploy an expensive asset, such as an aircraft, on a short-haul flight that is under 45 minutes when a bus can do it at a fraction of the cost, can be just as efficient, and/or can do it at a much lower price point? Point in case: Air France offers a service from Ottawa to Paris; however, the passengers don't fly out of Ottawa – they are bused to Montreal. This is done through one seamless multi-modal ticket, and there isn't much of a time variance in traveling by either mode.

Things are moving really fast. Changes are coming. Are you ready? We have not even factored in such things as the Hyperloop, virtual-reality holidays, robotics, flying cars, or drone deliveries, to mention a few. We are in the midst of a technological revolution, and, although we live in such exciting times, it is important to note that what worked in the past will most likely not work in the future.

Potential disruption #3 – terminal operations/concessions

Airports must remove barriers to travel efficiency, especially when competing with a car on routes that are 300 miles or less. With regard to commuter or short-haul flights, you could imagine a day when you are stimulated to buy an airline ticket via AI, your checked baggage is picked up from your house/office and is flown on an integrator such as FedEx to and from the destination. You check in remotely 24 hours in advance of your flight from a mobile device and perhaps get pre-cleared for screening so you don't need to remove your shoes, laptop, liquids, belt, and light jacket. How will this work? The day before your flight, you pay a $5 user fee to be pre-cleared; you enter your personal and flight information onto a portal; the algorithms process the information and pre-clear you. When you arrive at the airport one hour prior to departure in an autonomous vehicle or on a ride-sharing platform, you go directly to the pre-board screening; scan your bar code at an entrance to pre-board screening; and, because you are pre-approved, you are fast-tracked. Only if you had been notified would you be subject to the full screening process. With Google Maps to guide you to the aircraft, you pick up your pre-ordered meal, board the aircraft through an automated gate, and board the aircraft. No one wants to arrive at the airport three hours in advance of a domestic flight by choice. The reason they need to is that barriers have been placed on the consumer.

In the US, such an app was developed to process guests faster through US customs: The Mobile Passport (www.mobilepassport.us/) speeds you through US customs and border protection at 1 cruise port and 20 airports. You fill out your profile and answer CBP's questions – you then go straight to the "Mobile Passport Control" express lane at the airport!

Hopefully, one day such apps will be available to anyone. Other possible benefits will also accrue. Imagine a day when you can buy your duty-free products from this app, and then the duty-free products are drop-shipped from an approved warehouse/retailer not at the airport but to your home/office or location of choice. Why carry your duty-free products with you? The algorithms can verify how long you were out of the country, and the approved duty-free retailer can send you the products from the closest outlet to your preferred destination.

Potential disruption #4 – new aircraft types

Boeing and Airbus both have secured a majority of the aircraft orders required by airlines operating around the world in the coming years. Growth in emerging markets, such as China and India, and North American replacement orders are major contributors to this overall growth. Some of the aircraft being manufactured today and into the future by Boeing, Airbus, and Bombardier could lead to growth and new opportunities for secondary airports that were non-existent in today's market.

For instance, the Boeing 737 MAX could potentially shake up the transatlantic market and additional mature routes, due to its efficient design. Furthermore, it can open the door for low-cost carriers to more aggressively compete with legacy carriers on such routes. To date, legacy carriers have lost market share domestically to low-cost carriers, and now the same threat emerges on transatlantic flights and in other similar markets.

Norwegian Air Shuttle was the first airliner in the world to operate the 737 MAX, with the first aircraft arriving in May 2017. Norwegian has ordered 100 of these planes to aggressively and strategically alter the make of their existing fleet. Also, to coincide with the fleet mix, Norwegian recently announced several new transatlantic routes, starting in mid-2017. Many of the routes will service secondary airports in the US from Ireland and the UK. Two new routes will service Newburgh (serves New York City, 97 kilometers from Manhattan), and Providence (95 kilometers from Boston). This follows the proven concept of the lower the fare, the larger the catchment area and the greater the recognition. People will drive longer distances to capture greater savings. In line with this concept, Lars Sande, senior vice-president of sales at Norwegian, told *FlightGlobal*, "Instead of bringing people to the bigger airports, we wanted to bring them to these smaller airports, and our visibility there is a lot higher."[6]

Airbus and Bombardier are also on a similar path of disrupting the industry, respectively, with the Airbus A320neo family and the Bombardier CSeries aircraft types.

Another game-changing opportunity for an underserviced market could be the hybrid aircraft that are currently being developed by Zunum Aero, located in

Washington State. Zunum Aero is developing a small aircraft, which will have 10–50 seats, to transport people up to a distance of 700 miles starting in the early 2020s. As a part of this initiative, Zunum Aero is looking to serve the under-serviced airports. Also, Boeing's investment in Zunum Aero makes this game-changing opportunity seem more viable. "Boeing is investing in Zunum because we feel its technology development is leading this emerging and exciting hybrid-electric market space,"[7] explained Steve Nordlund, VP of strategy at Boeing. "This technology and customer approach has the potential to transform the market for small, short-haul aircraft that can use smaller regional airports."[8]

THE AVIATION WORLD IS CHANGING DAILY – IS YOUR AIRPORT READY?

Potential disruption #5 – infrastructure investments/planning

Several technological changes have been illustrated in the prior sections; with all these changes just years away, how is an airport operator supposed to plan? This is an area that airports should start focusing on now. "Build it and they will come" won't work in this technologically advanced era; airports, especially regional and secondary airports, will need to be careful about what they build. Some airports may become obsolete, because some airports are already headed in that direction, with the lack of economic generation. Airport infrastructure is very expensive to fund and is a long-term fixed investment, and moveable assets, such as cars, buses, and aircraft, can be shifted easily; with this in mind, the airport's planning processes can be disrupted relatively quickly, leaving an airport empty and in debt. However, on the other end of the spectrum, well-positioned airports can take advantage of this and attract growth; smart airport operators will try to create the future or be a part of the solution somehow, as compared to sticking to the status quo.

Technology has brought about disruption to many industries, let alone the travel industry. In all cases, technology can be altered in an instance to better position a company or an industry. Airport operators should take a hard look at the risks and threats in play and alter their business model to ensure they are agile, adaptive, and aligned to such upcoming changes. Lean innovations should be worked within existing infrastructures prior to large investments. Planning should follow suit on this principle of being sustainable. In the past, infrastructure upgrades/investments, along with planning, were based on peak-period traffic. Although the easy answer may be to continue to plan and invest in infrastructure based on peak-period demand, a better answer may be to speed peak flows through technological advancements, hence practicing lean innovation and doing more with less. We should begin to view infrastructure as no different than airplanes, where the goal is to ensure the building is always full of travelers, rather than focusing on it being full only during peak periods and making decisions based on those times. Once the facilities are at max capacity throughout the entirety of operating hours, we can then make large, sustainable fixed investments in infrastructure. Technological disruptions will push airport operators away from the "build it and they will come" model, thus ensuring the focus should be on breaking paradigms and shifting infrastructure investments away from the quantitative towards the qualitative value proposition. New ways of thinking will allow for new ways of hedging risk from the perspective of an airport operator, therefore allowing the airport infrastructure to complement the changes the technological era has brought and will bring to the industry.

How about a platform that leverages private $$$?

Another viable option for an airport operator to reduce risk and liability would be to focus on operating and expanding runways/taxiways/aircraft-maneuvering areas based on sustainable real-time demand. In the long run, and as technology makes aircraft and systems supporting aircraft more efficient, airport operators will not need to build longer runways or more taxiways. Aircraft will be able to land and take off at shorter distances and maneuver more quickly and swiftly. Airport operators will be able to do more with a skeleton runway system. Likewise, airports will be better positioned by renting land, so that private investors can fund hangars, roadways, terminal buildings, parking lots, shopping/showcase malls, hotels, and other infrastructure that is not tied to runways and taxiways. Under this platform, the airport would leverage its landmass as an economic enabler and empower investment entities to develop the airport lands. If there is money to be made, investment companies will find a way to fund the development. Another key benefit to the airport operator is that the airport's landmass can be built with other people's money; at the end of the day, whoever owns the dirt will own the assets upon expiration of the lease term. However, without losing sight, the original lease term would provide an ROI to the original investor, and the lease terms can always be extended based on additional capital being invested. This would allow the airport to be truly an economic enabler, as private sector funds would create jobs, economic activity, and investment opportunities; in short, the more money the private sector makes, the more they re-invest. This option would most certainly not be the most exciting for the airport operator, as this would reduce the airport operator's scope to operating runways and taxiways and renting land; most of the exciting and "sexy" things – route development, terminal expansions, setup of cargo operations, and so forth – would be done by other profit-driven entities. However, this option could be ideal for some airports and their regions in terms of organizational and regional prosperity.

Technology is changing fast, and so must we

If secondary airports can't innovate and create a value proposition that enables air carriers or technology companies to grow their airports, only the primary airports will continue to grow, leaving some secondary airports with no or very limited air service.

Airports and airlines will need to continue to embrace the technological changes as we move to a consumer-driven economy led by platforms such as Google, Facebook, Amazon, and others with data-rich platforms. End-to-end platforms will be the future. This will impact airlines, airports, and many others. End-to-end platforms will provide guests with more information; they will incorporate the entire journey: travel from home/office to the airport, the airport-processing time, the in-flight time, and travel to your ultimate destination. These platforms will continue to provide travelers with all the other goods or services they need as part of their travel experience. Travelers will continue to obtain real-time information on their trip (flight info, delays, directions, and so on). We are living in a world that is increasingly data-rich, and that information will be in the palm of your hand, or perhaps on an Internet-connected headpiece or watch.

If your airport doesn't make efforts to disrupt, your airport may be disrupted sooner than you think is possible.

Notes

1 A. Karp, "Analysis: Regional Airline CEO Says Pilot Shortage Getting Serious," *ATWonline.com*, 2017. Accessed April 25, 2017, from http://atwonline.com/opinions/analysis-regional-airline-ceo-says-pilot-shortage-getting-serious
2 Ibid.
3 *Hindu Business Line* Bureau, "DBS Bank Rolls Out Mobile-Only Bank in India," *The Hindu Business Line*, 2017. Accessed April 25, 2017, from www.thehindubusinessline.com/money-and-banking/dbs-launches-mobile-only-bank-in-india/article8523963.ece
4 "Forbes Welcome," *Forbes.com*. 2017. Accessed April 25, 2017, from www.forbes.com/sites/sethporges/2016/11/22/airbnbs-cofounder-opens-up-about-the-companys-new-experiences-features/#5e1e2b1a1444
5 S. Huntington, "How Tesla's Ridesharing Network Could Disrupt the Airline Industry," *TESLARATI.com*, 2017. Accessed April 25, 2017, from www.teslarati.com/tesla-ride-sharing-network-disrupt-airline-industry
6 "Norwegian Transatlantic 737 Flights to Begin in June," *Flightglobal.com*. 2017. Accessed April 25, 2017, from www.flightglobal.com/news/articles/norwegian-transatlantic-737-flights-to-begin-in-june-434464/
7 P. Sawers, "How Zunum Aero Plans to Revolutionize Air Travel With Electric Planes and Regional Airports," *VentureBeat*, 2017. Accessed April 25, 2017, from https://venturebeat.com/2017/04/05/how-zunum-aero-plans-to-revolutionize-air-travel-with-electric-planes-and-regional-airports
8 Ibid.

10   The changes and challenges affecting sales and distribution in the airline world

Trevor Spinks

Head of Sales and Distribution
Tigerair-Scoot

Thirty-plus years ago, if you asked people how many airline business models they could name, the answer would likely have been just one, the "full-service carrier" (FSC). The skies were ruled by BA, Singapore Airlines, American Airlines and the like. Ask that question today, and you are likely to get a range of answers, perhaps even into double figures. With models ranging from the traditional "full-service carrier" (FSC) through to the LCC, with a generous mix of hybrids in between. After the boom of the LCC, the LCC model was then further pushed to the extreme, by airlines such as Spirit in the US, with what is referred to as the "ultra-low-cost model" (ULCC).

The LCC business model also saw the LHLCC model prove itself a viable and profitable model just a few years ago. As with Scoot, Asia also has AirAsia and Jetstar running successful long-haul models. Interesting to note that AirAsia X was a natural step forward from AirAsia's short-haul model (also seen in Europe with Norwegian Air Shuttle) and both Scoot and Jetstar with FSC owners, Singapore Airlines and Qantas, respectively.

In the Singapore Airlines case, the reason for setting up Scoot was simple: to take on Jetstar and AirAsia which were slowly taking market share from them and eroding yields on overlapping routes. In Europe, while many would have thought EasyJet or Ryanair would be the first LCC to set up an LHLCC arm, it was Norwegian Air Shuttle that was the first, with Ryanair and EasyJet content to watch.

Perhaps the only certainty was that the airline business model was constantly changing, developing and merging to meet the ever-changing expectations and demands of the consumer. Technology had a significant part to play, for the consumer/sales channels as well as the aircraft itself. The aircraft was critical for the success of the LHLCC model, which prior to the likes of the Dreamliner had never succeeded. But now FSC airlines can shift loss-making routes to their LCC/LHLCC offspring and literally overnight see the loss become profit.

The now . . . copying the other guy, merging models and alliances

Full-service carriers now mimic many elements of the LCC model (realising the value of ancillary revenues, where a typical LCC would make 25% of the overall revenue). Singapore Airlines now charges for seat selection, or "preferred seat" as the airline calls it. A manager in Singapore Airlines would never have dared suggest this even just five years ago – it just wasn't the premium Singapore Airlines brand. But it's here and it's happening and likely to stay. And many more FSCs are following suit. The models are merging.

On the opposite side of the coin, LCCs now use distribution methods they would never have touched years ago (due to strict cost strategies), such as the GDS. When Scoot was set up, from the very start the sales strategy was to utilise all available channels as long as it is seen as incremental revenue. A far cry from the original LCC 100% web approach that helped the likes of EasyJet and Ryanair in their initial years.

As LCCs have grown, specifically when increasing route frequency, they have appealed more and more to the business traveller, especially those at small and medium businesses with a sharp focus on cost savings. EasyJet and Ryanair have had the schedules/frequency between major city pairs for years, enabling them to win share from BA specifically. This applies to pretty much all the top-tier cities. Tigerair in Singapore is another example, so it's not all about FSCs moving towards the LCC model.

No one can argue, though, that we are truly in the time of the LCC. The significant growth worldwide tends to come from the LCCs (admittedly many of these are owned by FSCs). It is the LCCs that are making capacity injections year-over-year and typically in double digits, while the parent airlines keep to a much more reserved growth strategy.

I see the birth of another airline model: the group model; for example, Singapore Airlines, SilkAir, Scoot and Tigerair. A group of four carriers with two in the LCC space and two in the FSC space but also covering short- and long-haul markets. But full integration will take some time, with different reservation systems—just one of the many areas to consider.

Sales channels

In the early days of air travel, consumers had very few choices, and those choices were really dictated to them. You had to walk into a store and book your holiday. Now, if an airline doesn't consider consumer behaviour, putting what consumers want first and how they want to shop, it is pretty much bye-bye to the sale. They will walk (or rather surf) to a competitor that offers what they need. So, an airline today must have a sharp strategy for each channel. For an international airline, this also needs to consider each and every country, because what works in one country will not necessarily work in the next country. In my role, I often say we need to get it right for each channel in each market. In a nutshell, if we focus too much effort on a channel that a market has little awareness of or penetration, it's a waste of time and effort. We need to understand the demand in each market (the same goes for payments; more on this later).

So, what are these channels? Web, mobile and API channels I will, of course, quote first due to my low-cost blood, but group sales, GDS, GSA and call centre are all in the mix. Any good airline today will be using all of these channels. There is no doubt. But I don't think senior airline managers can put their hand on their heart and say they are fully utilising and getting the best out of each and every one of these channels.

Web and mobile are of course well established. These are also continuously being re-worked and improved all the time, with many third-party improvement technology companies able to offer a seemingly endless supply of further optimisation tools and techniques. The hard thing is to figure out the good from the not so good.

The API channel has grown significantly in every market in which Scoot operates. Year-over-year percentage growth is in three figures, and by far it is the channel I see most growth as well as most future innovation occurring in. At Scoot, I split the "API" sales channel into three distinct areas.

A   Online travel agents (OTA), such as Expedia, Zuji and Ctrip. These are straightforward in that they are literally travel agent websites that sell our online fares/flights. They earn commission through confirmed bookings. OTAs have been around for a long time now; many have well-trusted brands and have grown to be truly global. They offer flights, hotels and car hire and, in more recent years, further expanded to attractions as they continue to cover pretty much everything.

B   Metasearchers, such as Skyscanner, Kayak and FareCompare. These are "search" websites that allow customers to search for and compare fares/flights between many different OTAs/airlines/hotels, etc. They do not make bookings directly (at least when they first set up) and refer the customer to the airline's website. They earn in one of two ways, either by "Cost-Per-Click" (CPC) when a customer clicks through from their website onto the airline's website, or by "Cost-Per-Acquisition" (CPA), once the booking is confirmed. No need to explain which of these payment methods makes the most commercial sense for the airline. I have seen the most innovation from the Meta players. They are already moving into the OTA space (more on that below with facilitated bookings).

C   Aggregators, such as Travelfusion. These are connected to various airlines and GDSs and serve as the distributors of the fares/flights to OTAs. They provide the connection and functionality to OTAs to book flights. Typically, OTAs with little or no technical background will approach an aggregator to help with the development work for the connection and very quickly have access to many airlines, hotels, etc.

APIs allow airlines to leverage well-known partners/brands on the other side of the world with next to no marketing spend, resulting in genuine incremental revenue. The downside being a higher cost than our own channels, but good negotiation should keep costs well within an acceptable range. As the API pool of partners ranges into the hundreds, the key is to work with the groups who deliver results and innovate. For example, Skyscanner's "facilitated booking" was thought through as a concept, commercials agreed upon and live all within six months, resulting in additional revenue for both Scoot and Skyscanner. But yes, this effectively moves the definition of Skyscanner from Meta to OTA. As I said, these groups innovate and are changing the game rapidly. Understanding and working closely with them will only benefit the airline and, importantly, result in additional revenue. It is also with API partners that the airlines are likely to make the most out of big data; the airlines continue to struggle with what they already have, let alone innovate using the unlimited possibilities big data can provide.

What does the future look like for the API channels? First the OTA. Their general importance and market share will only continue to increase in the short and medium term, but so will a) new competition, as barriers to market are low, b) competition from initially local OTAs expanding into foreign markets – for example, DeNA in Japan to Singapore, Ctrip of China to south-east Asia – these OTAs will eventually start fighting for the same customers. The metasearchers will also take share from the OTAs because they will become OTAs themselves – this is already happening. With Skyscanner.

Meta will be the fastest-growing API channel. But they need the consumer to believe in the advantage of metasearchers. This space is already turning into a two-horse race (but with separate local brands). Skyscanner (bought by Ctrip), Kayak and Momondo (bought by Priceline.com) have strong growth plans, as well as cash and technical expertise to support rapid growth. As the metasearchers strengthen their brands, their direct bookings will also grow, and, as already mentioned, they will merge into an OTA themselves. Ultimately there will be fewer and fewer differences between Meta and OTA (in e.g. the car rental market, there is already now no true Meta/OTA, only mixed players such as rentalcars. com). The joint OTA/metasearchers will focus more and more on the experience to differentiate themselves.

Aggregators will face a tough time. I cannot see where their future lies. Right now, there is a market for them, but the biggest OTAs/metasearchers will use direct connections to the airlines to save costs, so for now it is the smaller agents that aggregators will work with, if aggregators are smart. They will focus more and more on being an "alternative" to traditional GDS and focus on additional value (with payment to airlines to sell ancillaries). One day, when NDC is a truly viable option, the aggregators may cease to exist. But that's a long way off . . .

As for group sales, this channel has relatively low penetration in Europe but is huge in Asia. Yet there are very few technology solutions out there to help optimize this channel and automate what is effectively a straightforward demand on the consumer side.

GDS, the FSC's bread and butter, is being used more and more often by LCCs. One of the main reasons is that the GDS companies have moved with the times and have re-worked their offerings to the LCCs. Amadeus recently bought Navitaire and with this brought themselves into more than 60 LCCs that use the Navitaire reservation platform. Both Amadeus and Navitaire are also working on seamless ticketing to better serve their FSC and LCC clients. But this will take another few years at least.

Which brings us to GSA: general sales agents. When an airline moves into a new market, that airline has two options (sometimes also driven by regulation): a) set up a team from scratch or b) work with a GSA. The benefits of working with a GSA are instant understanding of the market and local intelligence, but at a higher cost and giving away part of your ticket sales. Typically, an LCC will use a GSA for the first few years then move to its own team once the airline better understands the market. However, FSCs will often work with a GSA for years, if not decades. While I don't see GSAs disappearing any time soon, it's becoming a less significant channel overall, and the older the airline the less reliant it will become on a GSA.

So, for anyone reading this, for your market, or multiple markets, have you got the right strategy per channel, by country? Because even if you have, and you feel on top of your market right now, the industry is fully expecting a truly coming-of-age experience in the not-so-distant future. The world-famous innovators Google, Amazon, Facebook, Alibaba, and Apple are already looking at the aviation industry; they certainly know and communicate with consumers better than any airline. They have more data and experience of using the data than any airline. What can the airlines do? To be honest, nothing. But certainly the airlines can work alongside these players, such as through Google Flights, which is a Meta API partner . . . for now.

Alliances

Low-cost alliances are coming. The FSC alliances – Star Alliance (1997), oneworld (1999) and SkyTeam (2000) – have been around for a while now, and although they certainly help build loyalty and, importantly, supply feeder traffic, very little has happened in the way of innovation. It seems they were all content with where things stood. The newly formed LCC alliances U-Fly and Value will certainly shake things up. Now it's the LCC's turn to look at alliances. The technology that allows LCCs to sell effectively one another's product bundles (always a complex issue to solve) has been developed over the last few years. This in fact led directly to Scoot founding the Value Alliance along with technology provider ABB. I'm certainly expecting to see big leaps in innovation in the LCC alliance space in the very near future.

ABB is primarily a technological sales and distribution platform that will allow consumers to book in one single itinerary flights from up to (currently) eight different LCCs directly from each airline partner's website. The technology overcomes the difficult areas of interlining and multi-carrier connectivity that exist behind the scenes and of course across different "passenger service systems" (PSSs), but also providing baggage alignment and mixed carriers as just two examples of additional benefits. But isn't that what the GDS does? Yes and no. The GDS does a very poor job of selling ancillaries, and this is where ABB delivers while other systems cannot. There are clear benefits for both airlines and the consumers. The airlines get a new platform to reach consumers not in their home markets (also a benefit of Meta/OTAs, and in this a future lower dependability on these channels). Feeder traffic will be generated from and to destinations they don't serve so as to keep passengers within the alliance rather than booking on other airlines. For the consumer, this means more destinations, more routing options and greater convenience in one seamless, connecting multi-leg journey without having to jump from website to website, making multiple bookings, payments and itineraries. The future will surely also provide a "manage my booking" functionality across all carriers simultaneously, as well as disruption management possibilities.

So why are LCCs looking now at alliances? Feeder traffic, cost reductions, less risk for new routes, improved traveller benefits. Both LCCs and LHLCCs are now often designing network plans around routes linked to feeder traffic; a passenger's profile could be as much as 50% or more connecting traffic. For example, Scoot's first move into Europe, in June 2017, was Athens. Could this route succeed based on just capacity from the population of Singapore (5.5 million)? Of course not. But linking this with its own Australian network was a significant part of the business case. Additional feeder traffic from surrounding countries via an alliance makes all the more sense.

In May 2016, Scoot and seven other airlines – the Philippines' Cebu Pacific, South Korea's Jeju Air, Thailand's Nok Air and NokScoot, Tigerair Singapore, Tigerair Australia and Japan's Vanilla Air – founded the Value Alliance, – the world's largest LCC alliance. It's still in the start-up stages, but it's truly an alliance formed by similar-thinking carriers. These carriers will supply passenger feed to each other's long- and short-haul networks.

The U-Fly Alliance was formed just a few months earlier, in January 2016. Founding members were HK Express, Lucky Air, Urumqi Air, and West Air. All four founding airlines are affiliated with the HNA Group, so clearly direction and strategy was coming from a group level. The fifth member, Eastar Jet, a South Korean low-cost carrier, joined the alliance in July 2016. The alliance currently focuses on Hong Kong, mainland China, and Southeast Asia and, like the Value Alliance, has huge potential to grow from both its own carriers as well as adding additional members.

Alliances within Europe? Certainly, EasyJet and Ryanair don't need this on their short-haul networks, but any carrier could see the benefits of linking up to such huge players, even just 1% of Ryanair's annual 120 million passengers means another 1.2 million passengers. It is hard to look at those types of figures and not want to be in the game. Norwegian is actively engaging both Ryanair and EasyJet to help support its long-haul network which will challenge the traditional and more established carriers. I can only see upside for all players if such an alliance can be formed – time will tell.

So LCC alliances will grow as both Value and U-Fly seek new members across Asia and then likely across the globe, and for sure loyalty schemes within such alliances will be hugely popular as well as revenue generating of a very small cost base. It is the LCCs that are more nimble, and it is the LCCs that turned aviation on its head, so I fully expect we have seen but a glimpse of what is to come in the LCC alliance space.

Merging models

Is an FSC/LCC alliance in the cards? Or perhaps it's best to refer to what I'll call the "group" model. This isn't really news, and it's already happening with Qantas and Jetstar, Singapore Airlines and Scoot and many more FSC/LCC carriers. An FSC "parent" invests/starts up an LCC to compete with existing LCCs so that the FSC can at least retain market share through the LCC.

What is extremely interesting is Singapore Airlines' current group strategy. On the premium business model side, Singapore Airlines and SilkAir are well established, with SilkAir's short-haul network connecting to Singapore Airlines' long-haul network and vice versa. They use the same reservation systems and same technologies (SilkAir employees even have Singapore Airlines email addresses). The strategy works; in fact, feeder traffic is critical on many routes that would otherwise not be viable.

But LCCs came along and took market share, then a little more, and more and more and more.

In 2004, Singapore Airlines responded by creating Tigerair Singapore, with an aim to compete with the LCCs. However, the years were far from kind for the Tigerair brand, seeing several brand extensions and partnerships all end in failure. 2007 saw Tigerair Australia launch, but that subsidiary now is 100% owned by Virgin (how long before this becomes Virgin?). 2007 also saw Tigerair Philippines fail to launch due to poor operational conditions. In 2012, Tigerair Mandala launched, but it ceased operations two years later. 2014 saw Tigerair Taiwan launch with the major stakeholder China Air, but Tigerair have now sold all remaining shares to China Air (will this Tigerair brand remain?). Finally, even Tigerair Singapore disappeared in 2017 when Scoot and Tigerair merged into just Scoot. The point I make is it is not easy getting one brand/model right, so how and why will the Singapore Airlines "group" model work?

So the Singapore "group" model will consist of Singapore Airlines (long haul), SilkAir (short haul) and Scoot (both long and short haul); this means they cover both the FSC and LCC/LHLCC in the market. But the plans don't stop there. The future will see full cross-selling across all the group's airlines, joint loyalty and many more areas that will make the consumer experience as seamless as possible (with just the small matter of different reservation systems to overcome). But you get the picture of what a group model could look like. In fact, it's already here, in its infancy, but with big plans to improve and grow.

What does this mean to the airline and to the consumer? For the airline, it means all airlines will sell each other's destinations. It means shared distribution costs as well as resources, simplification of settlements, feeder traffic across the whole group, joint sales incentives to OTAs and agents. . .the list goes on.

But, importantly, for the consumer it means seamless booking across multiple carriers, through check-in to destination as well as through checked bags. Cheaper pricing (rather than a standard sum of sectors approach, there can be well-thought-out OD pricing (origin/destination)), improved use of hub airports, shorter connection times and a loyalty programme that's effective across all the airlines in the group.

A last thought: an explosion in payments

For the consumer, payment isn't sexy; it just needs to be efficient, quick and easy. For a long time, it's been all about the debit and credit card. PayPal was one of the first "alternative payment methods" (APMs) in the early 2000s, and, for many years, it had little competition. Any international airline would of course have been aware of the local/unique forms of payment specific to countries that they flew to, and, hopefully, invested in ensuring the payment methods in question could be accepted. All it took was some local knowledge and some technical skills to set up the payment method. Overall, the payments area was something relatively straightforward and easy to set up for an airline.

Skip to the present day. We see that Scoot flies to 20 different countries, each now has several APMs, (let's, for argument's sake, say five significant payment channels per country). That's now 100 different payment methods, and a hell of a lot more complex to manage, track and set up. But, if you don't offer a payment type that a particular consumer wants, that consumer might go to your competitor. So, in this rapidly expanding area, there will be significant workload and complexity just to ensure that consumers are offered the method of payment they want to use.

In Europe, an airline that accepts direct debit and credit cards can be confident they are providing at least 90% of the population with a simple and easy way to pay. But in Asia this is far from the case. In Indonesia, for example, in 2014 only 36% of adults had bank accounts, only 7% had ever made an online payment, and only 2% had credit cards. For a population of over 250 million people, that leaves a lot of alternative payment methods to be desired. Currently in Indonesia this mostly involves cash. But in a country where there are 115 phone subscriptions for every 100 people (yet mobile payments are less than 0.1% for people with phone subscriptions), you would be foolish not to expect that changes are coming. It's only a question of when.

11   Shifting from asset management to customer value while building a new speed into the business

Chris Stevens

Managing Partner
Digital Frontier Partners, Melbourne Australia

Robin Barlass

Director of Corporate Services
Metro Trains, Melbourne Australia

Airlines and other companies, such as railways, airports and power utilities, have, over decades, had to invest in and maintain large-scale assets to operate their businesses. Despite the dramatic changes digitisation has brought about, the approach to creating value from large and often distributed assets used by these organisations is yet to fundamentally change. The digital era has made it possible for many businesses with large assets to use digital channels to connect and ultimately transact with customers. Although there is nothing wrong with this, often the lure of digital channels can overshadow the opportunities to create more value per dollar spent on the large assets used by the businesses. The money invested in asset lifecycle management out-numbers the money spent on digital channels by a considerable multiple. We are not saying that businesses should forget digital channels; rather, we suggest that there is significant opportunity to focus on leveraging more value from physical assets at the same time as investing in new digital value chains.

Large physical assets, such as car parks, trains, operational control systems, terminals and planes, all play a role in creating value for a customer. However, how these assets are used and maintained may not be optimally aligned to creating the highest possible customer value. In this paper, we will discuss challenges and approaches observed from working with various large-asset businesses, as well as the experiences of Metro Trains Melbourne in transforming to a digitally enabled business. Metro Trains is the franchised operator of the suburban railway network in Melbourne, Australia. It operates a fleet of 420 three-car train sets on 869 kilometres of track. There are sixteen regular service train lines and one special events train line. The train fleet travels over 30 million kilometres and provides more than 233 million customer boardings each year, over 14,000 services each week, and carries over 415,000 passengers each weekday. Metro Trains Melbourne is also responsible for 218 railway stations and employs a workforce of 5,000 rail professionals, including train drivers, mechanical and electrical engineers, network operations specialists and customer service representatives.

In a world where customers increasingly tangibly discern value, they can more easily seek out best value (with little effort, thanks to the power of the internet). Simply put, those organisations not demonstrating best value will be overtaken by those that do. Using the premise that a business exists only if it creates value that someone wants, the risks and opportunities are higher in today's environment than we have ever seen. The use of software and information, pervasive networks and smart devices allows almost anyone to create a value proposition for a consumer, on a larger scale than before.

Therefore, the urgency for established businesses to create more customer value is high, particularly if businesses are to remain relevant over the long term. Unlocking new levels of customer value from existing assets represents a significant opportunity for business growth, and recent technological advancements – in sensors, analytics and operational control systems – can help. Combine this with faster agile practices, and the ability to measure results and then adjust quickly – the means to maximise customer value – is theoretically easier than ever.

In the pre-digital 'industrialised' world, the settings for business were thought to be known patterns, and those achieving stand-out results (relative to their peers) were called 'best practice'. In a fast-moving connected world which thrives on disruptive change and innovation, a best-practice blueprint seems to have much less value. The focus on creating customer value is about understanding customers' needs and quickly adapting to provide value – somewhat akin to flying a rocket to the moon and being on course only 3% of the time, constantly course-correcting to deal with the myriad of variables.

The processes, systems, organisational model, culture, KPIs and style of decision making in a well-established organisation are a powerful force of control and containment. The interlock created by these characteristics requires an incredible force of change to make it into something else. An operational mind-set combined with short-term rewards can deny the organisation the space needed to create faster-moving digital practices that can unlock additional business and customer value. As a consequence, opportunities to extract more value from key assets are often not maximised.

A new style of organisation within the established business is needed to support a continuum of change (occurring at unpredictable and varying speeds) which does not disrupt the value that is still being produced by the well-established parts of the business. Throughout this chapter, we will share examples of how Metro Trains Melbourne addressed these challenges.

The tension between current constraints and the need to grow value

What's the predictable future if we don't sufficiently address this?

Any time large organisations try to plan improvements to their business model, some of the most senior leaders may struggle to comprehend the need to significantly refocus their business model for a different future. Perhaps it is an unconscious bias (but sometimes it can be conscious too). The bias sounds something like "We continue to be successful – we have a large customer base, a great brand. Revenues are good, and our strategy is well considered, so where's the burning platform?"

The problem with that mind-set is that it filters out the reality that the organisation is increasingly under threat from new service and product offers being presented to their customers, often by non-traditional competitors (e.g. a supermarket that offers insurance and credit cards!). Add in factors such as "We really don't know our customers as individuals, so we provide a generalised service offer", and the risk of the organisation losing its relevance to consumers increases.

When we take this all-too-common scenario into consideration and ask, "What is the predictable future if we do not embrace sufficient change?" in many cases the answer can reflect an absence of vision, an opinion in favour of the status quo. At Metro Trains Melbourne, though, we recognised the need to adapt our business model by digitising core aspects of the business. The approach to digitising the railway was not primarily just focused on direct customer value from customer-facing products or platforms. At an early stage in the development of the digital strategy, we also saw indirect opportunities from an internal perspective to enable and release capacity in the workforce to create more customer value from the resources we already possessed. Like many existing large and asset-heavy businesses, Metro Trains was stooped in clunky, onerous and time-consuming manual and paper-based processes built up over many decades. The adoption of apps and digital tools – for example, smart devices and automated workflow management – relieved the workforce of hours spent doing administration and reporting and redirected labour resources to more hands-on customer-facing interaction, to benefit the customer.

The connected consumer represents a massive opportunity for an organisation's focus and growth opportunities

Customers increasingly want it to be easy to find and use products and services aligned with their individual needs. Businesses that can master this are likely to attract more customers and often end up being class leaders. The connected consumers of today are more knowledgeable and can quickly research and compare many different data sets to inform their choices and hence purchase decisions. Once a supplier-consumer relationship has been formed and customer expectations have been met consistently over time, trust develops and other avenues can be opened for suppliers and service providers to generate additional forms of value for that customer. Some of which can then be commercialised and monetised as new revenue streams.

Many organisations limit their approach to addressing customer needs by not sufficiently leveraging what they can provide

The power of marketing and the influences from vendors can create an attraction to focus on the new tools of digitisation (e.g. moving data to the cloud, mobile apps, an improved website experience or even digital marketing campaigns that target the needs of customers as individuals). Although this is all relevant and necessary, a big component of the value equation often gets overlooked – the role of existing assets in creating customer value and business value. So, although investing in incremental digital capability is critical, a more balanced focus to consider key assets and their role in providing value to customers is equally critical.

'While frontline monetization opportunities tend to get the headlines, often the biggest, near-term gains are operational in nature. Data optimization helps reduce inefficiency.'

A McKinsey survey of more than 700 organisations worldwide found that spending money on analytics to gain competitive intelligence on future market conditions, to target customers more successfully, and to optimize operations and supply chains generated operating-profit increases by 6%.

In a recent conversation with one of us (the authors), an executive at a major bank in Australia said that, in an effort to become more customer-centric, the bank had recently hired a former Silicon Valley executive, and each area of the bank was being challenged to use digital practices, tools and channels more effectively to get closer to the customer. When asked a key question: "Out of your total budget for operating and changing the business, what percentage does the existing base-business consume?" he replied that they "spend something like 90% largely operating and maintaining the current business". Because the existing capabilities of assets such as processes, technology and people are what provides the services today, the greatest leverage for growing value should come from optimising *these*. If businesses focus mainly on the new digital layers, almost certainly they will be overlooking the larger-scale value that can be unlocked.

The style of many large established organisations is biased towards a 'control and operate' focus

Typical transport businesses have a significant focus on their assets. After all, it is the physical assets from which the service is provided. Transport businesses tend to be rich in assets but not good at aligning these assets for an integrated customer experience. The operating rhythm of these businesses, most of which were created in the industrial era, is heavily geared towards a 'control and operate' philosophy and is very much focused on operating these assets safely and efficiently to a predefined set of standards and service levels. From a risk-management and regulatory perspective, there is an absolute need to maintain this strict 'command and control' approach (let's call the existing business model Mode 1) to these elements of the business; however, the challenge facing transport operators is to understand that the fast-paced modern world of connected consumers will not allow organisations to continue to just operate at this slower speed or mode. Consumers want more value, and they want it quicker and often personalised to their needs. From our observations, leaders must understand and recognise that there are elements of every heavy-asset-focused business that require a different operating rhythm to thrive and create greater customer value (let's call this faster moving style of business Mode 2).

This then shifts the overall business focus from just managing assets to focusing on the areas where these two speeds (Mode 1 and Mode 2) come together and to integrating new customer value into the architecture of day-to-day operations. Commercialisation and monetisation can then follow.

Reassessing how you create value from your assets now becomes critical

Customers use the business's assets, yet we do not regularly and consciously link assets to 'customer experience' and 'customer value'. Changing the way we look at customers' needs through analysing how they use the assets can lead to adapting the use of assets to create new value for them.

Adopting a value-chain approach to the way in which strategic directions for a business are set makes the business think differently from the traditional vertical-asset view and shifts it to a horizontal view that looks across the business end-to-end and puts the customer at the center. This opens opportunities that may not have been noticed in the more straightforward asset-centric view. In a value-chain approach, divisions and departments look to their groups' contribution to the end customer result and how they can deliver a better set of outputs to the department/division downstream and create new customer value.

New digital business models and capabilities are challenging many company leaders with 'what it takes' to keep their organisations safe while continuing to grow customer and business value

The last decade has introduced profound changes that impact both our personal and our professional lives at the same time. "Smart" devices, fast broadband nearly everywhere, low-cost cloud computing, an abundance of low-cost or free apps, massive computational power available to anyone affordably – the list goes on. However, most senior executives learned their craft in the pre-digital era and have grown their careers within an industrialised business paradigm, which we refer to as Mode 1 (previously described). So, what does 'industrialised' mean in contrast to the digital world we are now in?

One way to look at the industrial and digital paradigms is to contrast the differences:

Industrial paradigm	Digital paradigm
Operational excellence	⟵⟶ Personalisation
Financial might	⟵⟶ Customer value over profit
Physical assets	⟵⟶ Software is the new tool set
Process driven	⟵⟶ Subscription models
Large employee base	⟵⟶ Leverage someone else's scale
High barriers to compete	⟵⟶ Low barriers to compete
Regulated industries	⟵⟶ Customer service over process
Control of the market	⟵⟶ Anyone can innovate

Figure 7.9 Industrial vs. digital paradigm

The digital era has a range of alternate and, to some extent, opposing characteristics for creating customer and business value. These new capabilities are challenging many company leaders to figure out 'what it takes' to keep their organisations safe and growing.

In a recent discussion with one of us, the CIO of a global materials manufacturer remarked that 'digital' is simply a buzzword and that the core business challenges still relate to getting the enterprise technology capabilities matured and doing their job well. He explained that the core technology such as the ERP systems and other enterprise technology all needed to play a role supporting supply-chain optimisation as well as order and supply management. He is partly right, in that the technology that powers the well-established (Mode 1) enterprise is more critical than ever, but it is also now part of an extended ecosystem where the internal enterprise technology must now interact with those technologies that engage with customers and suppliers in the outside world (Mode 2).

These two paradigms (industrial and digital) coexist, and we are in a transition period like none before. There is no roadmap, no blueprint or executive guide on how to lead a business across these coexisting paradigms or this bimodal approach. If we assume most senior leaders know that business must create value that someone wants (and is willing to pay for), then why does the transition from being an industrialised business to a digitally enabled one seem to be so slow?

Most often, rewards and incentives are short-term-focused, which tends to not influence leaders to change the status quo very much. Many executives still expect evidence on how changes can deliver assured success strategically before they commit to those changes. Ironically, most of the seismic shifts in business today are breaking ground with new business models and fundamentally different thinking on how value can be created for customers, so there simply is not the body of evidence yet in a way that will be familiar to experienced executives. Success for leaders in this new paradigm requires a willingness to accept that a bimodal business approach is no longer an option.

In most large, well-established businesses, there is a gravitational pull towards long-held enterprise practices

If we expand on this industrial-to-digital paradigm and the situation of most senior leaders in large organisations having come from the pre-digital era, it comes as no surprise that their bias is towards what they are familiar with and have therefore been successful with up to this point. Unfortunately, these biases can limit access to new or emerging practices, where customer value can be created through using software and information in conjunction with traditional business models. The challenge is to find a place for both Mode 1 (industrial/traditional) and Mode 2 (digital) to coexist and generate value in alignment with each other and at the same time, to some extent, independently from each other.

As confusing as that sounds, it stands to reason that the service or product offer to the customer needs to be as seamless as possible; however, the internal mechanisms of control and creativity are often in conflict. The different speeds which the traditional business model/Mode 1 uses for control versus the faster-moving 'discovery'-oriented practices which come from the digital/Mode 2 parts of the organisation do not align. Metro Trains Melbourne has its roots as a heavy-asset business, and prior to embarking on a digital transformation it was fully a Mode 1 business. Later in this paper, we will describe how the faster-moving Mode 2 capability was introduced.

To illustrate the contrast between traditional and faster-moving delivery approaches, let us look at two project-delivery mechanisms – 'waterfall' and 'agile' – that are well recognised in many businesses. Figures 7.9 and 7.10 demonstrate the contrast in these mechanisms. Traditional organisation approaches can tend to be biased towards a waterfall approach, whereas some styles of work could be delivered faster and more cost-effectively using an agile approach.

When we contrast this with an agile delivery approach which assumes we cannot know what the customer wants or will value, an iterative approach is used to 'discover' where the optimum value can be created within the investment and resourcing constraints.

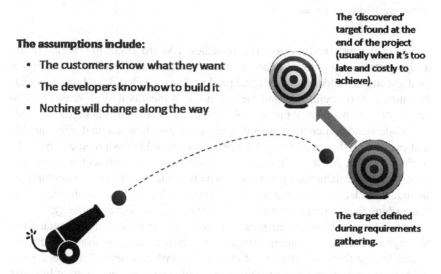

Figure 7.10 Traditional (waterfall) delivery has been compared to firing a cannonball

In this illustration, traditional delivery models are very 'plan and assumption' dependent, yet when used for a discovery situation, key value may be missed.

Source: Digital Frontier Partners Pty Ltd

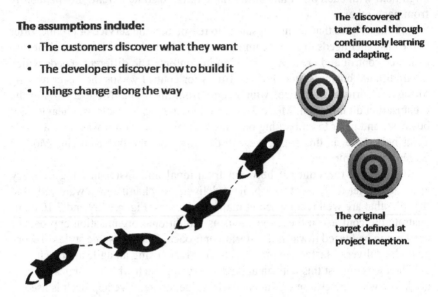

The assumptions include:

- The customers discover what they want
- The developers discover how to build it
- Things change along the way

The 'discovered' target found through continuously learning and adapting.

The original target defined at project inception.

Figure 7.11 Agile practices have been compared to a guided missile

This illustration shows that value is identified within a 'discovery' approach, using iterations to 'course correct' the path to value as learnings from the customer are captured progressively.

Source: Digital Frontier Partners Pty Ltd

One of the early and successful approaches at Metro Trains in bringing to life a digital strategy was to introduce a suite of internal sub-branding for its digital strategy and the underpinning digital product lines. Leaders found that by creating internal sub-brands that had their own visual identity and 'look and feel' in conjunction with an 'art of the possible' video, staff could quickly digest the strategy, understand and compartmentalise ideas and functionality, and align quickly and easily with the various product lines. This created its own momentum in the business, so that when staff came up with continuous improvement or innovation ideas of a digital nature, they were able to point to the sub-brands – "Shouldn't we include that idea in sub-brand X's development/build out"? Suddenly Metro was not pushing the strategy; internally, the business was pulling the strategy.

Once Metro had broader business buy-in to plot the path to implementation of the digital strategy, its leaders shifted their minds to the organisational design. It was known that the build-out of the digital platforms needed to operate at a different organisational cadence but co-exist alongside the heavy-asset business units. So, a separate business unit was established the sole purpose of which was to build out the digital strategy and product lines and operate in Mode 2 whilst the rest of the business continued to operate in Mode 1 delivering train services. At this point, it is worth noting Mode 1 included the traditional IT business unit that was transacting at a service level.

To set up the Mode 2 operation for success, product-management and product-development functions were built into the design that would work with the business in a partnership to build out the digital products and prioritise the features; product management being the link between the Mode 1 and Mode 2 worlds. Whilst this is nothing new and arguably is straightforward agile software development, the difference was that it was set up to co-exist within a Mode 1–style organisation.

An incremental approach to change where a fundamental approach is required

The quest for growing customer value and business value is one where the time taken plays a crucial role. If they take too long to adapt in an effort to remain relevant, organisations will be faced with an increasing risk of disruption or some form of erosion of value. A mind-set in which past successes are assumed to provide some certainty of a predictable future, often characterised by a change appetite which is at best 'incremental', is no longer good for the business. Because digitisation has created a new level of speed, for significant parts of the business model the question of 'incremental' to 'fundamental' change is critical. For large asset-based businesses, it is easy to focus on the 'big iron' and engineering aspects which are still critical; however, with each passing day, as in the 'boiling frog' analogy, the risk of value loss and disruption increases. In other words, a 'wash, rinse, repeat' approach to business could lead to irrelevance.

In Metro Trains, the consideration for 'fundamental' change was not confused with 'big bang' change in which there is a dramatic event, such as a switch to a new system or channel. Instead, leaders thought about how key parts of the business model could create additional value. A change-continuum mind-set was adopted, but it involved some areas of the model needing a 'reset' to establish the necessary enablers and capitalise on quick wins.

The customer decides what 'customer value' is

Customer value comes from a customer's personal definition of value, not what organisations choose to define for them. Being able to observe, measure and learn from customers in how they consume services can inform an extended value proposition from optimal asset management aligned to customer experience. In large heavy-asset businesses, customer value can be obscure. It can easily get lost between metrics such as 'mean distance between failure' and 'on-time running'. Whilst these are key measures of any reliable transport offering and represent the customer's known and stated needs for an on-time service offering, it is not enough in today's modern world when trying to meet evolving customer needs.

In Metro Trains Melbourne, the train, for example, is beginning to play a primary role in the overall customer experience. By giving a train an intelligent digital backbone, we have changed it from a moving 'steel tube' to an intelligent vehicle which can interact with customers as well as the environment that keeps the train operating (i.e. tracks, signals, electrical networks and the maintenance depot). This opens many opportunities to provide additional customer value such as:

- Observing customers' travel patterns, such as time of day travelled, origin, and destination, in real time to predict and optimise right-time departures and reduce station dwell times.
- Catering for additional services by running trains closer together.
- Predicting seating levels by car to point passengers to less-occupied carriages.
- Providing prior notification for special-needs-customer train access.
- Piping real-time disruption information straight from the customer-control centre into the carriage through handheld apps and the ability to provide direct compensation at the point of disruption.
- Providing predictive advice to the driver regarding conditions on the route, helping the driver to stay on schedule and reach the destination using the least amount of energy.
- Enabling passengers to locate people within their social networks who may be travelling on their train.
- Providing a safety and security presence at the press of a button.

Suddenly the train now becomes a vehicle for additional customer value that can be personalised at an individual customer level.

Considering this as the on-board train experience, and merged with a complementary on-station experience that includes WiFi, retail grocery shopping, parcel pickup and dry cleaning to name a few, the end-to-end customer value increases significantly. Imagine, for instance, that you could order the ingredients for your family dinner whilst on the station platform in the city and the order would be bagged and ready for collection at your destination station on the way home.

Ultimately time itself becomes the currency in which we exchange value. Convenience has and continues to be a significant driver of customer value. Most people are time-poor, and Metro Trains customers on average spend an hour of their day travelling with us. That is one hour as a captive audience and for which there are numerous opportunities to add value to their lives in a time that is otherwise unproductive. The opportunities are just enormous, but it takes a critical shift in mind-set to see the possibilities.

Metro Trains has a major focus on delivery and on-time running of services on its network. This is the key driver of customer satisfaction; however, there are many layers and facets to achieving consistent on-time running results. For example, there are a significant number of resources, assets, actions and events that need to be orchestrated in a sequence and all hold true to prepare a train for service ahead of its day of operation.

Early in the insights and analytics phase of the development of the product roadmap for one of the Metro product lines, it was evident that there was a significant opportunity to improve the customer experience through the service-delivery metric by improving and streamlining the preparation of the assets (trains) ahead of their first service run. By running an automated workflow across the process and having different resources interact with that workflow in the required sequence and within the time permitted for the task, and through digital enablement, it is possible to draw conclusions as to the value a consistent train preparation would deliver to the delivery metric and therefore cascade to an improved customer satisfaction metric.

A new mind-set and new approach are needed

Software and information have quickly become the most powerful means of exchanging value – like never been seen before

The means to create and grow business and customer value has been supercharged, given the power of software and the computational power for data analysis in recent years. Low-cost or free mobile and web apps, sophisticated software robotics, machine learning, chat bots, guided reality and more have unlocked a new order of human-to-machine capability. When this is further coupled with access to vast sources of data and use of data science, new forms of customer and business value are possible.

The speed at which these capabilities have evolved has been faster than most organisations can absorb and therefore adapt sufficiently to take advantage of. The situation for many companies, particularly large-asset companies, is that there is no safe middle ground. An organisation is either sufficiently moving ahead to take advantage of these new capabilities or is not and therefore, in a fast-moving competitive world, is falling behind!

Becoming an adaptive organisation

The Adaptive Organisation Manifesto in Figure 7.12 lists some characteristics that an adaptive organisation *has more of* and certain characteristics that it *has less of* compared to a non-adaptive organisation. The manifesto is styled similarly to the

An adaptive organisation is **more** of...	An adaptive organisation is **less** of...
• People being collaborative and self managing their own work to achieve outcomes.	• People working in a highly process-oriented environment where compliance is favoured over customer value and creativity.
• A healthy balance between Lean/Agile delivery practices and waterfall methods.	• A predominantly serialised delivery model with gated controls.
• A culture which holds client value and experience central to everything it does.	• A culture which is primarily shareholder and financially driven.
• An environment where leaders foster collaboration and innovation day to day.	• An environment where leaders are predominantly control and hierarchy oriented.
• Leverages modern technologies to gain a competitive advantage and speed.	• Takes a predominantly cost-minimised approach to technology investment.

Figure 7.12 Adaptive organisation manifesto

Source: Digital Frontier Partners Pty Ltd

Agile Manifesto (created in 2001 for agile software development) and aims to show a spectrum of behaviours where adaptive traits can be more or less.

In the case of Metro Trains Melbourne, the manifesto is being used by key leaders to communicate how the new digital approach is being styled. The manifesto does not intend to demonstrate right and wrong, but creates a realisation that different traits should be a conscious bias in how the organisation is designed to function.

Adaptive organisations reflect the traits of leadership that envision the future, inspire workers and shape the characteristics of the organisation to achieve its purpose. The culture is often 'by design' and therefore values the adaptive traits listed in the table above. As Charles Darwin said, "It is not the strongest of the species that survive, nor the most intelligent, but the one most responsive to change". Metro Trains Melbourne's digital transformation recognises the need to be not just an operating business, but an adaptive one as well.

Our observations show, though, that the path to fundamental organisational change is not just about having a model and a strategy. Above all else, it is a leadership challenge and one that requires courageous and visionary leadership. This is a challenge for top management, given the variety of conflicting forces to deal with in any large company. Without such leadership, the fundamental changes needed often cannot occur.

In 2014, Metro Trains Melbourne started to see the value technology could play in enabling its business strategy, but it needed something to start to shift its workers' mind-sets from an asset and operational culture towards one that had the customer at the centre and technology as the key enabler. A video was designed to start the conversation, create the momentum and explore the 'art of the possible' to digitising the railway. It put forward a view of the future of what the railway could become by leveraging technology for a better customer experience. The video was emotive and brought the strategy to life. Staff could engage more easily at any level in the organisation on the technology strategy. The possibility-led thinking broke through constraints and enabled staff and stakeholders to connect with the 'art of the possible'. Quite often in a larger and heavily regulated industry such as public transport it can become easy (almost as an unconscious bias) to come from a constraints perspective when assessing new concepts. The video broke through that and opened a discussion on how to make it happen rather than the barriers to getting there.

Being an adaptive organisation requires changes to the 'human system'

Metro Trains Melbourne realised that to become an adaptive and faster-moving organisation, the 'human system' was integral to the change. Although aligning the human system of the railway is a continuous change effort, certain enablers needed to be established. A Digital Services Unit (DSU) was established and holds the key skills needed inside the organisation to guide and align the key areas of the business. The DSU specialises in designing and co-creating changes to low-level operating models, labour models, use of digital tools, measures and how to introduce 'Mode 2' locally within teams.

An example of this was getting customer-service staff to feel comfortable with the use of "smart" devices to help them perform key tasks, such as supporting customers with train-arrival details as well as disruption information. In early attempts to roll out smart devices, it was discovered that the take-up by staff was inconsistent, and, in some cases, staff did not want to change from traditional work practices and were reluctant to use the device. Recognising that there is a wide span of age groups in Metro's workforce and therefore differing levels of aptitude for using technology such as smart phones, Metro Trains has developed a more proactive engagement approach, with representative groups who also became the early adopters and therefore the advocates for digital change locally. The central teams, such as the DSU, engaged with the local teams and, using a collaborative approach, agreed on the success criteria and steps to realise new value from digital change.

In addition to this collaborative approach, a capability to develop digital products was also introduced, and this formalised the disciplines of product management and product development central to Metro. Expertise from the commercial software industry was leveraged to help define these capabilities and the roadmap to embed them into Metro. The centralised and localised digital-team practices work in alignment to help deploy new digital solutions and practices and ensure the best possible alignment to staff expectations.

Extracting more value from assets, both customer value and business value

What was once considered to be only concrete and steel, possibly integrated with some form of control system logic (e.g. a car park or a train station), should no longer be considered as just a fixed asset. The introduction of sensors, WiFi, centralised control systems and real-time automation has enabled a means to extract more value from these assets. If we assume that an asset must perform more than its basic function (e.g. in the case of a car park, a space for cars to be parked), it must now play a role in contributing to both customer value and business value.

From a customer-value viewpoint, the value from a car park, as an example, may include that it is easily found online when people are searching for parking options and that it has ease of access, wide parking bays, competitive pricing, vacant space indicators, valet service, car wash service, etc. Knowing what customers value requires measurement and analysis. Measurement can be collected from environmental sensors to determine what parts of the car park are most sought after for convenience. Once customer preferences are clearer, a loyalty relationship can be created by offering things customers value.

Similarly, from an asset perspective, measuring utilisation levels, yield, maintenance and renewal costs helps determine the level of value the asset contributes. In the context of supporting the customer journey (directly and indirectly), a new perspective of value can be determined that each asset should seek to fulfil. If the utilisation of an asset is too low, or if the yield of income to pay for that asset is insufficient, then there is a dilution of business value. In developing an IT strategy in 2016, a major Australian airport identified a key opportunity to use sensors, analytics and the airport-control system to maximise passenger throughput. The assets involved were road access for vehicles, parking, and passenger flow in terminals through to aircraft boarding. The review team found that most of the capabilities were already in place; they were just not linked, monitored and managed for optimal passenger flow.

Similarly, when we look at the lifecycle costs of key assets, are we measuring maintenance and renewal investment based on utilisation, wear and tear or projected failure rates? All too often, maintenance can be applied based on a schedule of activities, regardless of the real maintenance needs of the asset. Using well-targeted measures, use of situation data from sensors, data science logic and analytics platforms allows for a more targeted approach to maintenance investment.

Conclusion

The approach to maximising value from large assets is often misunderstood or left unaddressed. Although digital tools can help organisations to connect, learn about and ultimately transact with customers, they can also enable organisations to extract more value from large assets.

In a fast-moving world, the connected consumer represents a significant opportunity to align assets and create greater levels of business and customer value than ever before; however, failure to address these gaps may leave organisations vulnerable to disruption and reduced relevance over time.

The style of most large established organisations created in the industrial era is biased towards a 'control and operate' focus, and many of these organisations have yet to identify how to create new levels of business and customer value through leveraging digital business models in conjunction with their long-established business capabilities. Many of these capabilities are centred on asset operation and management. The opportunities and risks in today's fast-moving environment are challenging many company leaders to determine 'what it takes' to keep their organisations safe while continuing to grow customer and business value.

Adopting an incremental approach to change, where a fundamental approach is required, can have severe strategic consequences in that the organisation may not sufficiently adapt in time and instil the maturity of capabilities needed to compete against those organisations that do get it right. Ultimately, the customer decides what customer value is, and software and information have quickly become the most powerful means of measuring customer needs and exchanging value beyond what industrialised business models can achieve alone.

Establishing new settings to balance the existing business model (Mode 1) and faster-moving digital capabilities (Mode 2) requires organisations to become more adaptive or bi-modal. Once this starts to occur, each organisation's natural, and to some extent, organic abilities will allow it to maintain alignment with the changing needs of the environment within which it operates. For large asset-based businesses, extracting more value from assets should be inextricably linked with addressing customer needs. When this alignment occurs, both customer value and business value can increase. When coupled with a more adaptive workforce model, driving even greater levels of business and customer value at greater speed is not just possible but should become the new business norm.

12 The evolving paradigm of interactive selling based on consumer preferences

B. Vinod

Chief Scientist / Senior Vice President
Research
Sabre Corporation

Overview

Demanding customers who have high expectations for personalized services is the new reality in today's competitive marketplace. Successful customer experiences are a fundamental driver for revenue growth for travel suppliers, such as airlines, hotels, rental cars and cruise lines. Customer loyalty can never be taken for granted, and insight into customer preferences in order to tailor offers has never been more important. The evolving paradigm of travel-product sales is advancing at a rapid pace, with a focus on displaying relevant content to a traveler during the shopping and booking process for a segment of one! Attracting and retaining profitable customers requires combining competitive market knowledge with consumer insights mined from structured and unstructured data to make the shopping and booking process effortless and memorable for a customer with relevant, targeted offers. Generating targeted, relevant offers is rapidly becoming crucial with the growth in adoption of chatbots and mobile, where screen real estate is at a premium.

To get closer to their customers and promote brand loyalty, travel suppliers need to understand customer preferences and purchase behavior patterns to better serve them across all channels of distribution. Toward this end, suppliers are investing in advanced analytics to understand customer traits, behaviors and preferences to support customer acquisition, maximize revenue generation potential from the customer base, and retain the most profitable customers. Conventional structured data sources such as booking and ticketing data can be augmented with the real-time collection and analysis of unstructured data such as shopping data, demographic data, survey data and social media data from virtual communities and travel sites to gain customer insights. Advanced analytics are then used to segment and target customers with relevant offers. Traditional statistical analysis can be complemented with natural-language processing of user-generated content, neural networks, machine learning and deep-learning techniques employed by data scientists. To enable customers with targeted options, new-generation applications collect information from customers in real time. Analytics has advanced from descriptive analytics to predictive analytics (what will happen) to prescriptive analytics (recommending options).

As an example, offer management has gone through this evolution. First came the data collection and visualization of airline ancillary sales data as a result of the unbundling of airline fares. This was followed by predictive modeling to forecast the sale of ancillaries by type and segment. Today we have augmented what we learned from data visualization and predictive analytics to develop advanced methods of recommending relevant offers (base fare plus ancillaries) to customers. Segmentation of customers based on purchase-behavior patterns is never a perfect science and should be refined periodically, preferably automatically learned and updated, as attitudes and customer behaviors change over time. In the competitive marketplace, travel solutions should focus on product offerings that resonate with customers to improve conversion rates and maximize revenues for suppliers with every customer interaction by offering the right product or bundle to the right customer at the right price at the right time.

The evolution of the sales process

This section highlights the key constructs to support the evolution of the sales process, with a focus on generating targeted offers to the customer base.

Segmentation – trip purpose and customer

From the advent of airline reservations systems (host CRS) and global distribution systems (GDS) in the 1960s, airlines have used the reservations booking designator (RBD), commonly referred to as a booking-class code, as a surrogate for customer segmentation in fare management, seat availability and inventory control, shopping, booking, pricing and ticketing processes. Although RBDs serve as the primary vehicle for product distribution, today airlines are looking beyond traditional RBDs for greater flexibility in customer segmentation, influenced by purchase-behavior patterns that cannot be encapsulated in a RBD.[1] Figure 7.13 illustrates an abstraction of the customer booking travel that leads to a personalized offer.

An approach that is more closely aligned with revenue management is trip-purpose segmentation based on *revealed preferences*. Trip-purpose segmentation is the first step toward targeted-offer creation and works even when the customer's identity is not known. The value of trip-purpose segmentation is based on the fact that a typical customer has multiple profiles based on the context for travel – business, romantic vacation, family vacation, visiting friends and relatives,

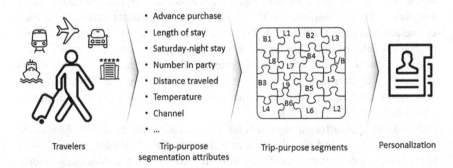

| Travelers | Trip-purpose segmentation attributes | Trip-purpose segments | Personalization |

Figure 7.13 Personalizing the travel experience

etc. – which represents variants of business and leisure travel (e.g. B1, L1, . . .) Trip-purpose segmentation is a practical step toward grouping of customers with similar purchase-behavior characteristics, for two reasons: First, not all customers are registered users and can be anonymous when they book with a travel agent or book on a website without cookies enabled. Second, the typical traveler has multiple profiles depending on the purpose of the trip. With knowledge of the context for the trip, determining the trip-purpose segment has a strong influence on customer preferences and price sensitivity. The trip segments are mutually exclusive and collectively exhaustive. Trip segmentation can be augmented with customer-specific data resident in a customer profile – name, credit card, frequent flyer status, past trips, etc. – when the customer is declared, to fine-tune the recommendation arrived at with trip segmentation.

Generating targeted offers to customers during shopping and booking requires advanced statistical techniques for trip-purpose segmentation. Trip segmentation is required when the customer has *not* been identified to generate relevant offers. When the customer has been identified, 1:1 personalization of offers is feasible and can be influenced by prior history.

Typical parameter ranges that are considered in combination to identify trip segments are advance purchase period, length of stay, Saturday-night stay, number in party, distance traveled, temperature differential between the O&D (origin and destination) and channel. This represents the first level of customer centricity, by personalizing, for example, the shopping experience, to provide the most relevant information during the sales process. Clustering techniques can be used to determine the trip-purpose segments from historical booking data.[2,3] Subsequently when the customer has been identified, recommendations can be refined by augmenting trip segmentation recommendations with past behaviors and stated preferences.

Trip segmentation is very different from customer segmentation, which is applicable only when the customer's identity is known. Common customer-segmentation techniques used in customer-relationship-management (CRM) applications are RFMTV (recency, frequency, monetary, tenure and value) or tiers based on the total or remaining customer lifetime value. Customer segmentation can work with trip-purpose segmentation to fine-tune the offer based on the customer's prior travel history. More modern techniques rely on natural-language processing (NLP) of user-review data for sentiment analysis of airline brands to recommend products that closely match the stated preferences on a customer's profile. For example, if someone shops for a flight from Chicago to Banff for two adults and a child, this trip-purpose segment will probably not be interested in Wi-Fi to respond to office email but would purchase advance seat selection to sit together. When a customer is declared, past travel history also plays a role in determining the components of the offer – products and price.

Power shopping – personalizing shopping responses based on trip segmentation

A typical shopping response generates itineraries that are based on the parameters of the shopping request. Shopping responses should be optimized to return itineraries by trip-purpose segment. For example, business travelers may prefer a short connection, whereas a family with children may want longer connect times for identical shopping requests. The definition of trip segments is a first step toward creation of rules or shopping parameters to narrow the search and return the most relevant set of options. For corporate travel, corporate compliance will also serve as a filter by augmenting the trip-purpose-segment shopping parameters. Establishing rules by trip segment requires validation with A/B testing to determine the best set of shopping parameters to be deployed to narrow the search and determine specific schedules for a trip segment that maximizes conversion rates. Trip segmentation is a learning process that needs to be fine-tuned and updated over time, because market conditions and customer behaviors change over time.

Attribute-based shopping

Attribute-based shopping is the first step in a journey to target customers with precise offers and generate incremental revenues. With the unbundling of the airline product, attribute-based shopping, pricing and booking represents the new reality. When a user specifies attributes specific to a trip, the search space needs to be refined to return content with the specified attributes. For example, for air travel, users like to select itineraries based on seat availability – premium (more legroom) seats, aisle seats, window seats, exit-row seats, seats together for a family, etc.; free bags, pre-reserved seats, schedule and fare preferences, loyalty tier, etc. In this new paradigm, the attributes specified by a user come first, before itineraries (e.g. flights) are returned. The unbundling of a fare to promote the sale of ancillaries has increased the complexity of shopping for air travel. Though there is a perception[4] that shopping for air travel should be as easy as shopping at an online retail store, there are significant differences and complexities with air travel! First, most customers when they shop are anonymous and usually declare who they are only at a later stage. Second, the context for a trip is very important – leisure, business, visiting friends and relatives, etc., which influences the types of itineraries a customer would be interested in.

Advances in revenue management with dynamic availability and dynamic pricing

In this age of schedule and fare transparency thanks to the Internet, suppliers are aware that customers shop across multiple sites before they make a booking. Suppliers therefore need to come to grips with market equilibrium and prevailing competitor fares to make informed decisions on revenue management and inventory control.

Revenue management has always been about what the supplier is willing to accept rather than what the customer is willing to pay. The key calculation in airline revenue management is the *bid price*[5,6] which is the opportunity cost of not having an incremental seat. The bid price for an itinerary serves as a threshold or hurdle for accepting a fare. Dynamic availability and dynamic pricing are the latest evolutions in revenue management, in which the objective is to dynamically determine the optimal inventory control or the dynamic price for a customer based on prevailing market conditions.

Similar techniques can also be applied to hotels to predict when hotel rates are expected to go up or down by star rating and neighborhood.

Dynamic availability is competitive revenue management by origin and destination to determine how an airline's existing inventory control recommendations need to be adapted and modified based on prevailing competitive market conditions.[7] This requires monitoring of competitive selling fares from shopping responses to determine an airline's competitive positioning with optimal inventory controls in the market based on bookings and seats available. For competitor insight, an airline can collaborate with travel marketplaces that provide shopping services to consumers or sources such as QL2, Infare and other third-party vendors. The attractiveness of each itinerary in a shopping response can be estimated, with a choice model calibrated from linked shopping request and response data, with pertinent variables such as departure/arrival times, travel time, fare and screen presence.

Dynamic pricing is closely related to dynamic availability. The term "dynamic pricing" frequently causes confusion when airline executives equate it to the millions of air filings that are made daily either proactively or in response to a competitor's actions. Dynamic pricing is a *sense and respond* capability and determines the optimal fare to quote to a customer, based on revenue-management principles and an airline's prevailing price competitiveness in the market, which may be different from a filed fare. Whereas dynamic pricing is airline-focused on computing the minimum fare the airline is willing to accept, there is a subtle difference with personalized pricing, which is a 1:1 fare based on the individual customer's travel characteristics and past behavior, which is stored on the customer's profile. Personalized pricing is not practiced in the airline industry today, but it may take root in the future.

Both techniques leverage competitive selling fares to arrive at an inventory-control or dynamic-price recommendation. They are big-data applications[8] due to the processing of unstructured data from shopping responses. The session-based fare optimizer determines the optimal price point for the host airline based on the tradeoff between the probability the itinerary will be selected from a set of competing itineraries and the yield. Instead of converting the optimal price point to an inventory-control recommendation, the dynamic price is used to approximate the ticketed price. Although dynamic pricing of opaque travel products[9] has minimal business-process changes, the potential impacts of deploying dynamic pricing on third-party systems can be significant.[10]

Dynamic pricing has the following advantages over dynamic availability:

i   Continuous vs. discrete price points
ii Works directly at the round-trip itinerary level (whereas dynamic availability is based on the best-fit solution across a range of different trip length-of-stays)

iii   Bridges the chasm between booking-class availability and pricing by ensuring that the dynamic price, which is based on bid prices by itinerary, is always greater than or equal to the total bid price for the itinerary

Offer management

Offer management is frequently used to describe an expansion of traditional revenue management of the base fare to include ancillary products that are bundled with the base fare to create a bundled offer. Surveys have shown that travelers are willing to pay for extra perks, such as more frequent flyer miles, pre-reserved seats and a seat with extra leg room. Indeed, ancillary revenues and new product offerings in the form of airline-branded fares, in which static ancillaries are included, have grown rapidly over the past decade, and new decision-support tools are emerging in this area.

Offer management is important for IATA's new distribution capability (NDC), and it extends across all channels of distribution. It is the process of determining the composition of the bundle when the customer is anonymous, followed with fine-tuning the bundle when the customer is known. Trip-purpose segmentation data can be analyzed against historical booking and ticketed data to determine the dominant ancillaries that resonate with each trip-purpose segment. (This is called market-basket analysis in traditional brick-and-mortar and online retailing.) This information can then be used to determine the composition of the most appropriate bundles for each trip segment. In summary, trip-purpose segments can be used to determine the bundled offer early in the sales process when the customer is not declared. Subsequent refinements to the bundle take place after the customer is declared, and past history and preferences can be used to fine-tune the offer. Before the final offer is created, it is important to consider airline-branded fares by mapping the ancillaries included in each branded-fare product to ensure that the lowest-cost option is offered to the customer, thereby promoting upsell of individual ancillaries.

Determining the price for the bundle requires estimates of a customer's willingness to pay, which should be calibrated for each trip segment. The customer's willingness to pay is an estimate that can be derived from A/B testing or surveys such as conjoint analysis. In general, A/B testing is more effective than surveys, due to bias caused when customers do not provide feedback based on what they really think. With the estimates of price elasticity by trip segment, the discount for the bundle can be determined to arrive at the price for the bundle. A/B testing can also be used to improve conversion rates on the proposed bundles. In an A/B testing framework, alternate versions – current (control) versus proposed (variation) split the incoming traffic and can be compared against each other to determine whether there is a positive, negative or neutral impact on a metric such as conversion rates. An alternate approach to A/B testing is deployment of the multi-armed bandit[11,12] which relies on trying out each alternative (arm) in an exploratory phase for a small percentage of the traffic (e.g. 10%) to find the best one and in the exploitation phase, sending the bulk of the traffic to the alternative (arm) that gives the best payoff.

Conclusions

Understanding customer preferences and generating pertinent targeted responses to customer requests during the sales process is the new reality. Customer preferences need to be used with attribute-based shopping and pricing. Generating a multitude of offers to customers who have to select among them slows down the sales process and leads to abandonment – an issue that is exacerbated with the growth in mobile bookings, where screen real estate is at a premium. A key to customer-centricity is the ability to offer the right product or bundle to the right customer at the right price at the right time, based on deduced or stated customer preferences. Displaying targeted offers that resonate with customers requires an investment in a data infrastructure and advanced analytics to understand consumer behavior and preferences to generate incremental revenues with targeted offers and ensure repeatable profitable customers.

Notes

1 B. Vinod, "The Continuing Evolution: Customer Centric Revenue Management," *Journal of Revenue and Pricing Management* 7.1 (2008): 27–39.
2 T. Bhaskar, A. Kothari, R. Ratliff, and S. Shebalov, "Multi-Dimensional Customer Segmentation," *54th Annual AGIFORS Symposium*, Dubai, October 2014.
3 A. Kothari, M. Madireddy, and R. Sundararajan, "Discovering Patterns in Traveler Behavior Using Segmentation," *Journal of Revenue and Pricing Management* 15.5 (2016): 334–51.
4 Henry A. Harteveldt, "The Future of Airline Distribution 2016–2021," *IATA – Atmosphere Research Group*, 2016.
5 B. Vinod, "Origin and Destination Yield Management," in: D. Jenkins (ed.) *Aviation Daily's Handbook of Airline Economics* (New York: McGraw Hill, September 1995).
6 Juan M. Chaneton and Gustavo Vulcano, "Computing Bid Prices for Revenue Management Under Customer Choice Behavior," *Manufacturing & Service Operations Management* 13.4 (2011): 452–70.
7 R. Ratliff and B. Vinod, "Airline Pricing and Revenue Management: A Future Outlook," *Journal of Revenue and Pricing Management* 4.3 (2005): 302–7.
8 B. Vinod, "Big Data in the Travel Marketplace," *Journal of Revenue and Pricing Management* 15.5 (2016): 352–9.
9 F. Zouaoui and B.V. Rao, "Dynamic Pricing of Opaque Airline Tickets," *Journal of Revenue and Pricing Management* 8.2/3 (2009): 148–54.
10 T. Fiig, O. Goyons, R. Adelving, and B.C. Smith, "Dynamic Pricing – The Next Revolution in RM?" *Journal of Revenue and Pricing Management* 15.5 (2016): 360–79.
11 H. Robbins, "Some Aspects of the Sequential Design of Experiments," *Bulletin of the American Mathematical Society* 58.5 (1952): 527–35.
12 J. Gittins, K. Glazebrook, and R. Weber, *Multi-Armed Bandit Allocation Indices*, 2nd edition (Hoboken, NJ: Wiley, 2011).

13   Leadership challenges in a disruptive era: rapidly changing market dynamics in airfreight as well as passenger air travel require a new leadership approach

Monika Wiederhold

Managing Director
Amadeus Germany GmbH

This thought-leadership piece discusses three major areas: (1) Market dynamics of the air-cargo sector and the passenger-air-travel sector, (2) Strategic direction: Is there a way out? and (3) Core leadership skills for the digital age in the airline sector and beyond.

1)   Market dynamics of the air-cargo sector and the passenger-air-travel sector

The commoditization of the airline industry is not a new phenomenon – however, its pace has accelerated in recent years. Ongoing yield pressure, overcapacities and aggressively growing low-cost carriers are typical challenges in both the passenger and the air-cargo business. This has led to a fiercely competitive situation between the airlines and airfreight carriers while, simultaneously, start-up as well as grown-up digital players are reshaping the market. The newly founded alliance around artificial intelligence between Amazon, Google, IBM, Facebook and Microsoft should be interpreted as well with regard to passenger travel and logistics. Most probably, in these sectors – as well as in others – extreme personalization and contextualization will appear, for example conversational commerce embedded in individual travel context. Pre-trained chat bots might assist or replace human travel agents in the near future, and plenty of other applications around travel and transport are thinkable.

The airfreight transportation chain is a very fragmented one, involving numerous players and lots of interfaces along the chain. It is still an extremely paper-based transaction, despite long-lasting efforts of the established market players to digitize the chain, and in comparison to other industries the degree of digitization is

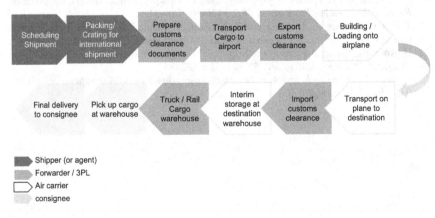

Figure 7.14 The airfreight chain

not satisfying. IATA recently launched an initiative foster the digital development and standards across the globe for air cargo.

In this context, the airlines – and all other players in the supply chain – need to work closely together and develop collaborative solutions, either through the IATA industry initiatives or through multilateral digital alliances, despite their tough competitive battle in the airport-to-airport segment of the airfreight transportation chain. The given market situation certainly is an opportunity for digital entrants connecting all the players and replacing, step by step, the analog world.

In comparison, the global integrators have invested huge amounts of money over decades into IT systems, enabling them to fully control the whole transportation chain of their shipments digitally. This is a clear competitive advantage in the parcel segment (up to 35 kg) compared to the fragmented airfreight chain. During the last few years, all integrators have shown revenue growth strategies not only by increasing peu à peu their fleet and aircraft sizes but also by eating into traditionally profitable airfreight segments:

- **Increasing the size of shipments**: Investments in infrastructure of the integrators' sorting hubs clearly prove their strategic direction. For example, DHL's Leipzig hub is now capable of sorting shipments up to 180 kg fully automatically. Also FedEx/TNT is investing heavily in the post-merger infrastructure at Paris's Charles de Gaulle airport, leading to a digitally seamless heavy-freight supply chain.
- **Focusing on special segments**: Integrators are also focusing on high-yield segments such as temperature-controlled solutions, which is a very important transportation need for the pharmaceutical industry. Also the focus on dangerous-goods transportation has increased.

Integrators putting even more pressure on the airfreight chain foster the need for digital collaboration and steering of companies across the traditional airfreight chain. The profit pool analysis provided in the World Economic Forum white paper "Digital Transformation of Industries: Logistics" indicates that the integrators' profitability (EBIT margin) has in the past and will over the next few years outperform the growth of the participants in the airfreight chain.

The big digital players have a clear focus on the logistics industry as well: One of Amazon's core competencies is logistics – in all aspects and with worldwide door-to-door ambitions. It certainly started with warehouse logistics, as well as to-door-delivery logistics, partnering with integrators. However, by now it is clear that Amazon's strategy is to create a global logistics network and to participate much more deeply in the transportation chain. Signs of this development are Amazon's massive entry into airfreight by leasing twenty 767Fs from Atlas Air, heavy investments in fulfillment centers in the US and forays into last-mile competencies by partnering with gas stations as delivery options for parcel pick-up – for example, in Germany. Assuming that the digital players, such as Amazon, are moving into the parcel segment, the parcel integrators will move into the heavy-freight and special-freight segments even faster and increase competitive pressure in the airfreight segment. Given the huge volume of Amazon's business, this move will put pressure on the integrators' parcel business – and their answer might be to focus even more on the traditional airfreight segments as their traditional express business is under attack.

Activity in the start-up scene focusing on logistics topics is accelerating as well. There is a clear sense in the ecosystem that logistics is ripe for disruption. The first professional accelerators for logistics start-ups emerged in 2016, and thousands of start-ups are developing. Unfortunately, we do not know which ones will become unicorns. . . . Evaluating their development, a focus on platform-related business models, is certainly a good start. Two interesting fast-growing candidates in this area are San Francisco–based Flexport (www.flexport.com) and Freightos (www.freightos.com). Quotes from their websites show their disruptive ambition: Flexport: "Freight forwarder for the internet age. Full-service air and ocean forwarder providing visibility and control over your entire supply chain through software." Or "90% of everything we eat, wear or use is shipped . . . But freight is stuck in the '90s. The Freightos Marketplace and freight rate management platforms are game-changers."[1]

And, as some food for thought, it might be interesting to project the digital possibilities as well as shared-economy and artificial-intelligence approaches into the future. Does this lead to quite disruptive scenarios?

Imagine the parts of the transportation chain totally fragmented into individual players fully organized by a digital platform – from pilots to documentation. This would lead to a global "Uberisation" of the airfreight chain far away from traditional asset-based business models. Or, imagine that the artificial-intelligence alliance of the "big five" tech companies (Amazon, Google, Facebook, IBM and Microsoft) manages to gain a massive advantage on data access. This would lead to an unbeatable treasure of freight data to train artificial intelligence and offer completely new levels of personalized predictive solutions for transport – currently a major weakness of the airfreight sector.

In passenger air travel, the competitive situation is different, especially the maturity of digital capabilities of the market players concerning inventory management and booking capabilities, yet with some interesting parallels between the sectors. The complete journey of a passenger is fragmented, with even more different players along the chain. Historically, for airlines there have been tour operators organizing and managing the complete journey for private travelers in the leisure segment (comparable to the integrators of the air-cargo sector). In the business travel segment, most organizations have professional-travel-management units organizing duty travel and negotiating on a company level. The development of distribution systems decades ago was the base for ongoing development of digital services for airline passengers. Online flight search and booking has been a feature of the market since the 1990s – whereas air-cargo efforts still rely heavily on direct phone contact with the carriers.

Given the level of digitization of the core processes and systems of the individual players (e.g., airlines) in the passenger segment, the threat of digital entries interconnecting them with a platform approach is clear. The digital technology now enables the complete virtual organization of the air-travel offer embedded in travelers' journeys. This includes not only the pure transportation chain, but other building blocks as well, from hotels, to restaurants to activities. This development is pushing airlines (and all other players in the journey!) into extreme commoditization by complete transparent offers and ongoing price and offer optimization and is a serious threat to traditional distribution systems as well.

Trying to reflect a customer-centric approach towards ultimately the shipper (industry) as the airfreight customer and the individual traveler do not have a comfortable, intuitive solution for their customers' core transportation needs, despite the need. A thesis is that those customers both would appreciate a holistic, **super-simple integrated digital solution** to solve their transportation needs across the different modes and market players. The chance is clearly there (Google is already into the travel segment), and the situation is similar in the airfreight and the passenger segment (see Figure 7.15):

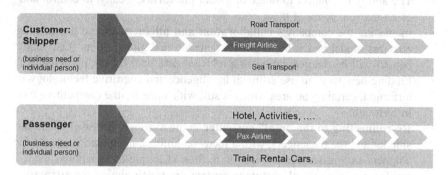

Figure 7.15 Customer-centric, integrated needs

2) Strategic direction: is there a way out?

What options do airlines have, given the increasing pressure on commoditization both in airfreight and in the passenger business? In principle, there are two basic strategies for getting out of the commodity trap:

One option is **price leadership**, and it makes a lot of sense to follow this road if an airline or airfreight carrier has the chance to become a cost leader in the market. Certainly, some Asian, Russian and Middle East carriers (as well as newcomers) are in a position to pursue cost leadership. It is realistic to challenge the legacy carriers if they have a chance of reaching a cost-leadership position, which is a prerequisite for sustainable price-leadership strategies. If not, the second option might be the right answer, and that is **differentiation**. Differentiation means innovation, and innovation in our current era means digital innovation.

The described – if not completely comprehensively – competitive challenges and dependencies are putting enormous pressure on airfreight carriers (and passenger airlines) to handle these developments simultaneously while securing the existing business mode. Several topics might feed into the digital agenda and will need top management focus-producing cost advantages, differentiation through digitization and generating transformational business models:

- Being always one step ahead in the airport-to-airport competition: Doing the homework and focusing on cost competiveness through standardization and digitization enabling **fast reduction of transaction costs**

- A focus on increased **cross-company-digitization and integration** starting from the shipper; connecting the forwarder and the airline is the core task in order to develop superior chains to defend against integrators' competitive advantage. Customer access to the shipper offering superior services will be a key success factor (similar for the participants in the passenger-travel sector)
- Actively searching for **digital service innovation** through systematic interaction up to M&A activities with the tech start-up scene
- The ability to connect to range of global **platforms**, ideally, to control and/ or co-manage some of them
- Increasing the company's **collaboration and alliances** around the existing business model and value chains to generate real global offers (One major benefit will be the generation of a relevant data pool for the participants.)
- Finding new ways to use artificial intelligence and **cognitive technology** in airfreight, certainly an area which is still wide open for the competitive race in airfreight
- **Re-connecting to the "real" customer** in the airfreight or travel chain: the shipper and the passengers, with a focus on holistic, integrated solutions for shippers and passengers in reaction to their changing expectations
- Implementing a radical **customer-centric approach** aiming for **attractive, super-simple and intuitive digital designs** of the offer portfolio of the future

Ultimately, the vision should be to create a truly digitally connected airline to solve the mobility and transportation needs of a passenger or a shipper. But if no airline is stepping in, other players will certainly do it.

3) *Core leadership skills for the digital age in the airline sector and beyond*

The digital era is changing the rules, the players and the forces in the airline sector. Therefore new leadership skills are needed, to help airlines not only navigate the changing global market but also cope with the very agile digital ecosystem to enable innovation.

A **"Think Big and Global"** attitude is necessary to build global alliances and to compete in a digital world on a global scale. One very important resource for success in a digital world is access to mass data on a global scale. "Big Data" is the oil of the digital age, and to generate it on a relevant scale it is necessary to cross the company's border and to find partners.

In the airfreight and logistics sector, no dominant player has succeeded so far in positioning itself as data generator and/or owner, which presents a great chance for the existing market players as well as for digital new entrants. In the travel sector, Google's activities have created already a massive advantage in access to travelers' data and behavior patterns. However, even Google is actively driving alliances to approach cognitive technology: One impressive recent example is the co-operation around artificial intelligence between Amazon, Google, IBM, Facebook and Microsoft. It will be – and most probably has been already during the design – an impressive challenge to bring the alliance of these big digital players to life. And cognitive products and services will certainly be highly relevant to the airline sector.

Another interesting example of collaboration between competitors in the mobility sector is the joint investments of Audi, BMW and Mercedes. The three German brands are traditional competitors in the automotive manufacturing sector and decided in 2015 to form a new alliance for their digital future: their acquisition of Nokia Here – a digital map provider – will put them in a position to collect mass real-time data, with their worldwide automotive fleet, on street layouts and traffic obstacles, which will lead to a competitive advantage for self-driving or assisted-driving vehicles of the future.

The **start-up ecosystem for digital innovation** is characterized by small players, a young generation, trial-and-error approaches, explorative but radically digital thinking and, last but not least: speed. Most of the established companies have developed approaches to connect efficiently with the start-up ecosystem – be it through venture strategies, co-operation with national or global industry-specific accelerators or their own start-up developments. One way or the other, a systematic approach for "building a bridge" between the corporate world and the start-up scene should be integrated into the company's strategy. The benefits will be found in new sources of ideas, fresh perspectives and access to know-how that is not available inside established companies. And, last but not least, the cultural impact of the contacts with start-ups should not be underestimated: it forces traditional companies into more entrepreneurial and experimental approaches. And these efforts will be a valuable resource for the externally innovative (re-) positioning of companies that need to differentiate. The technical possibilities seem to lead to a new kind of intermediation, where newcomers have a chance to develop into global players within a few years. In the airfreight sector, a lot of start-ups have this aspiration; they focus on the digital management of the very fragmented and still paper-based airfreight supply chain with lots of different players involved for each shipment. For example, San Francisco–based Flexport and Germany-based FreightHub are clearly positioned as digital forwarders – and it will be interesting to see how these newcomers will compete against the traditional legacy freight forwarders. Given their extreme focus on customer-centricity and simplification, there is a great chance that the names in the competitive landscape will change within a few years in airfreight logistics as well as in other sectors. And senior leadership in the established sector needs to find answers and ways of cooperation.

Of course, top management across the globe is aware of the forces of disruption and possible new entrants into their sectors driven by digital competence – big players as well as visionary start-ups with global leadership ambitions. The need for digital transformation of their respective businesses to safeguard the existing sector competence should drive most strategic thinking on the top level to put them into a future winner's position. As described, it is a challenging task for management to guide an organization through global approaches and in parallel to

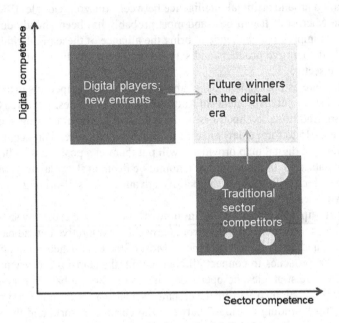

Figure 7.16 The changing competitive landscape in the digital era

connect to agile ecosystems of a new generation. However, what does this mean for their own leadership skills? Certainly there are additional skills necessary at the top to lead companies into the digital era, and I suggest three focus points for senior leadership development:

First of all, **visionary content leadership** is needed in a digital era: being able to create a cross-company digital strategy for business transformation and creating a system that nurtures the vision continuously. And this digital strategy is not meant to be a bottom-up collection of different function-oriented projects: A lot of different approaches in the airline sector have focused so far on bottom-up, process or product-related digital roadmaps leading to incremental digital improvements of the current business environments. The transformational digital strategies focusing on re-inventing the business, especially in traditionally asset-heavy environments, will need a much more holistic and radical approach, guided from the top of the organizations by a radical customer-centric perspective. Currently, less than half of the airline-related sector has a holistic digital strategy, despite the fact that 95% consider digitization as an opportunity (source: Bitkom Research 2016). The strategic positioning has to include an answer to the question of what mass data around their own capabilities can be controlled and have the potential to generate a competitive advantage using cognitive technologies. Additionally, senior leaders across different management functions will need solid digital capabilities to understand and transfer the technical developments creatively into their area of responsibility and transform it. The digital strategy will need two perspectives: (1) the digitization of the existing environment on a functional level and, in parallel, (2) the transformation of the business models to build new competitive advantages relevant in the context with new entrants into the respective sectors.

Second, it is necessary to develop **cross-company collaboration skills** in order to get the organization ready for much more interconnectedness than in the past: building networks and alliances with the traditional market players and industry associations to create industry standards and technical enablers as a base for competitive global solutions. As in other industries, it is most probable that former direct competitors will work closely together. Certainly, different partners participating in the value chain will need deeper relations and, given the developments of the last few years, it should come as no surprise that platform skills – meaning the management of and cooperation with a lot of different partners – will be key.

Collaboration with the start-up scene is worth considering. However, in looking at successful acquisitions or cooperation, the cultural/value fit seems to be very important, and unfortunately there is usually not a broad cultural fit between start-ups and corporate organizations. Thus working together may soon prove frustrating for the people involved. And that is exactly why management needs to carefully design and guide the organization through a new way of cross-company collaboration. Following is one suggested approach.

Internal preparation: Select a **core team** of frontrunners and forward-thinkers – ideally cross-functionally, but in any case including IT, product development and related digitization initiatives. Put **clear contacts**, **resources and processes** in place to facilitate the joint innovation efforts of the corporate organization and the start-ups. Prepare some **functional focus areas** in order to concentrate on start-ups contributing to your most urgent needs, and be aware of the required outcome.

Find and connect with start-ups: Establishing a transparent, publicly visible structure on how to contact and work with the corporate organization makes it much easier for start-ups to connect with the corporate organization.

The **screening process** in order to find promising start-up candidates is not an easy one. Especially because corporate managers are not familiar and somehow disconnected from that scene. However, it is necessary to find an appropriate screening approach – be it by dedicating some of your company's own resources or by using professional accelerator organizations (e.g., RocketSpace, Startupbootcamp).

Co-implementation: Once you have identified the entrepreneurs you want to work with, it is useful to connect personally to them with a real respect and interest for their efforts and ideas. The key to success – and simultaneously the biggest challenge for the corporate organization – will be the ability to create piloting opportunities typically much faster than a standard corporate planning cycle will allow. Connect to the start-up scene and prepare your organization to cope with fast-moving piloting approaches.

Additionally, collaboration with other **corporate partners** could be beneficial, helping your organization create broader global solutions, gain speed and world-wide data access and share the burden of re-inventing the industry.

The third core leadership skill is the most difficult, because it is usually not part of the corporate DNA. It involves the creation and nurturing of **agile innovation skills** not only inside the organization but also together with a foreign ecosystem – a culture that is vastly different from the typical corporate culture. The capability to implement an efficient innovation and start-up strategy is urgently needed. Such a strategy, which takes the organization in a new trans-formational direction, needs full backing from the CEO of the organization. To start with, it requires an appropriate – and most probably parallel – budget and execution process for innovation projects, accompanied by the willingness to accept more risk. The fostering of experimental and explorative approaches is highly recommended. This has to include a view of failures as a learning opportunity and a normal consequence of innovative activities. And, last but not least, super-simple and intuitive design in product and service development will be a key success factor not very common in traditional organizations. What with all the different needs, a major cultural change lies ahead for most organizations.

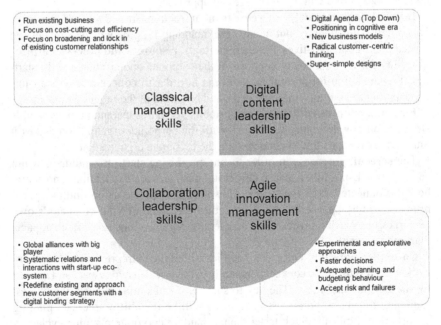

Figure 7.17 Leadership skills in the digital era

Reflecting on the challenging market dynamics I have described, and the need for strategic transformation and new leadership skills, the conclusion is obvious: Senior management needs to radically transform business models and foster a cultural change broadening the organizational mind-set to drop constraints. At the same time, safeguarding the existing business as the base for survival is certainly not an easy task. However, these are most exciting times for business leaders willing to re-invent their respective industries, thus shaping and contributing to a new way of life and business in the digital era.

Note

1 This is how Freightos introduced the company in its job listings. See, for example, https://www.freightos.com/careers/rd/F6.30C/senior-software-development-engineer/.

Index

About the author

Nawal Taneja, whose experience in the aviation industry spans almost five decades, has worked for and advised major airlines and related businesses worldwide. His experience also includes the presidency of a small airline that provided schedule and charter service with jet aircraft and the presidency of a research organization that provided consulting services to the air transportation community throughout the world. On the government side, he has advised worldwide departments of civil aviation on matters relating to the role of government-owned or government-controlled airlines and their management. Within the academic community, he has served on the faculties of the Massachusetts Institute of Technology (as an associate professor) and at Ohio State University (professor and later as chair of both the Department of Aviation and the Department of Aerospace Engineering).

He has served on the advisory boards of both public and private organizations. He continues to be asked to provide presentations at industry conferences worldwide and moderate panel discussions. He writes a Column in *Airline Leader*, the Strategy Journal for Airline CEOs (published by CAPA – Centre for Aviation). He advises senior executives in airlines and related businesses as well as senior government policy makers on the impact of following powerful and converging forces on the:

- radically changing behavior and expectations of connected and empowered passengers in the on-demand and sharing economies
- proliferation of smart consumer technologies that provide real-time information and services
- emergence of businesses with information and analytical skills to sell customized travel services to customers and to manage them
- rapidly evolving aviation regulatory policies, making the market more dynamic and more unpredictable, and
- emergence of platform-based and networked businesses.

At the encouragement of and for practitioners in the global airline industry, he has authored nine other books:

- *Driving Airline Business Strategies through Emerging Technology* (2002)
- *AIRLINE SURVIVAL KIT: Breaking Out of the Zero Profit Game* (2003)
- *Simpli-Flying: Optimizing the Airline Business Model* (2004)
- *FASTEN YOUR SEATBELT: The Passenger is Flying the Plane* (2005)
- *Flying Ahead of the Airplane* (2008)
- *Looking Beyond the Runway: Airlines Innovating with Best Practices while Facing Realities* (2010)
- *The Passenger Has Gone Digital and Mobile: Accessing and Connecting through Information and Technology (2011)*
- *Designing Future-Oriented Airline Businesses (2014)*
- *AIRLINE INDUSTRY: Poised for Disruptive Innovation? (2016)*

The first eight books were published by the Ashgate Publishing Company (now part of Routledge) in the UK and the ninth directly by Routledge.

He holds a Bachelors degree in Aeronautical Engineering (First Class Honors) from the University of London, a Masters degree in Flight Transportation from MIT, a Masters degree in Business Administration from MIT's Sloan School of Management, and a Doctorate in Air Transportation from the University of London. He is a Fellow of the Royal Aeronautical Society of Great Britain.

Printed in the United States
by Baker & Taylor Publisher Services